READING HOMER

READING HOMER

Film and Text

Edited by
Kostas Myrsiades

Madison • Teaneck
Fairleigh Dickinson University Press

Associated University Presses
2010 Eastpark Boulevard
Cranbury, NJ 08512

The paper used in this publication meets the requirements of the American National Standard for Permanence of Paper for Printed Library Materials Z39.48-1984.

Library of Congress Cataloging-in-Publication Data

Reading Homer : film and text / edited by Kostas Myrsiades.
p. cm.
Includes bibliographical references and index.
ISBN 978-0-8386-4219-1 (alk. paper)
1. Homer—Criticism and interpretation. 2. Homer—Influence. 3. Motion pictures—Plots, themes, etc. 4. Mythology in motion pictures. 5. Troy (Motion picture) I. Myrsiades, Kostas.
PA4037.A5R43 2009
883′.01—dc22 2009001421

PRINTED IN THE UNITED STATES OF AMERICA

Contents

Introduction: Why Read Homer?

Kostas Myrsiades

ALMOST 3,000 YEARS AGO, A BLIND POET(S) LIVING AT THE DAWN OF civilization recited/composed two epic poems, the *Iliad,* recounting the wrath of Achilles, and the *Odyssey,* about the ten-year-long adventures of Odysseus. Today the Homeric epics as they are known to us, are read and taught throughout our colleges and universities, and ultimately they will probably become known in one form or another to most educated people around the world. What is it about these two poems that makes them the most read works, except the Bible, in Western civilization?

The answers are many. Historians use Homer's works to piece together Mycenean society and the world as it existed during the poet's life, usually placed around the end of the eighth century B.C.E.; anthropologists and sociologists study the epics for their wealth of information on everyday Homeric life; psychologists focus on Homer's heroes to probe people's need for moral values and religion; and folklorists search the texts as an encyclopedia of classical mythology.

Alexander the Great reportedly carried a copy of the *Iliad* with him wherever he went because for him the poem represented the epitome of heroism and the way a warrior had to conduct himself. Leo Tolstoy believed the Homeric epics were the closest thing to nature itself. Victorian poet and critic Matthew Arnold found them the best cure for a headache.

Beginning with Aristotle, students of Homer tended to become bogged down with linguistic disagreements until 1795, the year the German philologist F. A. Wolf published his *Prolegomena ad Homerum,* which argued that Homer's epics were products of an illiterate age. With the publication of this book, Wolf was able to legitimize what up to his time was taken to be a heretical and minority view. Wolf's book defined the course Homeric studies were to take from that point on—that Homer was an oral poet (an *aoidos*) whose epics were preserved through memory until an alphabet came along to preserve them in writing. However, the *Iliad* and *Odyssey* were poems of too great a length for anyone to believe that a single bard could store them in his memory—the *Iliad* consists of 15,693 lines and the *Odyssey* of 12,109 lines. Thus, Wolf argued that Homer, or rather many Homers, orally composed and left behind a number of short lays, which were then stitched together at a later period when writing came into being. Wolf's theory was to occupy Homeric scholarship well into the early years of the twentieth century, dividing Homerists into two camps—unitarians who felt the epics were the products of a single mind and analysts who followed Wolf's theory that the epics were composed of smaller songs by a variety of bards and were stitched together. These arguments between unitarians and analysts abated to a degree as a result of the work of Milman Parry in the early part of the twentieth century. Parry demonstrated through linguistic analysis and fieldwork that Homer was an oral poet who composed his epics in performance. In other words, instead of reciting a memorized text, the bard composed as he performed, relying on a store of traditional techniques, formulas, stock phrases, and lines constructed to meet the demands of the dactylic hexameter line in which the epics were composed.

Earlier in 1870 a German businessman and avid unitarian, Heinrich Schliemann, began the excavation of Troy (modern Hissarlik, western Turkey) and convinced scholars to look at the Homeric epics in a historical light rather than as the unhistorical fictions they were considered to be up to that point. After the decipherment in the 1950s of Linear B, the early Mycenean alphabet, and the advancements made by archaeologists in Troy, scholars turned their attention to the epics' depiction of the Mycenean world in which they were set. In time, however, a generation of new Homerists concluded as K. A. Raaflaub states that "heroic epic is historical in appearance but contemporary in meaning" (1997, 628).

Although still concerned to a large extent with many of the issues that have plagued Homerists since Aristotle, the myriad books and articles appearing on Homer each year of the twenty-first century have shifted their emphasis. This time the emphasis is on the role of the narrator and narration itself, the poet's method of characterization and description, epic plot developments, the nature and purpose of epic type scenes, the nature of character speeches and "sound bites" and close readings of specific passages in both epics.

After 2,800 years on the best-seller list, Homer's *Iliad* and *Odyssey* in English translation are still required reading in most college/university basic world literature courses, judging from their appearance in most introductory world literature texts (including the *Norton Anthology,* the *Longman Anthology,* and the *Bedford Anthology*). Interest in Homer in the twenty-first century seems to be stronger than ever. The most recent of the over two dozen translations of Homer's *Iliad* and/or *Odyssey* in the last fifty years has just been published (Jordan 2008). Since 1990 there have been eight new English translations of the *Odyssey* and six of the *Iliad* (see appendix, 2. English Translations of the *Iliad* and the *Odyssey* in Circulation). New critical studies on Homer since 2000 seem to be on the rise, including a renewed interest among historians and critics in the question of the authenticity of the Trojan War and Troy, which has generated a number of new books in the last few years (Bryce, 2006, Burgess 2001, Castledon 2006, Latacz 2001, Lowenstam 2008, Strauss 2006, Thomas and Conant 2005, and Thompson 2004), and studies on Homeric influence on contemporary culture (Burgess 2008, Hall 2008, Macdonald 2003, Shay 2002, Tatum 2003; see appendix, 1. A Selected List of Critical Works on Homer's Epics since 2000). Even the graphic novel has appropriated Homer, as we see in the projected seven-volume series of Eric Shanower (2001–), of which three volumes (twenty-six installments) have already been published. Shanower is presently working on volume 4, having completed twenty-seven installments.

In her recent book, *The Return of Ulysses: A Cultural History of Homer's* Odyssey (2008), Edith Hall revisits the influence of Homer's epic on Western culture, a task first approached by W. B. Stanford in his classic *The Ulysses Theme* (1954), and finds that Homer's influence has pervaded all phases of contemporary culture. This is especially evident in film. Of the several versions of Homer's epics brought to the screen since the silent era, almost half have been produced in the late twentieth and early twenty-first centuries (*Troy,* 2004, *Helen of Troy* [TV miniseries], 2003, *The Odyssey* [TV miniseries], 1997, *Helen of Troy,* 1955, *Ulysses,* 1954; for a complete list of films see Winkler 2007). In addition to the film adaptations of the *Iliad* and *Odyssey* noted, both classic and contemporary world cinema have been studied for Homeric influences, especially in the American western film (see, for example, Goldhill [2007] and Eckstein and Lehman [2004], who supplement earlier work by Blundell and Ormand [1997] and Winkler [1996, 1985]). Works of fiction and nonfiction influenced by both of Homer's epics have also been at a record high ranging from John Barton's *Tantalus* (2000) to the popular final volumes of David Gemmell's Troy trilogy, *Troy: Fall of Kings* (2007); see appendix, 3. A Selected List of Works of Fiction and Nonfiction since 2000 Influenced by Homer's Epics).

The basic reasons why we still read Homer today seem to me to have remained constant, although each generation seems to find new ways of approaching the Homeric epics. As we see in the present collection of new essays on Homer's epics, the underlying issues of *timé* (honor), *kleos* (fame), *geras* (rewards), the psychology of Homeric warriors, the reevaluation of type scenes, the influences of Homer that have preoccupied scholars for millennia are still present but are revisited anew. Four of the essays collected in this book deal with fresh analysis of key passages and themes in the two epics in question while another four turn to Homer's influence on popular culture, specifically film. Since Wolfgang Petersen's *Troy* was released in 2004, Homerists have taken the opportunity not only to evaluate and critique this film but also to question the existence of Troy and to consider Homer's epics as film, war memorials, and the works of Homer in relation to politics (see Winkler 2007). Even before the release of *Troy,* scholars were finding Homeric influences in Clint Eastwood's *Unforgiven* (1992; see Blundell and Ormand 1997), John Ford's *The Searchers* (1956; Eckstein and Lehman 2004), the Coen Brothers' *O Brother Where Art Thou?* and Mike Leigh's *Naked* (Goldhill 2007), to mention only a few.

The present collection of essays on key scenes from Homer's epics and his influence on American cinema begins with a background essay by Shawn Ross, "Homer as History: Greeks and Others in a Dark Age," which argues that understanding Homeric epic as the product of a long-standing oral tradition facilitates its use as a source for early Greek history, which in turn illuminates the study of the beliefs, institutions, and ideologies of the eighth century B.C.E. when the *Iliad* and *Odyssey* as we know them were composed. The next four essays delve into Homer's texts themselves, focusing on a number of approaches to key passages and themes. Rick Newton's "Geras and Guest-Gifts in Homer" draws parallels between *xeineia* (hospitality and guest-gifts) in the *Odyssey* and *geras* (gifts from plunder) in the *Iliad.* Focusing on the Glaukos–Diomedes scene in *Iliad* 6, Newton establishes that this analogy is inherent in oral tradition and that the analogues function as interchangeable narrative components. John B. Vlahos in "Homer's *Odyssey,* Books 19 and 23: Early Recognition: A Solution to the Enigmas of Ivory and Horns, and the

Test of the Bed" tackles certain aspects of the *Odyssey* that have created problems for Homerists since the epics were composed. He first focuses on *Odyssey* 19 by posing two questions, "Why does Penelope ask Odysseus when he appears to her as a stranger to interpret a dream she supposedly had when the dream is self-interpreting?" and "Why does she decide to hold a contest with the bow, with her as the prize, at a time when she has been told that Odysseus is near?" For *Odyssey* 23 Vlahos asks, "What is the true purpose of the so-called test of the bed?" The answer he suggests for all three questions is that Penelope must already know the beggar to be her husband, Odysseus. Scott Richardson in "Conversation in the *Odyssey*" focuses on character conversation, which he claims tends toward "obfuscation rather than illumination." Focusing on Homer's language in the *Odyssey,* he illustrates that conversation in this epic is a game in which some play better than others, and playing the game properly requires not only a keen ability to convey meaning indirectly but also a sensitive awareness of what has been previously said. Conversation in the *Odyssey,* Richardson claims, creates a world characterized by distrust and uncertainty. Joel Christensen in "The End of Speeches and a Speech's End: Nestor, Diomedes, and the *telos muthôn*" turns back to the *Iliad* and offers a close reading of a crucial passage in *Iliad* 9 concerning the phrase *telos muthôn.* A clearer understanding of these two words, according to Christensen, enhances our understaning not only of this critical phrase, but more importantly of the dynamic of Homeric speech in general.

The second set of four essays turn from reading Homer's texts to Homer's influence on film. The first two contributions deal with Wolfgang Petersen's *Troy,* which has received a great deal of attention since its release in 2004 (see essays by Frederick Ahl, Alena Allen, Monica S. Cyrino, J. Lesley Fitton, Joachim Latacz, Robert J. Rabel, Stephen Scully, Kim Shahabudin, Jon Solomon, and Martin M. Winkler all in Winkler 2007; Hanna M. Roisman 2008). Jonathan S. Burgess's "Achilles' Heel: The Historicism of the Film *Troy*" argues that the film's weakness lies in its trying to portray a factual Trojan War rather than concentrating on the myth of the Trojan War. To navigate the film's uneasy negotiation of history and myth, Burgess concentrates on the motif of Achilles' heel in his death scene at the end of *Troy.* Charles C. Chiasson in "Redefining Homeric Heroism in Wolfgang Petersen's *Troy*" continues the discussion on the film by observing that by adding romantic love to heroism in battle and diminishing the power of the Homeric gods, the film intertwines the spheres of love and battle, which he believes are irreconcilable in the *Iliad.*

The final two articles in this collection turn to American classics and to genre films for Homeric influences. Critics and teachers of film have in recent years alluded to Homeric parallels in a number of films, including Preston Sturges's *Sullivan's Travels* (1942), Mervyn LeRoy's *Homecoming* (1948), Jean-Luc Godard's *Contempt* (1964), Stanley Kubrick's *2001: A Space Odyssey* (1968), Frank Perry's *The Swimmer* (1968), Barry Levinson's *The Natural* (1984), Lee David Zlotoff's *The Spitfire Grill* (1996), Victory Zunez's *Ulee's Gold* (1997), Joel Coen's *O Brother Where Art Thou?* (2000), Francis Ford Coppola's *Apocalypse Now Redux* (2001), and Anthony Minghella's *Cold Mountain* (2003). In "The *Odyssey* and Frank Capra's *It's a Wonderful Life,*" Bruce Louden emphasizes motifs shared by the *Odyssey* in one of the best known and loved American film classics. After tracing motifs such as the divine council, the hero's descent to the underworld, and *the vision,* Louden proceeds to demonstrate how *It's a Wonderful Life* Christianizes these mythical events to construct a distinctly American subgenre of myth. My own reading of a 1950s classic western film in "Reading *The Gunfighter* as Homeric Epic" examines the progress of the warrior through his pursuit of glory and his homecoming, comparing Henry King's *The Gunfighter* and Homer's two epics. It explores the themes of the hero's cunning, the destination, homecoming, and reunion in the *Odyssey,* and considers how the hero is condemned to glory, his self-recognition, and the roles of irony and fate in the *Iliad.*

Works Cited

Blundell, Mary Whitlock, and Kirk Ormand. 1997. "Western Values, or the People's Homer: Unforgiven as a Reading of the *Iliad.*" *Poetics Today* 18, no. 4 (Winter): 533–69.

Eckstein, Arthur M., and Peter Lehman, eds. 2004. *The Searchers; Essays and Reflections on John Ford's Classic Western.* Detroit: Wayne State University Press.

Goldhill, S. "*Naked* and *O Brother, Where Art Thou?* The Politics and Poetics of Epic Cinema." In *Homer in the Twentieth Centurty,* edited by B. Graziosi and E. Greenwood. Oxford: Oxford University Press, 2007.

Hall, Edith. *The Return of Ulysses; A Cultural History of Homer's* Odyssey. Baltimore: The Johns Hopkins University Press, 2008.

Homer. *The Iliad.* Trans. Herbert Jordan. Norman: Oklahoma University Press, 2008.

———. *The Odyssey of Homer*. Trans. Richmond Lattimore. 1965. Reprint. New York: Harper and Row, 1967.

———. *The Iliad of Homer*. Trans. Richmond Lattimore. 1951. Reprint. Chicago: The University of Chicago Press.

Raaflaub, K. A. "Homeric Society." In *A New Companion to Homer,* edited by I. Morris and B. Powell. Leiden: Brill, 1997.

Roisman, Hanna M. 2008. "Helen and the Power of Erotic Love: From Homeric Contemplation to Hollywood Fantasy." *College Literature* 35.4 (Fall): 127–50.

Shanower, Eric. *Age of Bronze* [Vol. 1, *A Thousand Ships,* Vol. 2, *Sacrifice,* Vol. 3, *Betrayal, Part One*]. Orange, CA: Image Comics, 2001.

Stanford. W. B. *The Ulysses Theme.* 1954. Reprint. Oxford: Blackwell, 1963.

Winkler, Martin M. "Classical Mythology and the Western Film." *Comparative Literature Studies* 22, no. 4 (Winter 1985): 517–40.

———. "Homeric kleos and the Western Film." *Syllecta Classica* 7: 43–54, 1996.

———. "The Trojan War on the Screen: An Annotated Filmography." In *Troy; From Homer's* Iliad *to Hollywood Epic,* edited by Martin M. Winkler. Oxford: Blackwell, 2007a.

———, ed. *Troy; From Homer's Iliad to Hollywood Epic.* Oxford: Blackwell, 2007b.

Appendix 1: A Selected List of Critical Works on Homer's Epics Since 2000

Adams, David. *Colonial Odysseys; Empire and Epic in the Modernist Novel.* Ithaca, NY: Cornell University Press, 2003.

Alden, Maureen. *Homer beside Himself; Para-Narratives in* The Iliad. Oxford: Oxford University Press, 2000.

Beck, Deborah. *Homeric Conversation.* Cambridge: Harvard University Press, 2005.

Benardete, Seth. *Achilles and Hector; The Homeric Hero.* South Bend, IN: St. Augustine's Press, 2005.

Beye, Charles Rowan. *Odysseus: A Life.* New York: Hyperion, 2004.

Brann, Eva. *Homeric Moments; Clues to Delight in Reading the* Odyssey. Philadelphia: Paul Dry Books, 2002.

Bryce, Trevor. *The Trojans and Their Neighbours.* New York: Routledge, 2006.

Buchan, Mark. *The Limits of Heroism; Homer and the Ethics of Reading.* Ann Arbor: The University of Michigan Press, 2004.

Burgess, Jonathan S. *The Tradition of the Trojan War in Homer and the Epic Cycle.* The Johns Hopkins University Press, 2001.

———. *The Death and Afterlife of Achilles.* Baltimore: The Johns Hopkins University Press, 2008.

Cairns, Douglas L., ed. *Oxford Readings in Homer's* Iliad. Oxford: Oxford University Press, 2001.

Castleden, Rodney. *The Attack on Troy.* Barnsley, England: Pen & Sword, 2006.

Dalby, Andrew. *Rediscovering Homer; Inside the Origins of the Epic.* New York: Norton, 2006.

de Jong, Irene. *A Narratological Commentary on* The Odyssey. Cambridge: Cambridge University Press, 2001.

———. *Narrators and Focalizers; The Presentation of the Story in* The Iliad. 2nd ed. 1987. Reprint. London: Bristol Classical Press, 2004.

Dougherty, Carol. *The Raft of Odysseus; The Ethnographic Imagination of Homer's* Odyssey. Oxford: Oxford University Press, 2001.

duBois, Page. *Trojan Horses; Saving the Classics from Conservatives.* New York: New York University Press, 2001.

Due, Casey. *Homeric Variations on a Lament by Briseis.* Lanham, MD: Rowman & Littlefield, 2002.

Finkelberg, Margalit, and Guy G. Stroumsa. *Homer, the Bible and Beyond; Literary and Religious Canons in the Ancient World.* Leiden: Brill, 2003.

Foley, John Miles, ed. *A Companion to Ancient Epic.* Oxford: Blackwell, 2005.

Fowler, Robert, ed. *The Cambridge Companion to Homer.* Cambridge: Cambridge University Press, 2004.

Friedrich, Wolf-Hartmut. *Wounding and Death in* The Iliad. Trans. Peter Jones and Gabriele Wright. London: Duckworth, 2003.

Goldberg, Michael J. *Travels with Odysseus; Uncommon Wisdom from Homer's* Odyssey. Tempe, AZ: Circe's Island Press, 2005.

Gotshalk, Richard. *Homer and Hesiod, Myth and Philosophy.* Lanham, MD: University Press of America, 2000.

Graziosi, Barbara. *Inventing Homer; The Early Reception of Epic.* Cambridge: Cambridge University Press, 2002.

Graziosi, Barbara, and Johannes Haubold. *Homer: The Resonance of Epic.* London: Duckworth, 2005.

Graziosi, Barbara, and Emily Greenwood. *Homer in the Twentieth Century; Between World Literature and the Western Canon.* Oxford: Oxford University Press, 2007.

Hall, Edith. *The Return of Ulysses; A Cultural History of Homer's* Odyssey. Baltimore: The Johns Hopkins University Press, 2008.

Hammer, Dean. The Iliad *as Politics; The Performance of Political Thought.* Norman: University of Oklahoma Press, 2002.

Hartog, François. *Memories of Odysseus; Frontier Tales from Ancient Greece.* Trans. Janet Lloyd. Chicago: The University of Chicago Press, 2001.

Haubold, Johannes. *Homer's People; Epic Poetry and Social Formation.* Cambridge: Cambridge University Press, 2000.

Heitman, Richard. *Taking Her Seriously; Penelope and the Plot of Homer's* Odyssey. Ann Arbor: The University of Michigan Press, 2005.

Holoka, James P., ed. and trans. *Simone Weil's The Iliad or the Poems of Force; A Critical Edition.* New York: Peter Lang, 2003.

Huler, Scott. *No-Man's Lands; One Man's Odyssey through the* Odyssey. New York: Crown, 2008.

Jenkyns, Richard. *Classical Epic; Homer and Virgil.* London: Bristol Classical Press, 2004.

Johnsons, Claudia Durst, and Vernon Johnson. *Understanding* The Odyssey. Westport, CT: Greenwood Press, 2003.

Kahane, Ahuvia. *Diachronic Dialogues; Authority and Continuity in Homer and the Homeric Tradition.* Lanham, MD: Rowman & Littlefield, 2005.

Kim, Jinyo. *The Pity of Achilles; Oral Style and the Unity of* The Iliad. Lanham, MD: Rowman & Littlefield, 2000.

Kitts, Margo. *Sanctified Violence in Homeric Society; Oath-Making Rituals and Narrative in the* Iliad. Cambridge: Cambridge University Press, 2005.

Latacz, Joachim. *Troy and Homer; Towards a Solution of an Old Mystery.* Oxford: Oxford University Press, 2001.

Lord, Albert B. *The Singer of Tales,* edited by Stephen Mitchell and Gregory Nagy. 2nd ed. Cambridge, MA: Harvard University Press, 2000.

Louden, Bruce. The Iliad; *Structure, Myth, and Meaning.* Baltimore: The Johns Hopkins University Press, 2006.

Lowenstam, Steven. *As Witnessed by Images: The Trojan War Tradition in Greek and Etruscan Art.* Baltimore: The Johns Hopkins University Press, 2008.

MacDonald, Dennis R. *The Homeric Epics and the Gospel of Mark.* New Haven: Yale University Press, 2000.

———. *Does the New Testament Imitate Homer?; Four Cases from the Acts of the Apostles.* New Haven: Yale University Press, 2003.

Manguel, Alberto. *Homer's* The Iliad *and* The Odyssey; A Biography. New York: Atlantic Monthly Press, 2007.

Maronitis, D. N. *Homeric Megathemes; War-Homilia-Homecoming.* Translated by David Connolly. Lanham, MD: Lexington Books, 2004.

Michelakis, Pantelis. *Achilles in Greek Tragedy.* Cambridge: Cambridge University Press, 2002.

Miller, Dean A. *The Epic Hero.* Baltimore: The Johns Hopkins University Press, 2000.

Minchin, Elizabeth. *Homer and the Resources of Memory; Some Applications of Cognitive Theory to* The Iliad *and* The Odyssey. Oxford: Oxford University Press, 2001.

———. *Homeric Voices; Discourse, Memory, Gender.* Oxford: Oxford University Press, 2007.

Morrison, James. *A Companion to Homer's* Odyssey. Westport, CT: Greenwood Press, 2003.

Nagy, Gregory. *Homeric Responses.* Austin: University of Texas Press, 2003.

———. *Homer's Text and Language.* Urbana: University of Illinois Press, 2004.

Powell, Barry B. *Homer.* 2nd ed. Oxford: Blackwell, 2007.

Price Salinas, Roberto. *Homeric Whispers.* San Jerónimo Lídice, Mexico: Scylax Press, 2006.

Rabel, Robert J., ed. *Approaches to Homer; Ancient and Modern.* Swansea: The Classical Press of Wales, 2005.

Schmidt, Michael. *The First Poets; Lives of the Ancient Greek Poets.* New York: Knopf, 2005.

Scodel, Ruth. *Listening to Homer; Tradition, Narrative and Audience.* Ann Arbor: The University of Michigan Press, 2002.

Shay, Jonathan. *Odysseus in America; Combat Trauma and the Trials of Homecoming.* New York: Scribner, 2002.

Strauss, Barry. *The Trojan War; A New History*. New York: Simon & Schuster, 2006.

Tatum, James. *The Mourner's Song; War and Remembrance from* The Iliad *to Vietnam*. Chicago. The University of Chicago Press, 2003.

Thomas, Carol G., and Craig Conant. *The Trojan War*. Norman: University of Oklahoma Press, 2005.

Thompson, Diane P. *The Trojan War; Literature and Legends from the Bronze Age to the Present*. Jefferson, NC: McFarland, 2004.

Vinci, Felice. *The Baltic Origins of Homer's Epic Tales*. Rochester, VT: Inner Traditions, 2006.

Walsh, Thomas R. *Fighting Words and Feuding Words; Anger and the Homeric Poems*. Lanham, MD: Lexington Books, 2005.

Weil, Simone, and Rachel Bespaloff. *War and* The Iliad. Translated by Mary McCarthy. New York: NYRB, 2005.

Willmott, Jo. *The Moods of Homeric Greek*. Cambridge: Cambridge University Press, 2007.

Wilson, Donna F. *Ransom, Revenge, and Heroic Identity in* The Iliad. Cambridge: Cambridge University Press, 2002.

Appendix 2: English Translations of Homer's *The Iliad* and *The Odyssey* in Circulation

The Iliad. Translated by E. V. Rieu. New York: Penguin. 1950.

The Iliad of Homer. Translated by Richmond Lattimore. Chicago: The University of Chicago Press. 1951.

The Odyssey of Homer. Translated by T. E. Shaw. 1935. Reprint. Oxford: Oxford University Press. 1959.

The Odyssey. Translated by W. H. D. Rouse. 1937. Reprint. New York: Mentor. 1960.

The Iliad. Translated by W.H. D. Rouse. 1938. Reprint. New York: Mentor. 1964.

The Odyssey of Homer. Translated by Richmond Lattimore. New York: Harper & Row, 1965.

The Odyssey. Transated by S. H. Butcher and Andrew Lang. 1950. Reprint. New York: The Modern Library. 1967a.

The Odyssey. Translated by Albert Cook. New York: W. W. Norton. 1967b.

The Odyssey of Homer. Translated by George Herbert Palmer. 1962. Reprint. New York: Bantam. 1971a.

The Odyssey. Translated by E. V. Rieu, 1946. Reprint. New York: Penguin. 1971b.

The Iliad of Homer. Translated by Alston Hurd Chase and William G. Perry, Jr. 1950. Reprint. New York: Bantam, 1972.

The Odyssey of Homer. Translated by Ennis Rees. 1960. Reprint. Indianapolis: Bobbs-Merrill. 1977.

The Iliad of Homer. Translated by I.A. Richards. 1950. Reprint. New York: W. W. Norton. 1978.

The Odyssey. Translated by Walter Shewring. Oxford: Oxford University Press, 1980.

The Iliad. Translated by Martin Hammond. New York: Penguin, 1987.

The Iliad. Translated by Robert Fagles. New York: Penguin. 1990a.

The Odyssey of Homer. Translated by Allen Mandelbaum. New York: Bantam. 1990b.

The Iliad of Homer. Translated by Ennis Rees. 1963. Reprint. Oxford: Oxford University Press, 1991.

The Odyssey. Translated by Samuel Butler, Reprint. New York: Barnes & Noble, 1993.

The Iliad. Translated by Michael Reck. New York: HarperCollins, 1994.

The Iliad. Translated Samuel Butler. 1942. Reprint. New York: Barnes & Noble. 1995.

The Odyssey. Translated by William Cowper. 1910. Reprint. London. J. M. Dent. 1996a.

The Odyssey. Translated by Robert Fagles. New York: Penguin. 1996b.

The Iliad of Homer. Translated by Alexander Pope. 1715–20. Reprint, New York: Penguin. 1996c.

Iliad. Translated by Stanley Lombardo. Indianapolis: Hackett, NJ: 1997.

Chapman's Homer; The Iliad. 1611. Reprint. Princeton, NJ: Princeton University Press, 1998a.

The Odyssey. Translated by Robert Fitzgerald. 1961. Reprint. New York: Farrar, Straus, Giroux. 1998b.

The Odyssey. Translated by Martin Hammond. London: Duckworth. 2000a.

The Odyssey. Translated by Stanley Lombardo. Indianapolis: Hackett. 2000b.

The Odyssey. Translated by R. L. Eickhoff. New York: Tom Doherty, 2001.

The Odyssey. Translated by Rodney Merrill. Ann Arbor: University of Michigan Press, 2002.

The Iliad. Translated by Robert Fitzgerald. 1974. Reprint. New York: Farrar, Straus, Giroux, 2004a.

The Odyssey. Translated by Edward McCrorie. Baltimore: The Johns Hopkins University Press, 2004b.

Iliad. Translated by Ian Johnson. Arlington, VA: Richer Resources, 2006a.

Odyssey. Translated by Ian Johnson. Arlington, VA: Richer Resources, 2006b.

The Iliad. Translated by Rodney Merrill. Ann Arbor: University of Michigan Press, 2007.

The Iliad. Translated by Herbert Jordan. Norman: Oklahoma University Press, 2008.

Appendix 3: A Selected List of Works of Fiction and Nonfiction since 2000 influenced by Homer's Epics

Atwood, Magaret. *The Penelopiad.* New York: Canongate, 2005.

Baricco, Alessandro. *An Iliad.* Translated by Ann Goldstein. New York: Alfred A. Knopf, 2006.

Barton, John. *Tantalus.* London: Oberon, 2000.

Clarke, Lindsay. *The War at Troy.* New York: St. Martin's Press, 2004.

———. *The Return from Troy*. New York: HarperCollins, 2005.

Cook, Elizabeth. *Achilles*. New York: Picador, 2001.

Gemmell, David. *Troy; Lord of the Silver Bow*. New York: Ballantine Books, 2005.

———. *Troy; Shield of Thunder*. New York: Ballantine Books, 2006.

———. *Troy; Fall of Kings*. New York: Ballantine Books, 2007.

George, Margaret. *Helen of Troy*. New York: Viking, 2006.

Geras, Adele. *Troy*. New York: Harcourt, 2000.

Hand, Judith. *The Amazon Warrior; a Novel of Ancient Troy*. New York: TOR, 2004.

Hughes, Bettany. *Helen of Troy; Goddess, Princess, Whore*. New York: Knopf, 2005.

Manfredi, Valerio Massimo. *The Talisman of Troy*. Translated by Christine Feddersen-Manfredi. New York: Pan Books, 2004.

Mason, Zachary. *The Lost Books of the Odyssey*. Buffalo, NY: Starcherone Books, 2007.

Rawlings, Jane. *The Penelopeia; A Novel in Verse*. Boston: David R. Godine, 2003.

Shanower, Eric. *Age of Bronze* Vol. 1. *A Thousand Ships;* Vol. 2 *Sacrifice;* Vol. 3. *Betrayal, Part One*. Orange, CA: Image Comics, 2001.

Simmons, Dan. *Ilium*. New York: HarperCollins, 2003.

———. *Olympos*. New York: HaperCollins, 2005.

Tobin, Greg. *The Siege of Troy*. NY: TOR, 2004.

Unsworth, Barry. *The Songs of the Kings*. New York: Doubleday, 2003.

Zimmerman, Mary. *The Odyssey*. Evanston, IL: Northwestern University Press, 2006.

READING HOMER

Homer as History: Greeks and Others in a Dark Age

Shawn Ross

Understanding that Homeric epic is the product of a long-standing oral tradition facilitates its use as a source for early Greek history. Oral tradition constantly evolves as poets interact with their audiences, retaining only such intangible elements of culture and society as remain relevant to its contemporary world. Although Homeric epic is of limited utility for understanding the Late Bronze Age, the *Iliad* and *Odyssey* constitute an invaluable source for the beliefs, institutions, and ideologies of the eighth century B.C. Homeric epic illuminates, for example, the beginnings of Panhellenism. Built through the extension of local identities, proto-Panhellenism was aggregative in nature. Yet it was oppositional in origin, spurred by intensifying contact between Greeks and the outside world. Homeric proto-Panhellenism reflected the cosmopolitan worldview of eighth century elites at the expense of the more parochial outlook of "middling farmers" like Hesiod. Such insights into the "Dark Age" would be impossible without recourse to Homeric epic as a historical source.

HOMER'S POETRY HAS BEEN VIEWED THROUGH MANY LENSES. IT HAS BEEN interpreted as a work of literature, analyzed as the end product of an ancient oral tradition, searched for insights into early Greek political, religious, or philosophical ideas. Deconstructed, reenvisioned, critiqued, or championed, the *Iliad* and *Odyssey* have been represented and retold, have fostered debate over the contents of the "Western" canon, and have been construed as an origin or archetype for modern ideas, ideals, and ideologies. But what use is Homer to the historian (or at least the historically minded student or scholar of the ancient world)? Most historians, after all, still seek to use texts to understand real societies beyond the bounds of their texts. It is not enough for the historian to treat the Homeric epics as self-contained artifacts, and the historian is, perhaps, rather more constrained than the literary critic in her interpretation—if not by authorial intent, then at least by the necessity of fitting the epics into a picture that contains other elements: nearly contemporary texts like Hesiod, later (classical) ideas about early Greece, comparative studies of analogous cultures, material evidence provided by archaeology.

At first the task seems daunting. Homer may have thought that he was singing about his own past, but the epics were not written as historical accounts. They were not initially written at all. As they were the product of an ancient (even in the eighth century B.C.E.) oral tradition, scholars agree on neither a date for the stabilization of the Homeric texts as we have them today, nor the date for any society that might be depicted in the epics. Even the very existence of a coherent, historical society underlying the epics remains in dispute. The epics reached more or less their present form at the very end of the an era still often referred to as the Greek "Dark Age," because of both the relative poverty of its material culture and, of more immediate concern, the lack of historical sources to illuminate it ("Dark Age" is a problematic term; *Early Iron Age* will be used here to describe the period ca. 1150–750; cf. Dickinson 2006, introduction, esp. 6–7, 12). Since history, narrowly defined, is the study of written texts, how can the historian study the history of a nonliterate culture at all? Despite the centrality of the Homeric epics to the canon of Western literature—not to mention the importance of the Early Iron Age as a formative period for Greek culture—relatively few *historians* study the Homeric world of the Early Iron Age and early archaic period (ca. 750–479 B.C.E,), especially compared with later eras of Greek history.

Still, as a graduate student I was drawn to Homer and his world. The challenge and novelty of studying early Greece as a historian, combined with the relative neglect and potential of the period, led me to believe that a young historian could still make a real contribution to its understanding in the closing years of the twentieth century. In the opening decade of the twenty-first, I have found that such attractions still draw students to the historical study of the Homeric poems. History, in my view, also offers a unique space to combine the insights of other disciplines—philology, oral theory, anthropology, archaeology, and others—to reconstruct and interpret the society behind the epics. Indeed, the sources (written and material) for the period are scant and problematic enough to require an interdisciplinary approach.

Sophisticated and responsible use of the Homeric epics as historical sources, however, demands a coherent and systematic methodology. The historian must demonstrate that the epics reflect a coherent, historical society external to the poems themselves. Once the basic historicity of Homeric society has been established, two chronological questions must be answered: when did the poems reach the form they take today, and when did the society depicted in the poems exist? Third, interpretation of the epics depends upon understanding the implications of their origin and nature as poetry produced by a long-standing oral tradition. Next, in order to contextualize Homeric epic, other early Greek literature (and traditions preserved in later sources) must be taken into account. Finally, archaeology must be considered, and material evidence integrated with the written—a fraught but extremely important task, especially considering that archaeology is almost certainly the only remaining source of genuinely new information about the world of Homer. Each component of a provisional historical methodology, moreover, will interlock with the others. The origin of the poems in an oral tradition, comparison with other early Greek poetry, and an understanding of material culture, for example, all contribute to dating the epics and the society that produced them. Even considered in isolation each component of the methodology I propose here probably stirs controversy; many will disagree with many of its individual elements, let alone the entire program. Still, I hope to demonstrate that each component is defensible, and that together they yield a reasonable approach to the study of the Homeric epics as history. Whether or not I succeed in making a convincing case, ongoing controversy over fundamental aspects of historical interpretation adds excitement to the study of the epics.

The Historicity and Date of Homeric Society

The rediscovery of Late Bronze Age, "Mycenaean" civilization in the late nineteenth century, initiated by Schliemann's excavations at Troy and Mycenae, forced archaeologists, philologists, and historians to face the possibility that Homer would have to be taken seriously as a historical source (Dickinson 1994, 1). In the early twentieth century, Homeric society was often thought to reflect realities of the Late Bronze Age in which the poems are set (Morris 1986, 94–95). By the early 1950s, however, such an interpretation had fallen out of favor. Dorothea Gray, for instance, could begin an article on metalworking in Homeric epic with an exasperated complaint that "belief in an historical 'Homeric Society' dies hard" (1954, 1).[1]

Two developments in the 1950s radically transformed the debate. First, Michael Ventris and John Chadwick deciphered the Late Bronze Age Greek script known as Linear B (Ventris and Chadwick 1973; Chadwick 1968). The tablets, produced by a small class of literate scribes, revealed centralized palace-states similar in certain respects to those of the contemporary Near East. Mycenaean civilization—excepting a few personal and place-names also occurring in Homer—bore little resemblance to the nonliterate, heroic world of the epics. Second, Moses Finley revolutionized the study of Homeric society with his publication of *The World of Odysseus.* Influenced by the historical sociology of the Frankfurt school and the economic anthropology of Karl Polanyi, Finley systematically analyzed the structures, institutions, customs, and attitudes of the society depicted in Homer (1978; Cartledge 1994). Finley's multifaceted examination led him to conclude that although the epics contain occasional anachronisms, "essentially the picture offered by the poems of the society and its system of values is a coherent one" (1978, 48). Finley, observing that the epics lack many aspects of later Greek society and culture, dates Odysseus' world to the tenth and ninth centuries B.C. (1978, 48; Morris 1986, 96–97).[2]

Finley's analysis did not convince everyone. Instead, the *World of Odysseus* has inspired a half-century of debate between supporters and opponents of a "unified and historical Homeric society" (Snodgrass 2006, 173–74). Opponents continue to argue, as did Gray, that the poems are a hopelessly tangled amalgam, "a mixture of practices, derived from a diversity of historical sources," which cannot be used to reconstruct a coherent society since it contains elements spanning from at least the thirteenth through the eighth centuries B.C. (2006, 180). Two examples will suffice. In the important article "A Homeric Society?" first published in 1974, Anthony Snodgrass answers Finley's anthropological arguments with a thorough analysis of inheritance, kinship, and marriage patterns. He finds two incompatible systems ("diverging devolution" versus "homogeneous devolution") improbably operating alongside one another in the epics. More recently, in an important 2006 discussion of the origins of city-state culture in Greece, Morgens Hansen complains that the cities described in the Homeric epics contain both palaces and temples (which never coexisted in any real Greek city), that warriors use physical objects (such as weapons) from a variety of periods, and that catalogues of place-names list both Mycenaean and later cities, thus yielding a muddled geography (2006, 42–43). Hansen sees a consensus building around the historicity of Homeric society but excuses himself from it, dissenting from "prevailing ideas of a 'Homeric Society' understood as a society of the early Iron Age described in the Homeric epics with an astonishing consistency and no disturbing anachronisms of any significance" (43). In an introduction to the 2006 reprinting of his 1974 article, Snodgrass sees no reason to modify his earlier skepticism and predicts that "the controversy [over the historicity of Homeric society] is one that will long continue" (2006, 174; cf. Dickinson 2006, 240, who is also skeptical of the value of the poems to the historian).

It is unnecessary to rehearse here specific responses that supporters of a coherent, historical Homeric society might make to the specific criticisms noted.[3] The best argument defending the existence of such a society depends not upon refuting alleged inconsistencies one by one, but upon asserting the implications of two facts: (1) that the Homeric epics are the product of an oral tradition, and (2) that the oral tradition behind the epics is comparable to oral epic poetry as it has been observed by anthropologists and historians elsewhere. If these two points hold true of the Homeric epics, then by their very nature they must depict—within limits and with certain predictable distortions—a unified and historical Homeric society (Morris 1986; Vansina 1985).

Just as the oral nature of Homeric epic is critical to a full appreciation of its structure and language (Foley 2007), it is also the key to using Homer as a historical source. In the first half of the twentieth century, Milman Parry, Alfred Lord, and their successors demonstrated conclusively that the Homeric epics are the product of an oral tradition. Since then, the idea that the poem arose from an oral tradition has underpinned most scholarly work concerning Homer.[4] This assumption is accepted even by critics of a historical Homeric society (e.g., Kirk 1962; Hansen 2006). Such critics usually deemphasize the strong comparative evidence by focusing on specific internal contradictions within the epics (as was the case with Snodgrass, mentioned previously).[5] The nature of oral epic poetry itself, however, explains many of these supposed inconsistencies, while those that remain are not significant enough to dismiss the weight of comparative evidence, which roots oral tradition firmly in the society that produces it.

Oral Tradition as History

Jan Vansina, in a comparative study of oral traditions, provides perhaps the best road-map for the use of Homeric epic as a historical source.[6] Vansina evaluates the typical origin and evolution of oral information, from eyewitness accounts of events, situations, and people to rich, fully mature traditions. Recognizing the diversity within oral tradition, he also discusses the characteristics of its various genres, from historical gossip to epic poetry.

The most important aspect of oral tradition in general and epic poetry in particular is that (with very few and limited exceptions) they are not memorized speech, repeated with little or no change generation after generation.[7] Instead, "oral tradition" represents a dynamic process, with stories or poems composed anew during each retelling or performance (Vansina 1985, 13–26; 33–55; Morris 1986, 83–86). Even a genre like epic poetry, which is supposed to be "true" in a way that prevents its contents from being altered at will by the poet changes continually (Vansina 1985, 83–84; Morris 1986, 89). Indeed, the fact that epic poetry makes extensive use of interchangeable formulaic elements ranging from the half-line noun-epithet names ("swift-footed Akhilleus") to stereotyped scenes (multiple-line descriptions of feasts or laments) to set story patterns (the return of the hero) appears to induce greater variability of content from one telling to the next when compared to orally transmitted prose accounts of the past (Foley 2007, 9–13; Vansina 1985, 52–54).[8] The formulaic elements of epic poetry can be rearranged almost endlessly, and thus contribute to the process of composition in performance, facilitating evolution of the poems over time.

Oral traditions are ever-changing. They convey and distort information over time in peculiar, but predicable ways. Oral traditions tend to have a particular shape, a three-tiered structure resembling an hourglass, common to diverse traditions across many societies (although invisible to participants in the tradition). The three sections of this hourglass are (1) a mythological, timeless past; (2) a "floating gap," usually two to three generations in the past; (3) a recent, historically bound period. For oral societies, "Historical consciousness works on only two registers: time of origin and recent times," separated by the floating gap (Vansina 1985, 24). Such a shape can be mapped onto the Greeks' view of their own past. In his synopsis of the Greek view of their own preclassical past, Dickinson observes that after the "vividly described" age of heroes, "there followed an ill-defined period about which virtually nothing was reported, which blended . . . into the period about which some information was preserved" (2006, 1).[9] Within the Greek oral tradition, the Homeric epics are set in the mythological past—what Hesiod, composing his own poetry circa 700 B.C.E., designated as the "Heroic Age"—yet they are profoundly affected by the recent period (Vansina 1985, 22–24; 168–69). Perhaps the latest major event assimilated back to the heroic age is the initiation of the Ionian migration in the eleventh century B.C.E. Most of the Early Iron Age falls into the floating gap, leaving bare genealogies like the Spartan king lists found in Herodotus (2.145.2; 7.204; 8.131.2; cf. Morris 1986, 92; Dickinson 2006, 11–12). Information begins to regain detail again in the eighth century with, admittedly hazy, events such as the first Olympic games, the Lelantine War, the Argive conquest of Asine, the First Messenian War, and the foundation of the earliest western Greek colonies, all of which Hesiod would have placed in his own "Age of Iron" rather than the heroic age (Dickinson 1–2, 11–12). Not coincidently, by about the third or fourth decade of the eighth century, the Greeks had adopted writing from the Phoenicians, and theirs was no longer a purely oral culture.

The mythological, timeless past that constitutes the age of origins within an oral tradition differs fundamentally from the present. Rich in detail and texture, stories about this age provide explanations of origin and may serve to validate or justify the bases of existing society (Vansina 1985, 22–23).[10] Such stories may contain kernels of fact reflecting once-extant people, events, or situations, incorporated into them as those events receded beyond the limit of a given society's horizon of chronological reckoning (24–29). Any seemingly genuine information, however, from such mythological tales must be viewed, at best, as data out of context, like an archaeological artifact of unknown provenance (examples from Homeric epic might include the presence of cities named Mycenae and Troy and the fact that the former fought a war against the latter). Decontexualized myths and legends from the age of origins are most useful to the historian as sources of considerable information about normative values, accepted beliefs, and general outlook at the time the tales are retold—sometimes for an entire community, sometimes for a particular group or class within that culture (31–32; chapter 4). Although epics like the *Iliad* and *Odyssey* may appear to have a "historical dimension," supplying a plausible narrative of events set within an internally consistent chronological framework, such coherence is illusory. They are part of the timeless, mythological age of origins common to oral traditions and as a result convey less information about any events from the distant past than they do about "existing situations in a recent past" (25).

Oral traditions tend to proceed from this richly detailed mythological age to the "floating gap," an ill-defined era when only a few names or a bare genealogy can be given, perhaps with some uncertainty. This hiatus gradually advances with the passage of generations. Often, it is compressed into one or two generations that separate the recent past from the age of origins (although not in the case of Greek legend, which recognizes a significant passage of time between the heroic age and the Homer's day, if leaving it short on detail). Sometimes, the floating gap is depicted as a normative period, a repetitive, cyclical, or static middle when society worked properly based upon models established in the mythological past; the middle period becomes a time when little of interest happened worth telling, when society functioned without the strains and conflicts often associated with the recent past in oral traditions. Whether the floating gap is compressed or idealized, the society producing the oral tradition is rarely conscious of its existence, although later, literate Greek historians were more troubled by it. For the historian, the gap might best be viewed not as a middle period, but rather as a reference to the capacity of different cultures to reckon time. Looking backward, beyond a certain time depth a horizon is met beyond which chronology can no longer be kept, when accounts begin to fuse and are ultimately forgotten or thrown back into the mythological past.[11]

Looking at the third and most recent tier of the past, in recent times oral traditions begin to supply more information again, tapering off as one looks backward toward the floating gap. Oral traditions about the recent period may be superficially similar to those about the age of origins, containing a wealth of seeming-plausible detail, but the former retain a chronological framework and can be used more directly by the historian. Generally speaking, the recent period may extend about three generations into the past, perhaps eighty to one hundred years at most (about as far as the stories told to the eldest living members of a community by their parents or grandparents when they were children), often less. Even within this horizon, however, a chain of transmission exists for all but the most recent events. Vansina likens the process of oral tradition after the floating gap to a succession of historical documents, all lost but the last. Just as each generation of historians reinterprets the past according to the needs and dilemmas of the present, each generation of storytellers reinterprets the received tradition so that it better speaks to contemporary listeners. A single line of transmission, however, does not exist, as it may in a manuscript tradition. Instead, the product of an oral tradition results from stories being told by many people to many people; it is communal, continuous, and dynamic. Compared with the age of origins, which establishes norms and values, or the static, properly functioning society of the floating gap, the recent past is often depicted as a time of change, decline, or tumult (Vansina 23–29).[12] Even though the epic tradition is set in the mythological past before the floating gap, it bears the imprint of recent times, as will be discussed later.

There are exceptions to the dynamic and relentlessly modernizing nature of oral tradition, its gradual, unconscious, but inexorable evolution from generation to generation. Oral traditions assimilate, forget, and modify different types of information at different rates. Things with external referents, such as physical objects, buildings, and places, may become fossilized within the oral tradition. The boars'-tusk helmet from the *Iliad* is attested in the Bronze Age archaeological record. Bronze Age sites like Mycenae are more prominent in Homer than their eighth century status would suggest. Early Iron Age and archaic heroons are often intentionally associated with Bronze Age sites (Hope, Simpson, and Lazenby 1970; Morris 1986, 89; Bennet 1997; Snodgrass 2006). Persons (the heroes of the epics, many of whom have names found in the Linear B texts or Hittite archives), events (like the Trojan War itself), and sometimes even the shell of political or social units (the name and approximate extent of kingdoms or kinship groups, like Agamemnon's domains as described in the *Iliad*) may also become embedded in an oral tradition, slipping beyond the horizon of living memory and assimilated into the age of origins (Vansina 1985, 10–11; 17–18; 24; Morris 1986, 89–91).[13] Finally, it is not impossible that under certain circumstances practices and ceremonies surrounding common occurrences like marriage, sacrifice, or burial might be retained in an oral tradition after they have changed in the broader society. Such retention is conceivable because audiences are familiar with analogous, contemporary events and could imagine similar events occuring differently in the distant past (Morris 1986, 90). Although I am skeptical about the frequency of this final class of retention, I concede that it may occur.[14]

Epic poetry is, moreover, a subclass of oral tradition accompanied by its own complications. Not only is it set entirely in the mythological past before the floating gap, but it also commonly displays the phenomenon of "epic distance" (Morris 1986, 89–91). Examples of epic distance in Homer include retaining and indeed highlighting the ancient physical objects and geography present in the oral tradition (see previous discussion), ignoring or suppressing (relatively) "modern" technological or social innovations (like iron weapons or the rise of the polis), using archaic or archaizing language, or asserting the categorical superiority of the heroes inhabiting this lost world (like Diomedes, who "easily" picks up a stone no two men "as they are today" could lift; Hom. *Il.* 5.303–04). Epic distance thus amplifies the general tendency of oral traditions to characterize the recent past and present as a period of decline. Homer assures his audience that everything in his epic poetry is bigger, better, and richer than things in the contemporary world, even inventing fantastic analogues to everyday objects (like the impossible "big round shield" at *Il.* 6.117–18; Van Wees 1992, 17–21). Hesiod's description of the "Ages of Man" perhaps best captures the intersection of epic distance and narratives of decline and is worth quoting at length:

> But when earth had covered [the third] generation [of Man] also, Zeus the son of Cronos made yet another, the fourth, upon the fruitful earth, which was nobler and more righteous, a god-like race of hero-men who are called demi-gods, the race before our own, throughout the boundless earth. Grim war and dread battle destroyed a part of them, some in the land of Cadmus at seven-gated Thebe . . . and some, when it had brought them in ships over the great sea gulf to Troy for rich-haired Helen's sake: there death's end enshrouded a part of them. But to the other father Zeus . . . gave a living and an abode apart from men . . . and they live untouched by sorrow in the islands of the blessed along the shore of the deep swirling Ocean, happy heroes for whom the grain-giving earth bears honey-sweet fruit flourishing thrice a year . . . and these last equally have honour and glory.
>
> And again far-seeing Zeus made yet another generation, the fifth, of men who are upon the bounteous earth.
>
> Thereafter, would that I were not among the men of the fifth genera-

> tion, but either had died before or been born afterwards. For now truly is a race of iron, and men never rest from labour and sorrow by day, and from perishing by night; and the gods shall lay sore trouble upon them. (*Works and Days* 156–78)[15]

Not only does this passage from Hesiod vividly illustrate the gulf separating poet and audience from the people of the heroic age, but it demonstrates that, despite the *Iliad*'s veneer of plausibility, the Trojan War is set firmly in the mythological past.[16] Epic distance may encourage retention of authentic but "old-fashioned" features of society to signal that events are taking place in the distant past, but it may also lead the poet to craft fantastic scenarios, in order to make the epic world feel different from and better than recent times, an era peopled by a "a god-like race of hero-men." As a result, it is often difficult to disentangle poetic invention from genuine, but archaic, information retained in the service of epic distance.[17]

Moreover, the ability of oral tradition to preserve certain types of information for long periods (either as a result of external referents stabilizing the tradition, or archaizing to produce epic distance) must be balanced against the extent to which such traditions are relentlessly modernizing. As discussed, oral traditions are dynamic, constantly changing through recomposition; as a result, they retain accurate details, chronological arrangements, and cause-and-effect relationships for only about three generations at most. After that, events and people slip out of historical time, traverse the floating gap, and reappear as part of the mythological past, taking with them some of their objects, homes, and other paraphernalia with external referents that oral tradition is good at remembering. More abstract information about institutions, practices, and values is, however, forgotten or transformed if it does not remain rooted in contemporary culture and society: "It would perhaps be an exaggeration to say that non-literate societies float in a kind of perpetual present, but it does seem to be the case that ideas that are no longer relevant to the present rapidly disappear from oral tradition" (Morris 1985, 87). Indeed, abstract information that does remain relevant to the contemporary world will not only persist in stories about the recent past, but will also imprint itself onto stories about the age of origins, before the floating gap. Oral poets, interacting with their audiences, continually reconfigure the heroic past in light of the contemporary world as they recompose their songs in each performance. The ideals, values, social structures, group identity, political practices, and other contours of the present continually transform the mythological past. At most, extinct institutions, practices, or values remembered by the eldest members of the poet's audience may be retained, often as part of the poet's attempt to provide epic distance. Oral tradition reveals the world and the worldview of the community that creates it; is part of the present even when it purports to describe the distant past (Vansina 1985, 24; 102–07; 114–23; 133–36; Morris 1986, 86–88).

In short, although oral traditions are capable of preserving certain types of information for extended periods, their content is also subject to rapid change as performers innovate and stories are retold in a way that makes sense to contemporary audiences. On the one hand, things with external referents become poetic artifacts that may endure for centuries. On the other hand, storytellers will quickly drop intangible aspects of society that no longer make sense to their audience. Meanwhile, abstract ideas and conditions relevant to the present imprint themselves on the mythic past. The modernizing tendency is somewhat tempered as the poet engages in intentional archaizing, ignoring or suppressing recent developments in society and retaining (but perhaps misinterpreting) defunct institutions described to him by the eldest members of his audience.[18] This process does not produce an unworkable amalgam, but instead creates poems that in general come to reflect contemporary near-society while retaining anachronistic names, places, and objects (and, with less certainty, activities that have contemporary analogues).

How does an understanding of oral tradition relate to the historicity of the Homeric epics? Because it is set in the mythic past and employs epic distance to differentiate that past from the everyday world, epic is "historical in appearance," but since it is also relentlessly modernizing, epic is "contemporary in meaning" (Raaflaub 1996, 628). The *Iliad* and *Odyssey* neither preserve nor recreate a vanished society. They present neither a world fabricated from whole cloth nor a hopeless mishmash of various historical periods. Instead, the epics reflect the fact that "the assumptions Homer made about the workings of society will have been based on those of the Greek world in which he lived" (Morris 1986, 89). Abstract social, cultural, and ideological information that was not immediately relevant to the society of Homer and his audience disappeared, entirely forgotten; the world of the poems is the world of poet and audience.

Epic, however, does not passively reflect contemporary society. Instead, it plays an active, structuring role in society. Oral traditions tend to be normative or pointedly etiological; those about the mythic past in particular frequently justify the bases of contemporary society.[19] Information contained in an oral tradition, for example, often expresses group identity or substantiates rights over land, resources, office, or property (Vansina 1985, 19–21).[20] Oral tradition may also provide an idealized model of society, justifying stratification, hierarchy, or domination: "To serve as an ideological tool to legitimize elite domination, presenting it as natural and unchangeable. This, the poet is saying, is how it was in the Heroic Age; this, he is implying, is how it should be now" (Morris 1986, 125).[21] More specifically, although it does not turn a blind eye to elite excess, Homeric epic serves as an ideological tool legitimating aristocratic rule.[22] Despite surface appearances, Homeric epic does not advocate monarchy. The fallibility of individual *basileis* ("rulers," pl. of *basileus*) like Akhilleus and Agamemnon drives the plot of the *Iliad,* for example, while their reconciliation serves as a model for integrating competitive individuals back into the *aristoi,* the community of ruling elites (Morris 124–25; Hammer 2002). It is this elite community that the epics critique yet endorse.

That the poems reflect an aristocratic perspective is not surprising. Oral poetry is composed in performance as the poet interacts with his audience; the desires and expectations of the latter, as indicated through their reactions to the performance, lead the poet to modify his song. The audience that mattered most to the poets consisted of elites, who held the banquets or the games at which poets would have sung and provided the poets with sustenance, prizes, and fame—if they approved the song (*Od.* 8.72–82; *W&D* 646–62). Homer considers poets, like prophets and builders, to be *demioergoi* ("workers for the people," pl. of *demioergos*) who are welcome guests in aristocratic *oikoi* ("households," pl. of *oikos*), and who perform a valuable service worthy of compensation (*Od.* 17.383–85; cf. *Il.* 21.441–57). Reward or censure, however, remains in the hands of the elite audience (Morris 1986, 91–94; see also Tandy 1997; Green 1984; Nagy 1996b, 1999). As a result, the Homeric epics constitute archetypes of aristocratic poetry, one of the two principal strains of preclassical Greek verse (with Hesiod serving as the archetype for the other, the antiaristocratic poetry produced by and for the *mesoi* ("middling farmers," pl. of *mesos,*) who were often at odds with the "bribe-swallowing *basileis*" that constitute the aristocracy (Donlan 1973, 1980; Kirke 1992; Hanson 1999).[23] Responding to the desires and expectations of its principal audience, Homeric epic does more than merely justify the dominance of the *aristoi* it reflects their entire worldview. As we shall see in the case of Greeks and others in the Homeric epics, this aristocratic worldview colors the way that many aspects of culture are portrayed.

First, however, after establishing that the Homeric epics reflect a coherent, historical society, it will prove useful to establish a date for that society. A wide range of dates, from the thirteenth to the seventh century B.C., have been offered in the past.[24] Again the origins of the Homeric epic in an oral tradition allow us to sidestep most of the details of this debate. Since oral traditions reflect the culture and society roughly contemporary with the poet and his audience, if we can determine the date when the Homeric epics reached approximately their present form, we will also know the date of the society behind them. As Foley's discussion indicates (2007, esp. 6–7), the task is not to date the *floruit* of a master poet, but to find the date when a tradition, for whatever reason, stopped its relentless evolution, stabilizing into a particular form. Such a stabilization probably, but not necessarily, involved the writing down of the poem.

Two compelling and independent lines of reasoning point toward a mid- to late-eighth-century date for the stabilization of the Homeric epics. Richard Janko, in a sophisticated comparison of epic language to that of other early Greek literature, arrived at a date of 750–725 for the *Iliad* and 743–713 for the *Odyssey* (2007, 228–31). Nagy, a student of Alfred Lord, developed an evolutionary model for the gradual stabilization of the Homeric oral tradition, involving a certain amount of feedback between a living oral tradition and the circulation of transcriptions. He concluded that the epics were so widespread and well known by the end of the eighth century that they could not have evolved much after that point.[25] Three further pieces of circumstantial evidence bolstering a later eighth century date for the stabilization of the Homeric epics are: (1) the development of alphabetic writing in Greece earlier in the eighth century, a likely prerequisite of the fixing of an oral tradition; (2) the compatibility of such a date with ancient knowledge, and lack thereof, about Homer; (3) the instability of late eighth-century Greek society and related challenges to aristocratic dominance, leading to a "sudden appearance of the past in the present" that included the crystallization of the Homeric epics (Morris 1986, 87, 91–94; cf. Hurwit 1985; Crielaard 2002).

I find a fifty-year window in the second half of the eighth century for the stabilization of the Homeric epics convincing. At most, archaizing by the poet might push some aspects of culture and society back two or three generations, describing a situation that existed within the horizon of living memory; social structures and cultural practices that passed away shortly before the oldest members of Homer's audience were born could have been passed down to them as "the way things used to be" and then employed by the poet to make his songs confirm to the collectively held view of what the past should look like. I doubt that more purely ideological—and therefore abstract—phenomena, communal identity, for example, would endure even that long, considering how subject they are to contemporary saliency and the active, structuring properties inherent to oral tradition.[26] At the risk of producing a false sense of accuracy, it may be helpful to translate this idea into exact dates. An epicenter around 735 (roughly averaging Janko's dates) and using the eighty-year horizon Vansina found in some African cultures yield an era for Homeric society of about 815–735; accounting for the full uncertainty inherent to dating the stabilization of Homeric epic might extend that range to something like 830–700.[27] Considering such uncertainties and the ability of oral tradition to retain information, not to mention intentional archaizing by the poet, I do not think that specifying a more accurate date is possible. Regardless of the uncertainties surrounding the date of Homeric society, the epics carry much of the eighth century B.C. out of the "Dark Age" and into the light of protohistory.

Finally, before turning to a historical "case study" of Greeks and others in the Homeric epics, it is worthwhile taking a moment to examine the existence of the epics themselves as an object of historical interest. The stabilization of the poems probably attests to a great degree of facility with writing before the end of the eighth century (especially when considered alongside internal evidence from the poems themselves about writing and papyrus). Indeed, Barry Powell has argued that writing was adopted by the Greeks specifically for the purpose of writing the epics (1991). The stabilization and widespread dissemination of the poems in the second half of the eighth century B.C. indicate that enormous efforts were made to transmit and probably transcribe them at that time, revealing that desires, needs, or pressures in contemporary society compelled their recording and fostered their popularity (Morris 1986, 122). Such widespread popularity also attests to the beginnings of a unified Greek cultural sphere; before 700 B.C. the poems became the common property of Greek speakers, signaling the beginnings of Panhellenism (Nagy 1999, 7; 115–17; 139–40). Whatever else the Homeric epics may reveal, they demonstrate that in response to some confluence of social and cultural factors, at the end of the eighth century B.C. a great deal of effort was expended across much of the Greek-speaking world on the process of stabilizing and disseminating these poems.

Homeric Panhellenism: Greeks and Others in the Early Iron Age

The question of preclassical Panhellenism is a vexed one. Historians who believe Panhellenism emerged mainly through opposition between Greeks and a barbarian "Other" tend to locate its origins in the Persian Wars.[28] If, however, Panhellenism emerged through the aggregation of disparate local and regional identities, then it may have arisen much earlier.[29] A third view has recently emerged, that oppositional identity may have begun to develop in the archaic period (or even the Early Iron Age) through intercultural contact brought about by Greek trade and colonization.[30] The Homeric epics potentially offer the earliest available literary evidence for Panhellenism. Judging from their subject—a war between a united Akhaian army besieging a foreign city in the *Iliad;* an Akhaian traveling among foreigners before returning home in the *Odyssey*—the poems seem poised to reveal what early Greeks thought of their collective identity and the differences between them and non-Greeks. The picture that emerges from the epic is ambiguous enough, however, to spark considerable disagreement.[31] On the one hand, Akhaians, under the rulership of Agamemnon, act in unison to wage war on the city of Troy (which no Akhaians help to defend). On the other hand, as Finley observed, Homer takes a universal view of humanity; there appear to be no regional, ethnic, or national dividing lines of genuine consequence as far as human nature or capacity is concerned—although social class, which cuts across all other boundaries, is critically important (1978, 135). No division categorically separated Akhaian lands from others; as soon as any traveler, Akhaian or not, left his own community, he was on foreign soil (102). Nor does a unique name designate the people who array themselves before Troy. Homer does not use *Hellene,* the term employed by

Greek speakers of later eras to describe themselves, in a Panhellenic sense. Instead, he employs the three apparently interchangeable names *Akhaian, Danaan, and Argive (18).* Akhaians and Trojans, furthermore, share customs, mores, and language; Diomedes (an Akhaian and king of Argos), and Glaukon (a Lykian hero fighting for the Trojans) need no interpreter to converse, and their gift exchange of armor, enacted on the battlefield, reveals that both understand the duties and privileges of *xenia* ("hereditary guest friendship"; *Il.* 6.232–36; cf. Finley 1978, 98–99; Donlan 1989b).

Although later Greeks, especially after the Persian Wars, might have heard or read the *Iliad* and directly equated Akhaians with Greeks and Trojans with barbarians, such a dichotomy had not yet developed in the eighth century. There are, nevertheless, indications of an emerging Panhellenic identity (I will use the term *proto-Panhellenism* to distinguish the variety found in Homer from the mature, opposition Panhellenism that emerged in the wake of the confrontation with Persia). Hillary Mackie, for example, has observed a consistent differentiation between Akhaian order and Trojan chaos. The common language of the Akhaians indicates that they, unlike the linguistically diverse Trojans, have forged a cohesive community.[32] Dean Hammer also sees the forging of a community as central to the narrative of the *Iliad,* with the Akhaians achieving cohesiveness through a dynamic of conflict and reconciliation unmatched on the Trojan side. Hammer sees the political norms, spaces, and performances, as they might have existed in a single, local community in the eighth century B.C., projected onto the entire Akhaian force before Troy (2002). Through such an analogy, the poet and audience show themselves able to extend the idea of a cohesive community beyond its operational limits at the local level to encompass all the Akhaians arrayed before Troy.

Still, such arguments hardly prove any widespread Panhellenic sentiment in the eighth century B.C.[33] After all, the unity displayed by Akhaian forces deployed before Troy in the *Iliad,* although reminiscent of individual communities at home, might be limited to the specific situation of an otherwise diverse group of soldiers waging a long war in a foreign land. Indeed, Walter Donlan has demonstrated the importance of impermanent warrior bands in the Early Iron Age, loyal to a particular leader so long as that leader could deliver appropriate rewards for service (1985 and 1989a). Is loyalty to Agamemnon on the battlefield the extent of Akhaian unity, or did some sense of a common identity transcend temporary military configurations? A range of evidence from the epics may indicate the latter.

Homer's identification of heroes, contingents, and armies; his depiction of linguistic diversity; and his deployment of collective terms such as *ethnos* ("contingent"; pl. *ethnea*) and *gaia* ("homeland"), all indicate the emergence of proto-Panhellenism.

First, as noted, Homer uses the terms *Akhaian, Danaan,* and *Argive* as interchangeable names for the "Greeks." Even in the same passage different terms may appear side by side: a retreating Eurypylos "shouts to the Danaans: 'my friends, leaders and rulers of the Argives'" (*Il.* 11.585). Although Homer uses three separate names, they are fully interchangeable and can apply to any individual hero or contingent in Agamemnon's army—or indeed to the army as a whole. By contrast, each of the collective names applied to groups of "non-Greeks," such as the Trojans, Lykians, or any of the other *epikouroi* ("allies," pl. of *epikouros*), designates specific and exclusive groups (compare, for example, Homer's introduction to the Akhaian Catalogue of Ships, *Il.* 2.484–93, to the preceding Trojan Catalogue, 2.802–06 and 811–15). Such designations are surprisingly consistent, especially considering the oral nature of the epics. *Akhaian, Danaan,* or *Argive* may modify not only Agamemnon's soldiers, but also Penelope's suitors, or anyone encountered by Telemakhos while he travels through the Peloponnesos in the *Odyssey. Trojan,* on the other hand, while occasionally used as shorthand when the poet needs a single word to describe all the warriors opposing the Akhaians, is strictly limited to the subjects ruled by the houses of Priam and Ankhises when it is applied to individual heroes or military contingents. Allies of the Trojans, such as the Lykians, Paionians, Thracians, or Mysians, are never referred to as Trojans or included in mixed groups referred to as Trojan. Mixed groups are instead consistently referred to by the phrase "Trojans and famed *epikouroi*" or a variation. A typical example occurs at the end of the recognition scene between Diomedes and Glaukos:

> There are plenty of Trojans and famed companions in battle for me
> To kill, whom the god sends me, or those I run down with my swift feet,
> Many Akhaians for you to slaughter, if you can do it.
>
> (*Il.* 6.227–29)

The terms *Akhaian, Danaan,* and *Argive* are, conversely, never combined with the term *epikouros* or an equivalent. Homeric nomenclature thus recognizes both the homogeneous nature of the Akhaian army and the composite nature of the army defending Troy. Second, as Mackie first realized, there is a fundamental difference in language between Akhaians and Trojans. Later, language became central to Hellenic identity. Speaking Greek is one of Herodotos's criteria for Panhellenism (Her. 8.144). Homer, however, indicates no language barrier between Trojans and Akhaians. Instead, the epics consistently portray Akhaian linguistic homogeneity against a backdrop of linguistic diversity among the Trojan allies. The Karians are, for example, described as *barbarophonos* ("barbar-speaking," i.e., unintelligible to Hellenes) in the Trojan Catalogue (*Il.* 2.867). Also in the Trojan Catalogue, Hektor is advised by the goddess Iris (disguised as the watchman Polites) to use interpreters to disseminate orders to his *epikouroi* (*Il.* 2.802–06). Even when linguistic diversity is recognized within "Greek" lands like Krete (*Od.* 19.172–77), groups traditionally considered "Greek" (Akhaians and Dorians) are not systematically differentiated from those who are not (Eteocretans, Kudones, Pelasgians). Selective recognition of the speaking of different languages contrasts Akhaian unity with non-Akhaian diversity, without establishing a simple dichotomy. Instead, linguistic diversity itself serves as a marker of alterity; the poet desires to cast the Trojan host as divided and chaotic, the Akhaian as unified and organized. This artistic device is effective because during the late eighth century, it resonated with—and perhaps even contributed to—an emerging sense of group identity; the audience found the linguistically homogeneous Akhaians familiar and perhaps heard in epic an extension or idealization of the "intercultural synthesis" emerging around them (see note 29).

Third, terms concerning place of origin and membership in a particular military retinue, which are normally only associated with restricted groups, are applied to the Akhaians as a whole. *Gaia* ("homeland") and *ethnos* ("contingent," pl. *ethnea*), are among the most important categories of identity in Homer, and both are used in a pan-Akhaian as well as a local or regional sense. In book 2 of the *Iliad,* for example, *ethnea* appears in the plural to denote the contingents of Akhaians preparing for battle (*Il.* 2.91; 464). Likewise, the Lykians and Trojans are each designated as an *ethnos* (12.330 and 13.495, respectively). Later in the *Iliad,* however, Homer applies *ethnos,* in the singular, to the Akhaians more broadly. When Athena visits the Akhaian army, she entered the "*ethnos* of the Akhaians" (*Il.* 17.52). Moreover, several uses of the phrase *ethnos hetaron* ("contingent of companions") indicate a broad application of the term. Eurypylos, for example, "shrinks in the tribe of his companions," but as he does so, he also "shouts to the Danaans: 'my friends, leaders and rulers of the Argives'" (*Il.* 11.585–86). The proximity of *ethnos hetaron* to "Danaans" and "Argives," as well as the use of both terms, emphasizes that Eurypylos considers any Danaan/Argive (or at least the "leaders and rulers" thereof) within earshot to be part of his *ethnos.* Likewise, when the Spartan king Menelaos's "eyes range over the *ethnos* of his companions" he is searching for Antilokhos, who is a Pylian rather than a Spartan; in the mind of poet and audience it seems that any two Akhaians belong to a single *ethnos,* regardless of specific origins. No parallel usage exists for Trojans and their *epikouroi.*

As with *ethnos,* Homer associates a *gaia* ("territory" or "homeland") with individual heroes or contingents of Akhaians, Trojans, or *epikouroi,* or with the Akhaians as a whole, but never with any combination of Trojans and *epikouroi.* Indeed, the phrase *Akhaiis gaia* (or the variant *Akhaiis aia,* "Akhaian homeland", singular only) appears four times in the epics (*Il.* 1.254, 7.124; *Od.* 13.249, 21.107). Nestor twice uses the phrase "Alas, a great sorrow visits the *Akhaiis gaia*" to introduce speeches censuring the Akhaians for disunity (*Il.* 1.254, 7.124). Likewise, when Agamemnon tests his forces by calling for a retreat, he proclaims, "Let us flee with our ships to our dear *patris gaia* ("paternal homeland," singular; *Il.* 2.140). Agamemnon then proceeds by invoking the Trojan *polis:* "For no more is there hope that we shall take broad-wayed Troy" (*Il.* 2.141). This juxtaposition balances the Akhaian *gaia* against the Trojan *polis,* implying that the former is as real and cohesive as the latter. Thus does Nestor emphasize the (potential) unity of the Akhaians by referring to their shared homeland immediately before castigating them for internal division; likewise, Agamemnon reprimands his army by comparing their entire homeland with the Trojans' single city.

Collective use of the terms *ethnos* (especially) and *gaia* could be situational, applied to the Akhaians because they followed Agamemnon to Troy and there fight as a single army. But why, then, are the Trojans and *epikouroi,* who also fight together and share a leader in Hektor, never described similarly? Throughout, Homer's consistency is striking. *Ethnos* and *gaia* are used only of individual contingents or of the Akhaians as a whole, never of any combination of Trojans and *epikouroi* or various groupings of *epikouroi.*[34]

This evidence from the epics—differential use of collective terms for Akhaians, Trojans, and *epikouroi;* Akhaian linguistic homogeneity versus linguistic diversity among Trojans and *epikouroi;* application of usually delimited terms like *ethnos* and *gaia* to the Akhaians as a whole—strongly suggests that proto-Panhellenism had arisen by the eighth century B.C. Other evidence corroborates an eighth century date. One implication of Nagy's argument about the proliferation of the Homeric epics in the late eighth century B.C. is that the broad acceptance of the epics at the time itself reveals an emerging "intercultural synthesis" that contributed to a nascent sense of Panhellenism (Nagy 1999, 6–7; see note 29). The contemporary emergence of the Panhellenic sanctuaries Delphi or Isthmia, as well as Panhellenic games like those held at Olympia, further attests to the emergence of such a synthesis (Snodgrass 1971, 419–21, and 1980, 55).[35] In a confluence of epic and ritual practice, in the ninth and eighth centuries B.C., cult offerings of large, expensive bronze tripods from other parts of Greece have been found in a cave on Ithaka—the cave where Odysseus supposedly hid similar gifts given him by the Phaiakians (*Od.* 13.1–15, 217–18, 361–71; Malkin 1998, chapter 3). These artifacts indicate that Ithaka was becoming a Panhellenic site, containing offerings dedicated by Euboians and Korinthians. These cult offerings also point toward a "Panhellenization" of Odysseus and Homeric epic in a way that inspired Greeks of diverse origins to commemorate the gifts given to Odysseus by the Phaiacians through the dedication of offerings on his island (which lies on routes to the west "pioneered" by Odysseus and used by Euboians and Korinthians in their commercial and protocolonial ventures). Material evidence, along with the dissemination of the Homeric epics themselves, reinforce internal evidence from the epics that proto-Panhellenism had emerged by the end of the eighth century B.C. Indeed, since identity arises through a discursive process, evidence from literary sources (including written sources based on an oral tradition) does much to verify what would otherwise be extremely speculative interpretations of material evidence.[36]

The epics can do more than confirm the eighth-century origins of Panhellenism and reveal something about the discursive process that produced it. The application of terms like *ethnos* and *gaia* to the Akhaian force as a whole, as well as to individual military contingents, supports the idea that Homeric proto-Panhellenism is aggregative in nature. Like the Archaic Panhellenism investigated by Jonathan Hall (based upon dialect and putative descent from a common ancestor), Homeric proto-Panhellenism was constructed from within through the merger of peer groups who saw cultural similarities among themselves (1997, 47–48).[37] At the same time, even though there is no strict dichotomy between "Greek" and other, the Homeric epics most often articulate their proto-Panhellenism by means of a contrast between Akhaian similarity or unity, on the one hand, and non-Akhaian diversity or disunity on the other. Such differentiation between Akhaians and others indicates that the rise of proto-Panhellenic may have been stimulated by interaction with non-Greeks.[38] Homeric proto-Panhellenism may have been *oppositional in origin* but *aggregative in nature.*

Is this interpretation of Homeric proto-Panhellenism plausible? It seems to me to conform to the broader context of the eighth century B.C., including the elite ideology that informed Homeric epic. First, the eighth century is generally seen as a period of state formation in Greece when, in a significant part of the Greek world, the small villages of the Early Iron Age gave rise to the larger *poleis* that dominated the archaic and classical eras (Hansen 2006, 43–46).[39] That transition involved a process of *synoikism,* by which smaller communities merged into larger, multiple villages jointing to form the urban core of a city-state.[40] Such a process, familiar to many Greeks, could have served as an analogy for the sort of aggregative Panhellenism seen in the epics.

Second, although Greeks of the Early Iron Age were less isolated from the outside world than once thought (Tandy 1997, 59; Thomas and Conant 1999, 93–94), Greek contact with non-Greeks increased substantially during the eighth century (Tandy 1997, chapter 3; Malkin 1998; Thomas and Conant 1999, 134–43). In Homer, Phoenicians and other non-Akhaians (such as the Taphian Mentes) conduct trade (*Od.* 1.178–84), while Akhaians such as Odysseus can be mistaken for traders (*Od.* 8.159–64, 9.252–54; cf. Finley 1978, 48). Akhaians and Phoenicians both engage in raiding.[41] Akhaians engage in *xenia* (paternal guest friendship) relationships and gift exchange with non-Akhaians. Such gift exchange established and maintained relationships, and may have served as a substitute for or supplement to market-based exchange in an aristocratic society that held merchants and trade in contempt (*Od.* 8.159–64; Donlan 1982; Morris 1986, 119; Tandy 1997, 114–18). Akhaians marry non-Akhaians (e.g., Bellerophon and the princess of Lykia, *Il.* 6.192; Alkinoos suggests Odysseus might marry his daughter, *Od.* 7.313). Archaeological evidence suggests that Phoenician trade with the Greeks began (or intensified significantly) in the late ninth and eighth centuries, the era when the Greeks borrowed the Phoenician alphabet (Thomas and Conant 1999, 109–10; Powell 1991). Soon, Greeks begin to conduct trade as well, emerging as the Phoenicians' primary mercantile and colonial competitors in the Mediterranean littoral (Tandy 1997, chapter 3; Thomas and Conant 1999, 134–43). The *emporion* (trading depot) at Al Mina in Syria was established at this time. Several *apoikia* (overseas settlements or "colonies") were also founded in Italy and Sicily in the eighth century, launching the era of Greek colonization that would spread hundreds of poleis along the Mediterranean, Aegean, and Black Sea coasts.[42] As opposed to (usually late) legends of colonial foundation that often report the simple expulsion of indigenous peoples, archaeological investigations conducted in the extraurban territories of *apoikia* like Taras (Taranto) have revealed intense and complex interactions between Greeks and natives.[43] Such environments may have provided the oppositional stimulus that initiated the development of proto-Panhellenism, but without instigating the hostility aroused by conflicts such as the Persian Wars (which led to a much more rigid dichotomy between Greek and "barbarian").

Third, certain aspects of the aristocratic worldview embodied in the epics would have provided fertile ground for proto-Panhellenism. Even though (or perhaps because) the epics depict every community beyond one's own as a foreign land and a place of potential danger, aristocrats maintained connections beyond their own communities (Kirke 1992; Donlan 1982; see also note 40). The unified Akhaian elite waging war at Troy, each hero leading his own contingent but bound to Agamemnon and Menelaus by oath and to one another through ties of guest-friendship, serves as a prototype for the aristocratic network. Intermarriage across, rather than within, communities also appears to be normal for elites, if not universal. Guest-friendship across communities among the *aristoi* is universal. Hesiod, by contrast, in giving voice to the *mesoi,* expresses a considerably greater investment in his humble *polis* of Askra. Such a pattern is not uncommon among premodern societies, where elites consider themselves part of a class that transcends local communities, while commoners live in a world bounded by those local communities (Gellner 1983, 8–14). Indeed, this cosmopolitan perspective, including guest-friendship and marriage ties with both Greek and (less frequently) foreign elites, represented a significant component of the early Greek aristocratic ideal (Donlan 1973, 1980; Kirke 1992; Hanson 1999). Considering their elite audience, it is not surprising that the Homeric epics reflect the cosmopolitan outlook of the *aristoi.*

Inasmuch as oral tradition actively shapes society, the epics agitate for cultural, if not political, Panhellenism.

An analysis of the Homeric epics as the product of an oral tradition, taking into account contemporary material evidence, points toward the emergence of proto-Panhellenism in Greek-speaking lands during the eighth century B.C. That proto-Panhellenism is oppositional in origin, spurred by intensifying contact between Greeks and others. Yet it is aggregative in nature, built through the extension of local identities, just as the villages of Greece emerged from their Early Iron Age isolation to form the *poleis* that would structure life in the most advanced parts of Greece for centuries. Finally, the proto-Panhellenism of the epics reflects and advocates a cosmopolitan worldview characteristic of aristocratic ideology.

Reading (and Teaching) Homer in the Twenty-first Century

Once the Homeric epics have been set in the historical realm, they offer considerable opportunity for rewarding study. Even fifty years after *The World of Odysseus,* many questions remain to be asked of the poems. Seeking the origins of later Greek institutions, practices, and ideas in Homer has been and remains an attractive line of inquiry. Continuing efforts to integrate Homer and the archaeological record in a meaningful and sophisticated way are needed, especially as new discoveries enhance our understanding of Early Iron Age and Archaic Greece. Over the past two decades, placing Homer's poetry and society in its wider Mediterranean context has generated what may be some of the most interesting research (see, for example, Burkert 1992, chapter 3; Malkin 1998). In my teaching, I have found that an excellent assignment for students new to ancient history consists of simply opening Homer to historical inquiry by asking students to read either the *Iliad* or the *Odyssey* with a single aspect of society (religion, the role and status of women, political institutions, etc.) in mind. For more advanced students, exploring interactions between Greeks and others, carefully illuminated through comparisons with contemporary or later intercultural encounters, is exciting and offers opportunities to introduce them to cultures, such as that of the Phoenicians, they would otherwise be unlikely to study.

In addition to opportunities for teaching and research, the historicity of Homeric society has some limitations. Evidence, written or material, for the eighth century B.C. is inadequate—even by the forgiving standards of ancient history and pre-Classical archaeology. Nevertheless, a coherent, historical society lies behind the Homeric epics, the existence of which constrains the range of possible interpretations. Although introducing fresh interests or concerns to the poems can be extraordinarily rewarding, lacunae in our knowledge of the era do not justify anachronistic projection of modern concepts to a society separated from us by 2,700 years and a vast cultural divide. To take examples I encountered while preparing this essay, I find it problematic to speak of capitalism in a society where even the significance of market exchange is debated, or imperialism in a society that had not yet fully developed the state and a culture that showed little interest in ruling non-Greeks. Even colonization must be carefully defined to take account of the cultural context and the differences between early (or even mature) Greek colonization and its modern counterpart.[44] Applying concepts such as these to Homeric society threatens to drain them of meaning or do violence to the evidence.

This is not to say that early Greece was not aggressive. The hundreds of *poleis* scattered across the Mediterranean and Black Seas beyond the Greek homeland did not arise through passivity. Yet in its aggression and violence early Greek colonization was hardly unique. The Phoenicians, as the Greeks, enthusiastically expanded their cultural and economic sphere by sea. Even excluding formal empires like Assyria or intrusive steppe nomads like the Cimmerians, the list of aggressive, expansionist land powers in the Early Iron Age Mediterranean is long and distinguished (Phrygians, Lykians, Thracians, Etruscans, Philistines, and Israelites were all contemporary with Early Iron Age and archaic Greece). What makes studying Greek colonization interesting is not the fact that it occurred or the violence that often accompanied it, but that it is an early and extensive example of expansion reasonably well attested in both written and material sources, and that it was accompanied by a peculiar intercultural dynamic that seems to have produced much equal and complex interaction, more "middle ground" than a student of early modern European colonization, for example, might expect (White 1991; Burgers 2004).

Similarly, if social and economic structures in Greece had been entirely just, there would have been no need for the critics and reformers, from Hesiod to Kerkidas, whom Greek society produced across 500 years of its history. The unusual characteristic of early Greek culture is not that it had a stratified society dominated by an elite class, as did almost all cultures that utilized plow-agriculture, but that ultimately in many *poleis* the *aristoi* capitulated to the *mesoi* at least in part. That compromise produced a *polis* culture that, alone in premodern world history, generated the expertise, wealth, and power of a differentiated, specialized society, while retaining some of the egalitarianism and participatory governance of village society—avoiding, to some degree, the exploitation, alienation, and unrest common in most cultures with economic specialization and social hierarchy (McNeill and McNeill 2003, chapter 3).

As a final example, although divisions between self and other might be expected in an epic tradition centered on stories about collective war against a foreign enemy, the extent to which such divisions are muted is somewhat surprising when compared to, for example, later Greek society (with its dichotomy between Hellenes and barbarians), ancient Egyptian society (the "people of the Black Land" vs. "vile foreigners"), or early Islamic society (the "Realm of Islam" vs. the "Realm of War"). The early archaic period is often called the "Orientializing Revolution" for good reason: Greek culture was reinvigorated largely through its willingness to adopt and adapt foreign ideas; Homer's poetry itself contains significant passages borrowed from or inspired by non-Greek literature (Burkert 1992, chapter 3).

I hope that my intentionally provocative conclusion illustrates the excitement and controversy that the study of early Greek society in general, and Homer in particular, can still generate. Students in ancient or world history courses often find the study of Homeric epic more interesting when it is used to explore issues like these, assessing how the world of the epics resembles or diverges from the patterns found in other civilizations—a line of inquiry that will also keep researchers occupied for some time to come. Situating Homer in the realm of history allows new and exciting questions to be asked, ensuring that Homer will continue to be read profitably in the twenty-first century and beyond.

Notes

1. Bibliographic references in this essay are illustrative rather than exhaustive, but should, I hope, offer a starting point for further study of the myriad issues treated here only briefly.

2. Specifically, Finley argues that there are "no Ionians, no Dorians to speak of, no writing, no iron weapons, no cavalry in battle scenes, no colonization, no Greek traders, [and] no communities without kings."

3. But see Morris (1986, 105–15), for a detailed rebuttal of Snodgrass's contention that the Homeric epics depict multiple, incompatible systems of marriage and inheritance.

4. Homeric orality has generated a large bibliography; key works include Parry (1971), Lord (1967, 1971, 1995, and 2000), Goody (1976), Kirk (1976), Janko (1982), Ong (2002), Havelock (1982), Nagy (1996a, 1996b, 1999, and 2004), Foley (1992 and 1999), Scodel (2002), Bakker (2005).

5. Snodgrass asserts that the Homeric epics are a special case, differing from other oral traditions attested in preliterate civilizations around the world. He admits that such an argument is subjective, based in some measure on belief in a unique genius behind Homeric poetry (Snodgrass compares Homeric epic to Germanic, Irish, and Icelandic oral traditions to make this point). Snodgrass ([1974], 2006 reprint, 190–91).

6. I base the following discussion primarily on Vansina (1985), which offers a useful and compelling explanation of the origins and nature of oral tradition, and one that has the added benefit of being derived independently from the Homeric epics themselves or the south Slavic epic studied by Parry and Lord when they formulated their models of oral composition.

7. For the exception of memorized speech, see Vansina (1985, 14–16).

8. Foley provides an excellent introduction to the formulaic yet dynamic nature of Homeric epic, which I have not duplicated here (Foley 2007). See also the bibliography in note 4.

9. Dickinson goes on to report the preservation of genealogies for some prominent families (2006, 1, 11–12). Overall, Dickinson's synopsis—written, so far as I can tell, without reference to the oral basis of that history—strikingly reveals the imprint of oral tradition on the Greek view of their own past. See also Raubischek (1989) but compare Whitley (1993, 226).

10. But see also Morris (1986, 123, citing Finnegan 1977), who notes that oral tradition may either sustain or critique the status quo.

11. Vansina (1985, 23–24). Vansina provides the following examples of the floating gap: "The shortest such time-depth I know is that of the Aka of Lobaye (Central African Republic), where it does not exceed one generation of adults. . . . For the Tio (Congo), c. 1880, the limit lay c. 1800, while in 1960 it had moved to 1880. If the Tio were still a fully oral society, the arrival of de Brazza in 1880 would now lie in the period of origins. As it is, he has become a culture hero, but can still be dated" (24).

12. Oral tradition does not suddenly end the moment writing is invented; oral and literate cultures can coexist for centuries, although the existence of writing may have an impact on living oral traditions (Vansina 1985). Herodotus's *Histories,* for example, preserve much information drawn from recent oral tradition (sometimes heard directly by Herodotus, sometimes preserved in other writings now lost, 31; Murray 2001a, 2001b). Early Roman history also reflects the three-tiered shape of oral tradition with the floating gap falling, perhaps, in the early third century B.C.. And of course the South Slavic epics analyzed by Parry and Lord in their reevaluation of Homer were products of a (partially) literate society.

13. For the boar's-tusk helmet, see *Il.* 10.260–65. The most striking examples of Mycenaean place-names can be found in the Catalogue of Ships and the Trojan Catalogue of *Iliad,* Book 2; cf. Hope-Simpson and Lazenby (1970), Benzi (2002) for Homeric and Late Bronze Age geography. Passages in Homer such as Mycenae's entry in the Catalogue of Ships (*Il.* 2.569–80) and Agamemnon's offer of cities to Akhilleus in exchange for his return to battle (*Il.* 10. 149–53) reveal the extent of Agamemnon's kingdom. For other Late Bronze Age survivals in Homer, see Bennet (1997), S. Morris (1997), D. F. Easton, et al. (2002), Mellink (1995). Wood (1998) contains a useful overview of the Late Bronze Age context for the Homeric epics and is particularly valuable for classroom use.

14. Practices in the Homeric epic that were once considered survivals from the distant past, such as "fairly lavish provision of possessions for the deceased, the occasional use of horse-sacrifice," have since been discovered in Dark Age archaeological contexts, such as the Toumba burial at Lefkandi on Euboia (Snodgrass 2006; Popham, Touloupa, and Sackett 1982). Usually, however, such "ancient" practices appearing in an oral tradition are likely the extrapolations of the poet to achieve "epic distance," as discussed later. For a more optimistic view of potential survivals of Bronze Age practices in Homer, see Janko and Kullman (2002, 653, which I have supplemented through personal correspondence with Richard Janko).

15. Translation from Evelyn-White ([1936] 2002 reprint).

16. But see Dickinson (2006) and Raubischek (1989), who emphasize another strand of Greek ideas about the past, exemplified by Thucydides, in which Greek civilization evolved slowly over time from modest origins without a particularly impressive Heroic Age or subsequent decline into an Age of Iron (Thucydides 1.2–12). I have focused on Hesiod's conception of the past because he was a near-contemporary of Homer. Dickinson characterizes Hesiod's narrative of decline as wholly moral in nature and purpose (2006, 2). Thucydides' narrative of slow progress can, however, be attributed to his desire to cast the Peloponnesian War as the most important conflict in history. His account, moreover, with its odd chronology and sparse information about the centuries between the Ionian migration and the Lelentine War also reflects the "floating gap" of oral tradition (cf. Dickinson 2006, 1, who comments upon "the general lack of information" available to Thucydides). See also Whitley (1993).

17. Different degrees of epic distance are even deployed in the *Odyssey* to distinguish the fantastic world of Odysseus's travels from the "real" world of Ithaka, Pylos, and Sparta (Vidal-Naquet 1981, Morris 1986, 91; cf. Giesecke 2007).

18. Examples of such archaizing in the Homeric epics might include those observed by Finley: absence of references to the Dorians, the Olympic Games, colonization, Greek trade with the Levant, and *polis* organization (1978, 48).

19. The period after the floating gap, by contrast, often shows society in a state of degeneration or decadence, such as is the case with Hesiod's "Age of Iron," for instance (Vansina 1985, 23–24, 100–07).

20. Vansina restricts some of the qualities of oral tradition discussed here to "historical" traditions, excluding epic, but it is clear that Homeric epic is historical in the sense that Homer believed that he was singing the truth about his own past, and the epics fit perfectly within the schema of Hesiod's Ages of Man, which is more self-consciously historical. See also Finley (1978, 45); Morris (1986, 120).

21. Cf. Vansina (1985, 102–06), Morris (1986, 122–27), Finnegan (1977), but see

also Mackie (1996, 3), who argues that more than one heroic code, and more than one model for social organization, can be discerned in the *Iliad.*

22. But see Finley (1978, 111), Morris (1986 123–24) for undercurrents of criticism aimed at the *aristoi;* cf. Rose (1992, 90), Nagy (1999), Haubold (2000).

23. While I agree that the epics advocate aristocratic authority, they are far more nuanced than Clark (1989) or Belski (2007), for example, contends. As noted, the errors of individual *basileis* (Akhilleus's wrath and withdrawal from society; Agamemnon's abuse of his power and position) provide negative examples of rulership that the poet clearly condemns; the eventual repentance of both leaders—after each pays a price for his errors—and in particular their reintegration into the broader community, typified by the evolution of Akhilleus over the course of the poem, illustrate that the epics do not give rulers carte blanche with regard to their prerogative; rather, they derive their authority through interaction with the people (Haubold 2000, Hammer 2002). As was recognized by Finley (1979, 111; cf. Nagy 1999, chapter 14), only an unsubtle reading of the Thersites episode excludes an implied criticism of the *basileis.* Moreover, an ideal of rulership is presented in the *Odyssey* that recalls Hesiod's statement concerning the good *basileus* (*Od.* 10.109–14, *W&D* 225–47). In short, the epics do not merely advocate aristocratic rule but also instruct and constrain the *aristoi,* providing a model for aristocratic behavior.

24. Even among those who accept the historicity of Homeric society, the dating of that society has generated extensive controversy, of which the following should provide an overview: Finley (1979, 48), Morris (1986, 91–93, 127–29), Talpin (1992, 33–35), Raaflaub (1993, 45 and 1996, 628).

25. Nagy argues that the poems did not reach a "definitive" form until the sixth century B.C. (Nagy 1996b, chapter 2, esp. 42), but the amount of acceptable variation among oral poets declined significantly after the end of the eighth century (Nagy 1996b, 20, 39–42). Nagy's evolutionary model, which he has developed over the past twenty-five years, is perhaps best explained in *Homeric Questions* (1996b, 29–112). Nagy allows for the creation of a number of transcriptions emerging in the latter half of the eighth century B.C., which interact with a still-living oral tradition until the Homeric epics become so widespread and well known that no more significant change is possible. For the dispute over whether or not the Homeric texts were dictated piecemeal or in one grand undertaking, see the exchange between Powell and Nagy in the *Bryn Mawr Classical Review* (Powell 1997a, Nagy 1997, Powell 1997b). See also Nagy (1996a, 31–34, 36–37, 100), Powell (1991, 221–37).

26. See Donlan (1989a, 7). Beginning his discussion of the terms *oikos, demos,* and *laos* ("household," "homeland plus people," and "people"), Donan writes, "In any body of hearers, at any given time, they would have aroused universally shared images; for it is difficult to conceive how, even in the deliberately archaizing epics, a singer's evocation of these concepts would not have approximated his audience's experience of them" (cf. Ross 2005).

27. Complicating matters further is the fact that the Homeric epics were, as Nagy has demonstrated, essentially Panhellenic. They are drawn from oral traditions from across the Greek-speaking world, various parts of which were evolving at different rates, some displaying considerable innovation while others remained conservative. An archaic or archaizing passage in the epics, therefore, could represent contemporary features of more conservative regions of Greece (my thanks to Professor Carol Thomas for pointing out this possibility to me).

28. The consensus holds that the dichotomy between Greek and barbarian arose during and after the Persian Wars and that any Panhellenic identity based upon it, therefore, does not precede the advent of the classical era. Cartledge, for example, contrasts the archaic period, when there is no such oppositional identity, with the classical era, when "Greeks . . . construct their identities negatively, by means of a series of polarized oppositions of themselves to what they were not" (Cartledge 1993, 12–13, cf. Cartledge 1995, 75–82, esp. 77–78). E. Hall (1989) agrees; in her discussion of Greek tragedy, she explores the absence of the barbarian in early Greek thought (chapter 1), the "discourse of barbarism" that arose in poetry after the Persian Wars (chapters 2–3), and finally solidification of the barbarian as the antithesis of the Hellene (chapter 4). See E. Hall (1989, esp. 4–5; 76–79, 117–21, 177–79). Choosing a contemporary of Aiskhylos, Morgan (1993, 18, 36) argues that Panhellenism in Pindar's poetry is a novel development. The Greek-barbarian dichotomy reaches maturity in Herodotus, where Hartog finds evidence for an oppositional identity in Herodotus's depiction of the Skythians' "otherness," especially their nomadism. According to Hartog, Herodotus implicitly and negatively contrasts this lack of a settled, agricultural city life with the rooted (indeed, autochthonous), agricultural, and *polis*-oriented existence of the Athenians; Hartog (1988, esp. 10–11, 193–99, 206).

29. Snodgrass and Nagy find a nascent Panhellenism in the eighth century B.C. built from, but beginning to transcend, local identities. Both recognize, for example, the Olympic games, the Delphic Oracle, and the Homeric epics themselves as indicators of eighth-century Panhellenism. See Snodgrass (1999, 55–57, 419–21, 434–36), Nagy (1999, 6–7, 115–17, 139–40). See also Mackie (1996, 7–8, 19). J. Hall, who explicitly views archaic Greek identity as "aggregative" in character, places the emergence of proto-Panhellenism somewhat later, but still prior to the Persian Wars. According to J. Hall, the sixth century B.C. constitutes a critical juncture in the slow evolution of aggregative proto-Panhellenism, marked especially by the founding of the Hellenion at Naukratis and the first well-attested use of collective names (*Hellenes* or *Panhellenes*) for the Greeks as a whole (1997, 47–51; see also 2002, 130–34.)

30. For example, Morris has argued that Greeks constructed a "negotiated periphery" with the Near East during the late Dark Age, which engendered rejection of outside influences among some Greeks, while others actively sought out eastern goods (1996, 1–8). J. Hall (2002, chapter 4) discusses early Greek knowledge of and interaction with non-Greeks, but does not yet see the reductive stereotyping characteristic of later oppositional modes of thought (see esp. 121–24 and cf. chapter 6). Kirke (1992, 91–120), while agreeing that Greeks did not define their identity in opposition to a barbarian other before the Persian Wars, argues that during the sixth century B.C., interaction between Greeks (especially Ionians) and non-Greeks (especially Lydians) did foster the development of a widely shared aristocratic ethos of virtuous luxury. This ethos was then rejected after the Persian Wars, replaced by the rise of the civic ideology of *isonomia* and the feminization of Eastern customs that accompanied the "invention" of the barbarian.

31. Although no one argues for a mature Panhellenism in the epics, a wide gulf still separates scholars who demand evidence for a well-developed sense of Greek versus Other before admitting the saliency of Panhellenism, and those who already see a shared Hellenic identity superseding intra-Hellenic social and cultural diver-

sity in the epics. Largely on the basis of the lack of the term *barbarian* or an equivalent, Cartledge argues against any sense of Panhellenism in Homer (1993, 12; cf. Cartledge 1995, 77–78). Konstan extends this line of thought, contending that the contrast between civilized and uncivilized worlds underlying books 9–12 of the *Odyssey* is never conceived of in terms of Greek versus non-Greek (2001, 31–32) but also admits that while "it seems impossible, on the basis of the epics themselves, to discriminate Greeks from non-Greeks" on the basis of language, religion, customs, geography, or even genealogy, it is nevertheless "Achaeans and only Achaeans who mobilize to carry on the siege of Troy, whereas Priam draws his allies from among [only] non-Achaean populations." On the other hand, Finley (1978, 18) both respects the heterogeneity of Homer's Akhaians and sees in the epics the beginnings of Greekness. He sees Homer's use of (multiple) common names for the Akhaians as a metaphor for early Panhellenism: "The presence of a common name (or names) is a symbol that Greek history proper had been launched. But there was more than one name, and that serves as a symbol, too, of the social and cultural diversity which characterized Hellas both in its infancy and throughout its history, little though it is to be seen in the two Homeric poems." See also Haubold (2000, 43–45). Although he is a supporter of an early emergence of proto-Panhellenism, the "softness" of Finley's belief in Homeric Panhellenism is evident when he later asserts that there are no local, regional, or national dividing lines of genuine consequence in Homer, and that while individuals and classes vary in capacity, peoples do not (1978, 135). Compare Mackie (1996, chapter 1, esp. 20), where she argues for "complex unity" of the Greek army before Troy.

32. Mackie (1996, 21, 19, cf. 11–12; 15–16; 92; 97; see also chapter 4, esp. 127–35 and 158–59). See also Konstan (2001, 31), Ross (2005, 210–11). Mackie also sees systematic differences between the speeches of Akhaian and Trojan heroes, with Akhaian speeches being aggressive, public, political, and censuring, while Trojan speakers are introspective, private, and poetic and prefer praise to blame. Overall, Mackie sees this distinction as marking the difference between political community and household (reconciled successfully by the Akhaians; 1996, chapter 1, esp. 1, 5, 12).

33. Indeed, Mackie in particular is reluctant to extend her argument beyond "an imagined, artistic version of ethnic and cultural difference" (1996, 44).

34. I plan to expand this analysis elsewhere and extend it to the terms *demos* (a term designating a people and/or their territory), *laos* (a people), and *genos* (lineage). *Demos* is used in a pan-Akhaian context at least once, and *laos* appears to follow a similar pattern. By contrast, *genos* is rarely used in a regional context, and never in a Panhellenic context; as argued by Jonathan Hall, the rise of ethnic groups based upon putative descent from a common ancestor appears later than Homer (Hall suggests the sixth century B.C.; cf. Haubold 2002, Hall 1997; 2002).

35. See also Morgan (1993), Malkin (1998, 94), Scodel (2002, 45–46).

36. Hall (1997, chapter 1, esp. 2, see also chapter 5). The epics provide the emic criteria for ethnic identity that is very difficult to interpret from material evidence alone; cf. Hall (1997, chapter 2, especially 18–21; 2003).

37. But often such groups also retained their local identities, creating "nested" intra-Hellenic and Panhellenic identities; see Hall (1997, xiii). The practice of constructed larger (fictive) kin groups from smaller ones was known as *syngeneia*, "joining of *genea*" (*genea* is the plural of *genos*, lineage group; 36–37).

38. See note 29. Cf. Hall (1997, 44–46).

39. See also Snodgrass (1981; but see Runciman 1982 for a contrary view).

40. Hall also notes a process of *syngeneia* (see note 34).

41. Clark (1989, 125) is mistaken in singling out Polyphemos's identification of Odysseus as a raider as something unusual or significant; such interrogations were common when meeting unknown strangers, who could always pose a threat; indeed, Nestor greets Telemakhos with exactly the same question about being a pirate that the Kyklops uses (*Od.* 3.73 versus 9.254; see Finley 1978, 101–02). Nor do Akhaians attack non-Akhaians with any more enthusiasm than they raid other Akhaians; yes, Odysseus raids the Cicones (allies of the Trojans during the war; *Od.* 39–44, *Il.* 2.846–47), and in the "Kretan Lie" Odysseus talks about a (failed) raid on Egypt (*Od.* 14.261–72), but Nestor also tells the story of how he won glory when the Pylians launched a retaliatory raid against the Elians after the latter had stolen Pylian cattle (*Il.* 11.670–84). Nor are the Greeks alone in this aggression; Taphians raid Phoenicians (*Od.* 15.425–29) and in Odysseus's "Kretan Lie," a Phoenician tries to enslave an Akhaian (*Od.* 14.290–97). Piracy, brigandage, fear of strangers, and uncertain treatment outside networks of kin or guest-friendship all characterize the epic tradition, but I see no evidence that these follow any sort of Akhaian versus non-Akhaian fault lines.

42. The Greeks had no term exactly equivalent to the Latin *colonia* or English *colony*. The Greek terminology of *apoikia* and *emporion* is retained here, although archaeological evidence from sites like Pithakussai on the island of Iskhia off the Bay of Naples indicates that there was not always a clear distinction between a trading depot and a colony; Greeks at *emporia* often engaged in agricultural activities while most *apoikia* were also involved with trade.

43. Excavations indicate that l'Amastuola in the territory of Taras seems to have arisen spontaneously as a mixed community of Greeks and Messapians, with hybrid burial practices and multifaceted material and cultural exchange. Archaeological surface survey of the surrounding region has also revealed the foundation and growth of new indigenous settlements in response to Greek colonization, attesting to constructive change stimulated by the encounters with newcomers. Indeed, Greek colonization in southern Italy was not a simple unidirectional process, whereby the incoming Greeks imposed their culture on the Messapian natives. Instead, it reveals diversified models of cooperative and even indigenous-dominated interaction (Burgers 2004; Burgers and Creilaard 2007).

44. For the ancient economy see Finley (1999), Scheidel and von Reden (2002), Manning and Morris (2005), Tandy (1997), Silver (1995). For "imperialism" and colonization, see Runciman (1982), Boardman (1999). Like *capitalism,* the term *imperialism* seems in danger of becoming merely pejorative; when teaching comparative imperialism I have found Doyle (1986) a good starting point for exploring a more precise definition. For the difficulties inherent to discussing "colonies" and "colonization," in an early Greek context, see note 41.

Works Cited

Bakker, E. J. *Pointing at the Past: From Formula to Performance in Homeric Poetics.* Cambridge: Center for Hellenic Studies and Harvard University Press, 2005.

Belsky, S. A. "The Poet Who Sings through Us: Homer's Influence in Contemporary Western Culture. *College Literature* 34, no. 2 (2007): 216–28.

Bennet, J. "Homer and the Bronze Age." In *A New Companion to Homer,* edited by I. Morris and B. Powell. Leiden: Brill, 1997.

Benzi, M. "Anatolia and the Eastern Aegean at the Time of the Trojan War." In *Omero tremila anni dopo: atti del Congresso di Genova; 6–8 luglio 2000,* edited by F. Montanari. Roma: Ed. di Storia e Letteratura, 2002.

Boardman, J. *The Greeks Overseas.* 4th ed. New York: Thames & Hudson, 1999.

Burgers, G.-J. "Western Greeks in Their Regional Setting: Rethinking Early Greek-Indigenous Encounters in Southern Italy." *Ancient West and East* 2 (2004): 252–82.

Burgers, G.-J., and J.-P. Crielaard. "Greek Colonists and Indigenous Populations at L'Amastuola, Southern Italy." *Bulletin Antieke Beschaving* 82 (2007): 77–114.

Burkert, W. *The Orientalizing Revolution: Near Eastern Influence on Greek Culture in the Early Archaic Age.* Translated by M. E. Pinder and W. Burkert. Cambridge, MA: Harvard University Press, 1992.

Cartledge, P. *The Greeks: A Portrait of Self and Others.* Oxford: Oxford University Press, 1993.

———. "The Greeks and Anthropology." *Anthropology Today* 10, no. 3 (1994): 3–6.

———. "'We Are All Greeks'? Ancient (Especially Herodotean) and Modern Contestations of Hellenism." *Bulletin of the Institute of Classical Studies* 40 (1995): 75–82.

Chadwick, J. *The Decipherment of Linear B.* 2nd ed. London: Cambridge University Press, 1968.

Clark, M. "Adorno, Derrida, and the *Odyssey:* A Critique of Center and Periphery." *boundary 2,* 16, no. 2/3 (1989): 109–28.

Crielaard, J.-P. "Past or Present?; Epic Poetry, Aristocratic Self-Representation and the Concept of Time in the Eighth and Seventh Centuries B.C." In *Omero tremila anni dopo,* edited by F. Montanari. Atti del Congresso di Genova 6–8 Iuglio 2000. Con la collaborazione di P. Ascheri. Roma: Edizioni di Storia e Letteratura. 2002.

Dickinson, O. *The Aegean Bronze Age.* Cambridge: Cambridge University Press, 1994.

———. *The Aegean from Bronze Age to Iron Age: Continuity and Change between the Twelfth and Eighth Centuries BC.* New York: Routledge, 2006.

Donlan, W. 1973. "The Tradition of Anti-Aristocratic Thought in Early Greek Poetry." *Historia* 22: 145–54.

———. *The Aristocratic Ideal in Ancient Greece: Attitudes of Superiority from Homer to the End of the Fifth Century BC.* Lawrence, KS: Coronado Press, 1980.

———. "Reciprocities in Homer." *The Classical World* 75 (1982): 137–75.

———. "The Social Groups of Dark Age Greece." *Classical Philology* 80 (1985): 293–308.

———. 1989a. "The Pre-State Community in Greece," *Symbolae Osloenses* 64 (1989a).

———. "The Unequal Exchange between Glaucus and Diomedes in Light of the Homeric Gift-Economy." *Phoenix* 43 (1989b): 1–15.

Doyle, M. W. *Empires.* Ithaca, N.Y.: Cornell University Press, 1986.

Easton, D. F., J. D. Hawkins, A. Sherratt, and E. S. Sherratt. "Troy in Recent Perspective." *Anatolian Studies* 52 (2002): 75–109.

Finley, M. I. *The World of Odysseus.* Rev. ed. New York: Viking Press, 1978.

———. *The Ancient Economy.* Updated ed. Berkeley: University of California Press, 1999.

Finnegan, R. *Oral Tradition: Its Nature, Significance, and Social Context.* Cambridge: Cambridge University Press, 1977.

Foley, J. M. *The Theory of Oral Composition: History and Methodology.* 1988. Reprint. Bloomington: Indiana University Press. 1992.

———. *Homer's Traditional Art.* University Park: Pennsylvania State University Press, 1999.

———. "'Reading' Homer through Oral Tradition. *College Literature* 34, no. 2 (2007): 1–28.

Gellner, E. *Nations and Nationalism.* Oxford: Blackwell, 1983.

Giesecke, A. L. "Mapping Utopia: Homer's Politics and the Birth of the Polis. *College Literature* 34, no. 2 (2007): 194–214.

Goody, J. R. *Production and Reproduction: A Comparative Study of the Domestic Domain.* Cambridge: Cambridge University Press, 1976.

Gray, D. H. F. "Metal-Working in Homer." *Journal of Hellenic Studies* 74 (1954): 1–15.

Green, P. "Works and Days 1–285: Hesiod's Invisible Audience." In *Mnemai: Classical Studies in Memory of Karl K. Hulley,* edited by H. D. Evjen. Chico, Calif.: Scholar's Press, 1984.

Hall, E. *Inventing the Barbarian: Greek Self-Definition through Tragedy.* Oxford: Oxford University Press, 1989.

Hall, J. *Ethnic Identity in Greek Antiquity.* Cambridge: Cambridge University Press, 1997.

———. *Hellenicity: Between Ethnicity and Culture.* Chicago: Chicago University Press, 2002.

Hammer, D. *The Iliad as Politics: The Performance of Political Thought.* Norman: University of Oklahoma Press, 2002.

Hansen, M. H. *Polis: An Introduction to the Ancient Greek City-State.* New York: Oxford University Press, 2006.

Hanson, V. D. *The Other Greeks: The Family Farm and the Agrarian Roots of Western Civilization.* Berkeley: University of California Press, 1999.

Hartog, F. *The Mirror of Herodotus: The Representation of the Other in the Writing of History.* Translated by J. Lloyd. Berkeley: University of California Press, 1988.

Haubold, J. *Homer's People: Epic Poetry and Social Formation.* Cambridge: Cambridge University Press, 2000.

Havelock, E. A. *Preface to Plato.* 1963. Reprint, Cambridge, MA: Belknap Press of Harvard University Press. 1982.

Hilary, Mackie. *Talking Trojan: Speech and Community in the* Iliad. New York: Rowman & Littlefield, 1996.

Hope Simpson, R., and J. F. Lazenby. *The Catalogue of the Ships in Homer's* Iliad. Oxford: Oxford University Press, 1970.

Hurwitt, J. M. *The Art and Culture of Early Greece, 1100–480 B.C.* Ithaca, N.Y.: Cornell University Press, 1985.

Janko, R. *Homer, Hesiod, and the Hymns.* 1982. Reprint, New York: Cambridge University Press, 2007.

Janko, R., and W. Kullman. "Concluding Remarks." In *Omero tremila anni dopo: atti del Congresso di Genova: 6–8 luglio 2000,* edited by F. Montanari. Roma: Ed. di Storia e Letteratura. 2002.

Kirk, G. S. *The Songs of Homer.* New York: Cambridge University Press, 1962.

———. *Homer and the Oral Tradition.* New York: Cambridge University Press, 1976.

Kirke, L. "The Politics of *avrosyni* in Archaic Greece." *Classical Antiquity* 11, no. 1 (19792): 91–121.

Konstan, D. "To Hellenikon ethnos: Ethnicity and the Construction of Ancient Greek Identity." In *Ancient Perceptions of Greek Ethnicity,* edited by Irad Malkin. Cambridge, MA: Harvard University Press, 2001.

Lord, A. B. 1967. "Homer as an Oral Poet." *Harvard Studies in Classical Philology* 72 (1967): 1–46.

———. "Homer, the Trojan War, and History." *Journal of the Folklore Institute* 8 (1971): 85–92.

———. *The Singer Resumes the Tale,* Ithaca, N.Y.: Cornell University Press, 1995.

———. *The Singer of Tales.* 2nd ed. Cambridge, MA: Harvard University Press, 2000.

Mackie, H. *Talking Trojan: Speech and Community in the* Iliad. New York: Rowman & Littlefield, 1996.

Malkin, I. *The Returns of Odysseus: Colonization and Ethnicity.* Berkeley: University of California Press, 1998.

Manning, J. G., and I. Morris. *The Ancient Economy: Evidence and Models.* Stanford, CA: Stanford University Press, 2005.

McDonald, W. A., and Thomas, C. G. *Progress into the Past: The Rediscovery of Mycenaean Civilization.* 2nd ed. Bloomington: Indiana University Press, 1990.

McNeill, R., and W. H. McNeill. *The Human Web: A Bird's-Eye View of World History.* New York: W. W. Norton, 2003.

Mellink, M. J. "Homer, Lycia, and Lukka." In *The Ages of Homer: A Tribute to Emily Townsend Vermeule,* edited by J. P. Carter and S. P. Morris. Austin: The University of Texas Press, 1995.

Morgan, C. "The Origins of Pan-Hellenism." In *Greek Sanctuaries: New Approaches,* edited by Nanno Marinatos and Robin Gägg. New York: Routledge, 1993.

Morris, I. "The Use and Abuse of Homer." *Classical Journal* 55, no. 1 (1986): 81–138.

———. "Negotiated Peripherality in Iron Age Greece." *Journal of World-Systems Research* 2, no. 12 (1996): 1–8.

———. "'Homer and the Iron Age." In *A New Companion to Homer,* edited by I. Morris and B. Powell. Leiden: Brill, 1997.

Morris, S. "Homer and the Near East." In *A New Companion to Homer,* edited by I. Morris and B. Powell. Leiden: Brill, 1997.

Murray, O. "Herodotus as Oral History, II." In *The Historian's Craft in the Age of Herodotus,* edited by N. Luraghi, 16–44. New York: Oxford University Press, 2001a.

———. "Herodotus as Oral History Reconsidered." In *The Historian's Craft in the Age of Herodotus,* edited by N. Luraghi. New York: Oxford University Press. 2001b.

Nagy, G. *Homeric Questions.* Austin: University of Texas Press. 1996a.

———. *Poetry as Performance: Homer and Beyond.* New York: Cambridge University Press. 1996b.

———. Response: Nagy on Powell on Nagy, An Inventory of Debatable Assumptions about a Homeric Question. *Bryn Mawr Classical Review* 97.4.18, 1997, http://ccat.sas.upenn.edu/bmcr/1997/97.04.18.html (2007).

———. *The Best of the Achaeans: Concepts of the Hero in Archaic Greek Poetry.* Rev. ed. Baltimore: Johns Hopkins University Press, 1999.

———. *Homeric Responses.* Austin: University of Texas Press, 2004.

Ong, W. J. *Orality and Literacy.* 2nd ed. New York: Routledge, 2002.

Parry, M. *The Making of Homeric Verse: The Collected Papers of Milman Parry.* Edited by Adam Parry. Oxford: Clarendon Press, 1971.

Popham, M., E. Touloupa, and L. H. Sackett. "The Hero of Lefkandi." *Antiquity* 56 (1982): 169–74.

Powell, B. *Homer and the Origin of the Greek Alphabet.* Cambridge: Cambridge University Press, 1991.

———. Review of G. Nagy, *Poetry as Performance, Homer and Beyond. Bryn Mawr Classical Review* 97.3.21, 1997a. http://ccat.sas.upenn.edu/bmcr/1997/97.03. 21.htm

———. RESPONSE: Powell on Nagy on Powell on Nagy (Schluss). *Bryn Mawr Classical Review* 97.4.24. 1997b, http://ccat.sas.upenn.edu/bmcr/1997/97.04. 24. 1997b, html

Raaflaub, K. "Homer to Solon: The Rise of the Polis: The Written Sources." In *The Ancient Greek City-State,* ed. M. H. Mansen. Copenhagen: Munksgaard, 1993.

———. "Homeric Society." In *A New Companion to Homer,* edited by I. Morris and B. Powell. Leiden: Brill, 1996.

Raubitschek, A. "What the Greeks Thought of Their Early History." *Ancient World* 20 (1989): 39–45.

Rose, P. W. *Sons of God, Children of Earth.* Ithaca, N.Y.: Cornell University Press, 1992.

Ross, S. A. "*Barbarophonos:* Language and Panhellenism in Homer." *Classical Philology* 100, no. 4 (2005): 299–316.

Runciman, W. G. "Origins of States: The Case of Archaic Greece." *Comparative Studies in Society and History* 24, no. 3 (1982): 351–77.

Scheidel, W., and S. von Reden, eds. *The Ancient Economy.* New York: Routledge, 2002.

Scodel, R. *Listening to Homer: Tradition, Narrative, and Audience.* Ann Arbor: University of Michigan Press, 2002.

Silver, M. *Economic Structures of Antiquity.* Westport, CT: Greenwood Press, 1995.

Snodgrass, A. M. *The Dark Age of Greece.* 1971. Reprint. New York: Routledge. 1990.

———. "An Historical Homeric Society?" In *Archaeology and the Emergence of Greece.* Ithaca, N.Y.: Cornell University Press, 2006.

Talpin, O. *Homeric Soundings.* Oxford: Clarendon Press, 1992.

Tandy, D. W. *Warriors into Traders: The Power of the Market in Early Greece.* Berkeley: University of California Press, 1997.

Thomas, C. G., and C. Conant. *Citadel to City-State: The Transformation of Greece, 1200–700 B.C.E.* Bloomington: Indiana University Press, 1999.

Van Wees, H. *Status Warriors: War, Violence, and Society in Homer and History.* Amsterdam: J. C. Gieben, 1992.

Vansina, J. *Oral Tradition as History.* Madison: University of Wisconsin Press, 1985.

Ventris, Michael, and John Chadwick. *Documents in Mycenaean Greek.* 2nd ed. Cambridge: Cambridge University Press, 1973.

Vidal-Naquet, J. P. "Land and Sacrifice in the *Odyssey:* A Study of Religious and Mythical Meanings." In *Myth, Religion and Society,* edited by R. Gordon. Cambridge: Cambridge University Press, 1981.

White, R. *The Middle Ground: Indians, Empires, and Republics in the Great Lakes Region, 1650–1815.* Cambridge: Cambridge University Press. 1991.

Whitley, J. "Response to Papadopoulos: Woods, Trees and Leaves in the Early Iron Age of Greece." *Journal of Mediterranean Archaeology* 6 (1993): 223–29.

Geras and Guest Gifts in Homer

Rick M. Newton

The heroic currency of the *Odyssey* (guest gifts: *xeineia)* is parallel to that of the *Iliad,* where distributed plunder *(geras)* determines a warrior's worth. The Glaukos-Diomedes scene in *Iliad* 6 establishes that the analogy is inherent in oral tradition and that the analogues function as interchangeable narrative components. As the poet interweaves type scenes from battle and *xeneia,* the poems' parallel heroics become part of a parallel poetics in which Odyssean hospitality assumes the ethical complexity of Iliadic warfare. When, in *Odyssey 10,* Odysseus's sailors transform Aeolus's guest gift into *geras,* they unleash the poetic syntax of a wronged hero who wills his comrades' destruction. Just as Achilles in *Iliad* 1 longs for the slaughter of the Achaeans who allow Agamemnon to seize his prize, Odysseus wills the death of his comrades when he lets eleven of his twelve ships sail into the deadly Laestrygonian cove. The glory of both heroes entails the loss of countless souls.

IN *ODYSSEY* 5 ZEUS ISSUES A PRONOUNCEMENT ON ODYSSEUS'S FATE AMONG the Phaeacians:

> They will honor him in their heart as if he were a god
> And send him to his dear homeland in a ship
> With gifts of bronze, gold, and fabrics in such abundance
> As Odysseus would never have taken from Troy
> If he had arrived home unscathed with his share of booty.
> (*Od.* 5.36–40)

This declaration establishes an analogy between the two currencies of the *Iliad* and *Odyssey*. The guest gifts (*xeineia)* of the one poem are likened to the war prizes (*geras)* of the other.[1] In the *Iliad,* the warrior who fights with his comrades to take Troy also tries to stand out among his peers by accumulating plunder. Iliadic war has two goals: victory for the group and the amassing of individual honors. Similarly, the hero of the *Odyssey* has two goals: he wants to reach Ithaca and to collect gifts. It is widely recognized in scholarship on the *Iliad* that the warrior's quest for honor, materialized as *geras,* generates deadly tensions among the ranks. Stripped of his prize by Agamemnon in *Iliad* 1, Achilles abandons the expedition and "casts countless heroes' souls to Hades" (*Il.* 1.3). This paper will propose that, in the *Odyssey,* the same analogy generates equally severe tensions between Odysseus and his men. Indeed, the identification of gifts as tokens of honor lies at the core of two highly problematic aspects of Odysseus's *nostos:* he reaches Ithaca late and alone because, as a glory-seeking hero, he pursues gifts along the way.

The equation of guest gifts and *geras* also invites a comparative perspective on the poetics of the two epics. For, if *geras* and *xeineia* are interchangeable currencies, we may expect a poet skilled in the oral tradition to take advantage of the flexibility. This approach would be especially productive if the analogy articulated by Zeus is not an invention for this one poem but, rather, part of the traditional inventory. This paper will therefore also pursue questions of poetic composition and audience reception. Does the *Iliad* provide indications that gifts and war prizes are analogous? Does the *Iliad* poet invoke this analogy as he innovates within his tradition? If so, does the *Odyssey* poet utilize a similar poetics? Does he build on audience expectations raised by the parallel and manipulate them for effect?

An Iliadic Foundation

Zeus's equation of guest gifts and *geras* is adumbrated in *Iliad* 6. On the verge of combat, Glaukos and Diomedes lay down their weapons and exchange armor. The two stand face to face, when Diomedes abruptly inquires after his opponent's identity:

> But who among mortals are you, my good man?
> For I have never before seen you in battle that brings men glory . . .
> But if you have come from heaven as one of the immortals,
> I would not fight against the heavenly gods.
>
> (*Il.* 6.123–24, 128–29)

What ensues at this point—in lieu of a duel—is a dialogue that seems perhaps more fitting in a hospitality scene. For Diomedes' inquiry after Glaukos's name is the first question a host asks of his guest.[2] Especially puzzling is Diomedes' speculation that Glaukos may be a god: Athena has recently removed the mist from his eyes (*Il.* 5.124–32) so that he can distinguish human from divine combatants. Aristarchus explains the problem by positing that Diomedes' clairvoyance is only partial.[3] Others have assumed that it is no longer in effect.[4] The text does not encourage either assumption.[5] But if the poet is constructing the battle scene with a specific conclusion in mind—the friendly exchange of armor—he may be incorporating elements from a hospitality scene, taking advantage of a compositional flexibility provided by a gifts-as-*geras* equivalence inherent in the tradition.

Diomedes' question is triggered by something unusual about Glaukos. To the surprise of Diomedes, from whom human and mortal opponents have been scurrying throughout his merciless *aristeia,* Glaukos has shown the "boldness to step out far in front of his companions" (*Il.* 6.125–26) and challenge him from an offensive position. The Lycian brazenly "awaits Diomedes' long-shadowing spear," the very weapon with which this "savage spearman instills dread terror" (*Il.* 6.97). Diomedes may find such eagerness puzzling, and his question "Are you a god?" may be tongue in cheek, suggesting that only a god would display such temerity.

Vision-enhanced, he knows Glaukos is no god: his question is rhetorical. Though it is understandable within its context, the Homeric audience would have found the question also remarkable. For this is the first instance in the *Iliad* in which a warrior asks his opponent's name. Pausing over a stranger's divinity, furthermore, is especially typical of hosts in hospitality scenes. Diomedes' question is not only rhetorical: it is formulaic.[6] The same wording (with a shift from second to third person) appears in the *Odyssey* when Alcinous invites the Phaeacian noblemen to a banquet for a stranger who may be a god:

> But if he has come from heaven as one of the immortals (= *Il.* 6.128)
> The gods must be contriving something different for us.
> For, until now, the gods have always presented themselves to us in full view
> Whenever we offer them glorious hecatombs.
>
> (*Od.* 7.199–203)

The textual analogue is apposite: both Diomedes and the Phaeacians can see gods head-on. The *Odyssey* provides several instances of hosts' pondering the divine nature of guests. In *Od.* 4.27, Eteoneus announces the arrival of two strangers who "resemble the offspring of great Zeus." In *Od.* 16.183, Telemachus addresses the transformed beggar in the swineherd's hut, "O stranger, you must be one of the gods who dwell in heaven." After Athena-Mentes leaves through the palace roof in *Od.* 1.319–23, Telemachus surmises and then concludes (*Od.* 1.322, 420) his visitor to be a god. When Diomedes therefore interrupts the fighting in *Il.* 6.123–29 to ask whether Glaukos is a god, Homer's audience would likely detect an innovation from hospitality scenes.[7] Specifically, it sounds as if the narrative is conflating two types of scenes. One heroic endeavor—the pursuit to kill an enemy and strip his armor—is juxtaposed to another—an exchange between strangers that will end in traded gifts.

The introduction of the hospitality motif heightens the audience's perception of Diomedes' amusement. By asking of his challenger's identity and divinity, Diomedes himself introduces the conflation into the narrative of his own *aristeia.*[8] The theme enters via direct speech, not through a poetic aside. Glaukos has entered Diomedes' house, identified here as the space between the armies in which Diomedes has been freely ranging. Exceptionally eager for a fight, Glaukos has burst into this zone and stands at the threshold of Diomedes' domain. The Achaean finds the brashness amusing and patronizingly addresses his opponent as a newly arrived guest. Toying with his prey before pouncing, he in effect says, "Who are you, stranger? Are you a god? For only a god would have the audacity to come into *my* house! In fact, I have just now been wounding gods!" Oral tradition is consistent in terms of who asks the first question in a hospitality scene: the host always asks the guest's name, not vice versa.[9] The irony is dense: Diomedes has crossed the Aegean Sea to fight on Asian soil, which includes Glaukos' home territory of Lycia, but he now behaves as a host. Just as this warrior breaks the barrier between gods and men in his *aristeia,* he now crosses the line between host and guest.[10]

The suggestion that Diomedes and Glaukos are engaged in a hospitality scene is expanded by Glaukos's reply,

> Great-hearted son of Tydeus, why inquire after my lineage?
> Like the generation of leaves, so are the generations of men.
> The wind blows leaves to the ground, but the flourishing woods
> Give rise to others when springtime follows.

> So too with the race of men: one generation sprouts up, another dies.
> But if you want an answer to your question so that you can learn
> My lineage, there are many who know it.
>
> (*Il.* 6.145–51)

Glaukos answers that he is anything but divine: a frail mortal, he is doomed to death as is every creature of nature. Only after declaring his lowly human status does he begin speaking of himself boastfully as a man of distinction. Many indeed know his name, for he is of noble ancestry, his family hailing from Ephyre. This speech pattern—a humble admission of wretched humanity, followed by a declaration of social prominence and a boasting of a hometown—is observed in hospitality scenes. In *Odyssey* 9, Odysseus finally gives his name to Alcinous:

> Your heart is bent on my telling you my pitiable troubles
> So that I may lament all the more.
> What am I to list first, what last?
> For the gods in heaven have given me many sorrows.
> But I will first give my name so that you too
> Can learn it, and so that, if I survive my day of doom,
> I may become your guest, though I live in a home far away.
> I am Odysseus, son of Laertes, known to all mankind
> For my wiles, and my fame has reached heaven.
> I dwell in sunny Ithaca.
>
> (*Od.* 9.12–21)

The theme of hospitality, introduced by Diomedes, is still in play. The conflation is undergoing protraction. In response to a hostlike question, Glaukos gives a guestlike answer, formulating his statement according to the syntax of a hospitality scene. Like Diomedes, Glaukos is conversant in the diction of the tradition, and he takes on his opponent in the new game. Glaukos is a confident warrior, as evidenced by his jumping into the fray, but he is also a confident guest: if Diomedes wants to play host, Glaukos will gladly play along.

As we reflect on Zeus's declaration in *Od.* 5.36–40 and pose the question whether the gifts-as-*geras* analogy is an innovation of the *Odyssey* poet or an inherited feature of oral tradition, it appears as if the *Iliad* poet invokes the comparison with the assumption that his audience would detect and appreciate it. Indeed, the suggestion arises that *geras* and guest gifts are more than material equivalents acquired in two different heroic endeavors. On a poetic level, they are narrative components. Each analogue (gifts and prizes) draws into the poem the syntactical sequence of events found in type scenes of its respective genre (hospitality and battle). Diomedes' heroics and Homer's poetics are intertwined.

This suggestion is borne out in the ensuing dialogue. Now that the context of hospitality has been introduced by the one speaker and expanded by the other, the anticipated narrative sequence takes its course. For, in a hospitality scene, a guest typically follows his declaration of name and birthplace with a family story highlighting his social standing. Glaukos heeds the syntax, tracing his descent from Bellerophontes, slayer of the Chimera, and imbuing his name with an aura of distinction to impress his "host." He tells the story, furthermore, so that his interlocutor may join the ranks of the many who know him ("so that you can learn my lineage"). But as Glaukos follows the narrative rules of a hospitality scene, he speaks of hospitality itself: both the syntax and the content of his words focus on *xeneia,* and he describes the hospitality his grandfather once received from the king of Lycia. In the course of that reception, the rules of *xeneia* were duly observed: the host asked his guest's name after nine days of feasting, and exceptionally lavish gifts were offered at the end (including the hand of the princess and half a kingdom: *Il.* 6.191–95). By setting the story of his grandfather's slaying of the Chimera within a hospitality narrative, Glaukos replies in kind to the dual challenge posed by Diomedes, who is both foe and host. Descended from accomplished fighters and heroic guests, Glaukos presents himself as a worthy match on both fronts. The Lycian is as bold in word as he is in deed.[11]

While listening, Diomedes deduces that he and this stranger are grandsons of men who were *xenoi* to one another. Form and content are thus both still in operation when he replies that his own grandfather hosted Bellerophontes. In fact, Oineus provided twenty days of hospitality to the same man. Diomedes raises the stakes just set by Glaukos: the Lycian king provided nine days of feasting, but Diomedes' grandfather doubled the stay. If Glaukos is the descendant of an impressive guest, Diomedes is the descendant of an even more impressive host. During those twenty days Oineus offered the requisite entertainments. For, in the syntax of a hospitality scene, the guest's life story is followed by host-provided entertainments.[12] As conversant as Glaukos in the syntax of the tradition, Diomedes knows what to do and say at this point. But he is not at liberty to furnish songs, baths, or beds on a battlefield. He meets his obligation therefore by boasting that his grandfather followed the protocol with twice the magnanimity of the original host. The mere reporting of hospitality appears to be an acceptable substitute for the real thing.

The giving of gifts traditionally follows entertainments, and Diomedes—in keeping with audience expectations—now recounts the grandfathers' gifts: Oineus gave a red belt and received a golden two-handled cup. But Diomedes does not stop with mere description, for nothing on the battlefield prohibits a real gift exchange. As a good host, therefore, he takes the initiative and suggests swapping armor. The two men "jump down" from behind their horses—an act that in a battle scene would indicate the commencement of hand-to-hand combat (cf. *Il.* 3.29, 5.13)—and, instead of fighting, clasp hands in a pledge of friendship. Two features have puzzled commentators about the armor exchange: the men remove all their armor (instead of trading selected pieces, as Hector and Ajax do in *Il.* 7.299–305), and the poet describes the items' worth. G. S. Kirk summarizes the difficulties: the incident is "bizarre," showing an "unexpected change in ethos"; Diomedes' enormous profit marks

> a cheap success . . . out of key with the episode as a whole; the action and its implications are . . . intended to be humorous . . . and certainly not serious or heroic in the normal epic sense. . . . The poet . . . withdraws for a moment from his regular narrative mode and proposes a typical folktale-type transaction containing . . . fantasy and exaggeration that are . . . "alien to the normal epic genre." At the same time, it is admitted, "Such an effect would be virtually unique in the *Iliad,* a rare intrusion into the epic of an individual flight of fancy." (Kirk 1990, 190–91)

If this assessment is correct, we may ask why Homer ends the *aristeia* of Diomedes in an anticlimactic mode that compromises the dignity of epic.[13]

Let us consider the full suits of armor. In battle scenes, the removal of armor marks the conclusion of the confrontation. Once an opponent is killed and stripped, the victor's mission is accomplished and hostilities are over. Since Diomedes has been raging for an exceptionally long time and with exceptional skill, an amplified ending is required: he must emerge with more than an ordinary prize. On the narrative level, the poet must conclude with a climax: this inordinately long *aristeia* (over 1,200 lines that began in *Il.* 4.419) calls for an extraordinary ending. The exaggerated gesture of trading full suits of costly armor meets both needs.[14] The Diomedes who moments ago converted a battle scene into a hospitality scene finds himself trumped by the very rules he initiated: his Lycian foe has been transformed into a genuine, not mock, guest-friend (*xeinos philos, Il.* 6.224). He announces the end of hostilities by plunging his spear into the ground, a gesture that his opponent—and Homer's audience—would recognize as signaling peace.[15] Battle over, the armor must come off. All the armor must be removed, furthermore, since the men can never again be enemies: for the rules of *xeneia* dictate that the guest-host bond is an inherited obligation that progeny of the clans are bound to uphold.[16] Diomedes, no longer free to combat Glaukos, now consoles his amusingly eager opponent by pointing out that there are other enemies for them both to kill. Irony is present in this surprising closure. The armor is removed by the wearers themselves, and they are both still alive. Fighting has ended, but there is no corpse. A battle scene has been transcended by something else.

When we compare the exchange of sword and belt between Hector and Ajax in *Il.* 7.299–305, we find no context that signals a permanent change in relationship between the contestants. On the contrary, Hector proposes swapping trophies as a way of ceasing hostilities temporarily,

> Let us now cease our fighting and hostility,
> For today. We will fight again in the future, when some god
> Will choose between us and grant victory to one of us.
> (*Il.* 7.290–92)

Hector proposes a truce, not a treaty. But the moment of *xenos*-recognition between Diomedes and Glaukos calls for something magnificent. Anything less would be anticlimactic.

What of Diomedes' "cheap success"?[17] This question finds an answer in hospitality scenes. In *Od.* 4.614–19, when Menelaus promises Telemachus a Sidonian bowl, he declares its value: it is silver with a gold rim, the work of Hephaestus, a gift originating with King Phaidimos. He calls it the "most beautiful and most expensive" of his treasures. Odysseus tallies up his take from the Ismarian priest of Apollo as seven gold talents, a silver crater, and twelve jars of magically potent wine (*Od.* 9.197–207). Similarly, when the Phaeacian noblemen shower their gifts, they follow Alcinous's instructions for each to provide a large tripod and cauldron (*Od.* 13.10–15) in addition to the previously mandated cloaks, tunics, and talents of silver (*Od.* 8.389–93). "We will recover our losses with a tax on the deme," Alcinous consoles the donors. In hospitality scenes, therefore, guest gifts are routinely "assessed," itemized as so many items of precious metals, rare fabrics, and talents of silver and gold. They tend to be things that can be stored as family heirlooms.[18] Diomedes looks on Oineus's souvenir from Bellerophontes in the same terms: he recalls the golden cup among his grandfather's holdings. Read within this light, the evaluation of the armor is not so much puzzling as it is intriguing. The exchange between the fighters ends as it began: as a conflation of type scenes in which hospitality and warfare are juxtaposed. In the course of the juxtaposition, battle has given way to hospitality. What began as *geras* has been transformed into guest gifts that will stay in each recipient's family for generations.

We observed earlier that Diomedes presumptuously postured as Glaukos' host, perhaps to toy with him. By the end of the scene, however, it occurs to Diomedes that he owes his friend an apology. After posing as a host on foreign soil, he knows he is a mere stranger. The real host in the now-hospitable encounter has proven to be Glaukos, a native of the region. Diomedes acknowledges the role reversal when he explains, "So now I am your friend and host in the midst of Argos, but you are mine in Lycia" (*Il.* 6.224–25). But the apologies of epic heroes entail qualifications. Warriors who make amends also reassert their superiority. Agamemnon in *Il.* 9.160–61 concludes his catalogue of compensatory gifts to Achilles, "And let him submit to me, since I am more kingly and many years his senior." An apologetic Agamemnon reclaims his higher status over even Achilles. A similar dynamic informs the end of the Glaukos-Diomedes exchange. On the one hand, Diomedes compensates with a gift. On the other, he remains Glaukos' superior by receiving over ten times the value of what he gives. Diomedes' *aristeia* on the battlefield has been transformed into an *aristeia* of *xeneia:* Glaukos can outperform the son of Tydeus neither in the actual outdoors of real battle nor in the mock indoors of pretend hospitality. This is still Diomedes'—not Glaukos'—finest moment.

Read within the context of a hospitality scene, the description of the value of the armor sheds light on another detail commentators have found "out of place" and "rather forced."[19] Recalling the grandfathers' gifts, Diomedes claims firsthand knowledge of Oineus' cup and hearsay knowledge of the belt given to Bellerophontes: "I left (*katelipon*) the cup in my house when I came here. But

Tydeus I do not remember, since he left (*kalliphe*) me when I was a mere child when the Achaean army perished at Thebes" (*Il.* 6.221–23). Applying the same verb—*kataleipein* —to the cup he "left behind" and the child his father "left behind," Diomedes draws an analogy between his own and his father's actions. What point, on the contextual level, does the son of Tydeus make with this allusion to his father, who was not involved in the grandfathers' transaction? On the narrative level, what does the *Iliad* poet accomplish with this seemingly extrinsic detail? An answer emerges when we read the scene as a conflation of a military *aristeia* and a hospitality scene. Although Diomedes has seen the cup, he knows of the belt only through stories he has heard growing up "in his house." For along with Oineus' souvenir, the story of his hosting Bellerophontes—that is, the narrative context of the cup—has entered the house as an orally transmitted heirloom that likewise spans generations. In similar fashion, Glaukos' house resounded with tales of the military exploits of his forebears (Bellerophontes slew the Chimera) and their heroic hospitality (Bellerophontes was royally hosted in Lycia). Even within the context of a war poem, tales of ancestral hospitality are esteemed, preserved, and handed down.

Raised to prove himself a fighter worthy of his father, as he has been hearing from both gods and men who recount Tydeus' exploits (*Il.* 4.370–400, 5.800–13), Diomedes is also conditioned to look on hospitality as a competitive arena—not only with his "guest" on a synchronic level but also diachronically with his ancestors. He speaks of his grandfather's "left-behind" cup as analogous to himself, "left behind" by Tydeus, because he is thinking of heroic legacies: Diomedes is still competing with his father. Claiming not to remember Tydeus the person, he does know of the hospitality Oineus extended two generations ago: Oineus received the most precious of metals from a guest who revered him. Oineus himself gave a leather belt, an item of value to be sure, but worth considerably less than a golden vessel. This tale of his grandfather's profitable *xeneia* is as well known to Diomedes as are the accounts of Tydeus' accomplishments in war, for both activities have been celebrated in the oral tradition in which he was raised. Similarly, as we have observed, Glaukos knows—through tales of his ancestors—that his grandfather was both decorated fighter and honored guest. Looking on Glaukos' golden armor, therefore, Diomedes takes advantage of a rare opportunity to outperform his forebears with a gesture that would have elicited their beaming admiration. Proving himself a worthy grandson of Oineus by making an astounding profit from the grandson of Bellerophontes, he trades bronze for gold—a full set of armor, not a single cup—and makes an instant 1,000 percent return on his investment. This is not a "cheap success" lacking in the dignity of epic. For a hero's worth in the Homeric world is measured in material possessions, both those won in war and those received in hospitality. Indeed, Glaukos has just boasted of Sisyphus of Ephyre, "the most profit-making of men" (*kerdistos andrôn, Il.* 6.153) as the founder of his family line. Diomedes has outprofited Glaukos' entire clan!

The value of items exchanged at *Il.* 6.234–36 is significant, therefore, on two counts. First, in giving Glaukos armor worth nine oxen, Diomedes observes the protocol of transgenerational hospitality. As descendants of former *xenoi* receive one another, the gifts are expected to equal or surpass the value of earlier presents.[20] Glaukos' grandfather received leather, but Oineus' grandson now gives bronze. A generous transgenerational host, Diomedes not merely matches but significantly increases the value of the gift his ancestor gave. Second, receiving gold in exchange, he strikes an even better deal than his grandfather did years ago. Oineus' cup is an impressive memento, but his grandson now receives the weight of many gold cups. Diomedes' *aristeia* is still in operation, therefore, and in outdoing his own grandfather in gift exchange he proves himself more measurably heroic than the *father of Tydeus.* Tydeus "left behind" his son for battle in Thebes, leaving a legacy of oral heirlooms celebrating his military excellence (the *klea andrôn).* Now Diomedes earns his place in this line of hosts who pride themselves on striking profitable transactions with guests. He has "left behind" his grandfather's gift to return with a better one. Diomedes thus takes even his own *aristeia* to unprecedented heights. He does more than match his father: he outmatches his own grandfather. By the climactic end of the episode, this hero proves himself an exceptional performer in both arenas. This son of Tydeus has wounded gods, and this grandson of Oineus has won the worth of one hundred oxen in a single gift exchange. In Homer's world, hecatombs are reserved for the gods themselves (cf. *Il.* 1.99, 309). In receiving a hecatomb equivalent from Glaukos, therefore, Diomedes imbues himself with a divine aura similar to that with which Athena has graced him, enabling him to pursue Apollo in battle and even wound Ares and Aphrodite. This ending is not merely climactic: it is virtuoso.

Most significantly for our appreciation of the poetics of the episode, Diomedes' *xeneia* unfolds in such a way as to draw audience attention to the poet's accomplishment as an innovator within his tradition. For, besides the armor that will become Diomedes' material legacy, this hero has given rise to a new narrative tradition about himself. Future generations will hear of his hostlike victory over Glaukos and his surpassing of his father's father as a performer of hospitality on the battlefield. The proof lies in the Homeric text itself, an oral heirloom celebrating the innovative juxtaposition of two heroics: the heroics of warfare *and* the heroics of hospitality. The poet revels in his own *aristeia* with a rare metanarrative comment: "Zeus, son of Kronos, robbed Glaukos of his wits, for in exchanging armor with Diomedes, son of Tydeus, he gave gold for bronze, the worth of a hundred oxen for nine" (*Il.* 6.234–36). Mark Edwards (1992, 288) observes that "type scenes may be closely related in form": the sequence a fighter follows in donning armor, for example, may resemble a woman or goddess putting on her finery, or a messenger may be received into a house as if he were a guest.[21] But in *Iliad* 6 the poet raises type scene conflation to new heights. For the sequence of events in a battle scene does not readily translate into those of a hospitality scene: these are not inherently analogous undertakings, and the likening of a blood-thirsty Diomedes at the height of his physical prowess to a host is a most unexpected comparison for the audience of a war poem. The poet's juxtaposition of these two traditions may therefore occur "contrary to audience expectations" (*para prosdokian; para doxan:* cf. Aristotle, *Poetics* 52a4).[22] The audience would likewise have found Diomedes' opening question unexpected. But, composing within the genre of military epic, the poet has done what Diomedes himself has done. The warrior has transformed himself from a fighter into a host. The poet has transformed a battle scene into a hospitality scene. In the process, both poet and hero have surpassed what has been handed down to them: Diomedes improves on the multigenerational accomplishments of his clan, and the poet improves on the oral tradition he has inherited. As an *aristeia* in its own right, *Il.* 6.119–236 constitutes an *aristeia* among *aristeiai.*

In conclusion to this discussion of the heroics and poetics of this Iliadic scene, we may reasonably surmise that the tradition in which the *Iliad* poet composes does indeed allow the equation of prizes taken in war with gifts received in hospitality. The analogy announced by Zeus in *Odyssey* 5 therefore articulates explicitly what the *Iliad* presents in implicit terms. The equivalency exists on two levels.

On a contextual level, war prizes and guest gifts are analogous currencies. We may therefore expect to find characters in the *Odyssey* treating guest gifts with the same earnestness that characters in the *Iliad* assign to plunder. Throughout the *Odyssey*, Odysseus displays keen interest in acquiring and guarding his presents. At times, he goes out of his way to procure more, jeopardizing the safety of his comrades. Such "acquisitiveness" and "cupidity" have been interpreted as expressions of an "untypical hero's" less-than-dignified character when it comes to his belly and insatiable appetites.[23] His valuing of gifts over the welfare of his companions has been read as a sign of his deficiency in leadership.[24] But now we may look on it as an expression of a traditionally heroic, and therefore ethically complex, nature.

The analogy also has implications for our appreciation of Homeric poetics. These currencies are especially intelligible to an audience steeped in oral poetry when the poet presents them within recognizable contexts. Such contextualization lies within his control, for he is free to move from one genre of type scenes to another, crossing even from war into hospitality. *Geras* and guest gifts are thus compositional elements that the poet can manipulate for effect as he performs. When he subtly introduces guest gifts into a war narrative (as in *Iliad* 6), he introduces the theme of hospitality, giving himself the opportunity to play on audience expectations from type scenes in that genre. When he openly introduces war prizes into a poem about hospitality (as in *Odyssey* 5), he introduces the theme of warfare, giving himself the opportunity to play on audience expectations from type scenes in that genre.

Unlikely Analogues

In the *Iliad*, the value of *geras* is directly dependent on an amassed and intact soldiery. Plunder from battle is distributed openly to the fighters. As Achilles explains with resentment in *Il.* 1.163–68, the portion of honor always goes to the commander in chief (Agamemnon), and the rest is distributed, the best items designated for the best fighters. Whatever the prizes' intrinsic worth, their value is augmented by the award ceremony itself. M. I. Finley (1982, 126) observes that these ceremonial "acts [are] an added touch that would have been needless were possession sufficient unto itself . . . in fact, both counted greatly, the wealth as wealth on the one hand, and the wealth as symbol on the other." Achilles especially esteems Briseis because (*Il.* 1.162, 392) "the sons of the Achaeans gave her" to him. The fact that she is chosen by the troops for the "best of the Achaeans" increases her worth in everyone's eyes. She holds a "value-added" status that puts her on a par with Chryseis, daughter of the priest of Apollo: Agamemnon thus looks on her as a fair replacement for his own concubine. At the same time, however, *geras* has a negative side, for it engenders a jealousy that can destabilize the community. Achilles resents that the lion's share goes to a commander who is a lesser fighter than him. Prizes are so equated with status, furthermore, that their seizure is tantamount to a public shaming. Thus, Achilles complains to Thetis,

> Wide ruling Agamemnon, son of Atreus,
> Has dishonored me: he has taken my prize himself and keeps it.
> (*Il.* 1.355–56)

This dishonoring triggers the consequences that an audience of oral poetry readily recognizes: as "a wronged hero seeks revenge in the death of his colleagues," Achilles goes off alone to enlist the help of Thetis.[25]

Achilles' anger, it is important to note, is not restricted to Agamemnon. He is enraged with his comrades on a pan-Achaean level for standing idly by. So contemptuous is he of his comrades' passivity that he publicly demeans them as "nobodies" (*outidanoi*) as he abuses Agamemnon:

> You, king who feed off your people, since you are lord over nobodies (*outidanois*).
> Otherwise, o son of Atreus, this would be your final outrage. . . .
> For I would be called a coward and a nobody (*outidanos*)
> If I were to defer to you in every matter, no matter what you say.
> Go and give your orders to others, but don't tell me what to do.
> (Il. 1.231–32, 292–95)

Achilles then physically separates from his peers in refusing to become a cipher. This is why, when he specifies to Thetis the punishment he wants Zeus to mete out, he directs his ire against the men:

> As for the soldiers, (ask Zeus) to pin them against their sterns along the sea
> As they are slain, so that they might all take joy in their king

And so that wide-ruling Agamemnon may come to know of his
Outrage in showing no honor whatsoever to the best of the Achaeans.
(Il. 1.409–12)

Achilles envisions a punishment that fits the crime. "Wide-ruling Agamemnon" has based his right to seize Briseis on the fact that he rules more men. Since these widely ruled troops have failed to stand up for Achilles, he demands a punishment that will engulf them along with their king. He wants the men to die an ignominious death, pinned in by the ships after retreating, so many "nobodies," from the storming enemy. Achilles wants the men to be—as he is—disgraced. This is the precise form of revenge that Zeus will initially contemplate (*Il.* 2.3–4) and eventually execute (*Il.* 11.93–94) in the course of the poem.

There is a reason why Achilles attaches life-or-death importance to *geras*. The hero who accepts war prizes is obligated to risk his life for others. This obligation finds its clearest articulation in *Iliad* 12, where Glaukos tells Sarpedon:

Glaukos, why have we two been especially esteemed
With places of honor and cuts of meat and the fullest cups
In Lycia, and all look on us as if we were gods? . . .
This is why we must now take our stand in the front ranks of the Lycians
And go out to meet the heat of battle.
(*Il.* 12.310–16)

Herein we see the symbiotic relationship between the leader and his troops that is materialized in *geras*. Separating from the others to fight in the front, the hero furthers the communal cause. At battle's end, the comrades reciprocate with prizes that, appropriately, single him out. To accept prizes thus carries the obligation to continue plunging into the fray. This duty is so pronounced that prizes can be offered even in advance. Agamemnon' gifts are promised only if Achilles will rejoin the war (*Il.* 9.299). Similarly, in *Il.* 10.303–12, Hector assembles the Trojan leaders and offers Achilles' horses to whoever will venture out on a particularly risky night spying mission. In the *Iliad, geras* is a public matter: the warrior must have a group to defend so that, after battle, the same group can distinguish him with honors they validate in ceremony. An Iliadic hero is necessarily "invested" in his comrades.

The same cannot be said of guest gifts. *Xeineia* are bestowed privately, within the confines of the host's house. They are not put on display, and no onlooking troops oversee their distribution. On the contrary, an item's value increases with its interiority and obscurity. We have already commented on Menelaus' gift to Telemachus. This bowl has moved from the indoor forge of Hephaestus to a Phoenician palace, where the "concealed" (*amphekalypse, Od.* 4.618) heirloom was then transferred to the king of Sparta. It will now join the treasures of the Ithacan royal family. Also in Sparta, Helen gives Telemachus her most ornate *peplos,* a wedding gown for his future bride. The dress, Helen's own handiwork, lies beneath her other valuables at the bottom of a chest (*Od.* 15.108).[26] The intimate nature of these items increases their value, for a gift is a token of the private relationship that arises between guest and host during hospitality. Odysseus boasts of this when he recounts his "gleaming gifts" from the Ciconian priest (*Od.* 9.205–07): the twelve jars of special wine were from a private reserve known only to Maron, his wife, and one female steward. Odysseus next takes this *xeineion* "to the inner recesses of Polyphemus's cave" (*Od.* 9.236).[27] Upon reaching Ithaca, furthermore, he will conceal his holdings in a cave, thereby preserving their secrecy. We may also recall from the Glaukos-Diomedes episode that Diomedes recounts "leaving behind" his grandfather's cup "in the house." This gift does not travel to Troy: it stays home.

Throughout the career of a regifted item, gazing troops have no bearing on its value. Amassed soldiers do not validate the objects. Instead, *xeineia* confer honor when the traveler returns home. Odysseus declares to Alcinous,

> If you were to bid me to stay here a full year
> And provide me escort and give resplendent gifts,
> I would prefer that, and it would be far more profitable
> To return to my dear homeland with fuller hands.
> I would be more respected and loved by everyone
> Who would visit me after I return to Ithaca.
>
> (*Od.* 11.356–61)

Odysseus expects to dazzle future house guests with his trophies. Telemachus's awe (*sebas*) at the interior of the Spartan palace is in keeping with this pattern: beholding the showpieces Menelaus collected on his seven-year return trip, the wide-eyed youth wonders whether this is the palace of Olympian Zeus (*Od.*4.71–75).

Odysseus's confession to Alcinous suggests another distinctive feature of guest gifts. The pursuit of *xeineia* may prolong the journey.

Odysseus declares that he would gladly remain an entire year in exchange for a more lavish send-off. Telemachus in Sparta tactfully declines Menelaus's offer of a twelve-day stay by invoking the same words in *Od.* 4.595–96: "I would gladly stay with you a full year, if I did not miss my house and parents." It is interesting to note that Telemachus invokes the formula as a prelude to declining his host's offer. His allusion to missing his (plural) "parents," with only his mother at home, suggests that he may be invoking a formula from a polite *decline* of extended hospitality (such as "I would love to stay, but I must get back to the folks at home"). Telemachus seems to be using the formula "typically." Odysseus, by contrast, applies it in "atypical" fashion to a profitable end: he invokes it as prelude to *accepting* Alcinous's invitation to postpone the send-off ("I would love to stay, but I expect more presents if I do"). The contrast between father and son is telling: Telemachus is a novice in these heroics; Odysseus is a professional.

A homecoming delayed to amass gifts poses problems especially if the traveler has comrades in tow. Delays jeopardize the welfare of the party.

The longer the journeyers travel, the greater the risks they face. Hosts must be sought out for practical reasons: relying on the kindness of strangers, travelers must receive sustenance, replenish supplies, and repair ships as they make their way. Stops are necessary, then, but not lengthy ones. Indeed, overly kind hosts may induce forgetfulness of the homecoming goal. Odysseus must forcefully retrieve his scouts from the narcotic Lotus Eaters (*Od.* 9. 92–104), and his own comrades must prod him to leave after he languishes for a full year in Circe's bedroom (*Od.*10.467–74). The longer Odysseus prolongs his *nostos,* the more men he loses. The relationship between guest gifts and homecoming, therefore, is not a symbiotic one. The glory-seeking hero of hospitality is at cross-purposes with his companions as he turns necessary stops into prolonged award-winning performances at the hearth. In battle, the prospect of *geras* induces soldiers to fight for the common good. Guest gifts, by contrast, do not play an analogous role in homecoming. A traveling party can be superfluous. Paradoxically, the hero's pursuit of *xeineia* prolongs and thereby jeopardizes the *nostos* of both him and his companions.[28]

Comrades can be worse than irrelevant. Their sheer numbers can impede. Even in Homeric hospitality, no mortal host can comfortably provide meals, baths, beds, and gifts for some six hundred sailors aboard twelve ships—the original size of Odysseus' retinue. As in warfare, therefore, the hero must part from the group to single himself out. But, instead of standing protectively "in the front ranks," he leaves them to fend for themselves while he heads for the new "front" of a strange house. Hospitality is a one-on-one affair—conducted not on an open plain before onlookers but deep inside, behind closed doors. When Telemachus sails to Pylos, he seeks hospitality only for himself and Athena-Mentor. When Nestor invites the two to stay the night, Athena-Mentor replies that s/he must tend to the crew, and Nestor does *not* open the invitation: he puts up Telemachus alone (*Od.* 3.342–70). When Telemachus then travels by land to Sparta, he is accompanied by Nestor's son. The Ithacan crewmen do not join him, and whatever gifts Telemachus collects remain his private property.

Though analogous, therefore, guest gifts and war prizes are not identical in terms of their implications for the heroics of the two poems. They call for drastically different social stances between the leader and his men. The Iliadic hero needs companions to grant and validate prizes. Properly observed, the reward system of *geras* preserves the soldier community. Only if the rules are breached, as they are by Agamemnon, is the community set at risk. The loss of Achaeans to Achilles' withdrawal is directly attributable, therefore, to the breakdown of the *geras* system. In rejecting Agamemnon's gifts, Achilles concomitantly expresses his rejection of his comrades (*Il.* 9.630). In the *Odyssey,* by contrast, the delays in the hero's homecoming and the destruction of all but one of his ships are attributable to his successful pursuit of the heroic currency of his poem. Long before his seven-year detention by Calypso and long before the Ithacan remnant consume the Thrinacian cattle (the crime curiously identified in the proem as causing the mass deaths), this leader opts for detours and delays that gain him—and him alone—prestige and profits.[29] Among the Ciconians, his first postwar stop, he lets the men run amok on the shore while he pursues hospitality in the home of Apollo's priest: he returns the next morning with "gleaming gifts" (*Od.* 9.201), but at the cost of seventy-two comrades (six per ship).[30] In the Cyclops episode, he leaves eleven ships at goat island to return with eighteen rams and Polyphemus' enormous pet, but at the price of six comrades eaten alive. He then spends a full month with Aeolus, during which the sailors stay by their ships and seethe with jealousy.

From Aeolus to the Laestrygonians

When Odysseus visits Aeolus, hospitality is offered only to him. His account employs the first-person pronoun (here, italicized) four times in seven lines,

> (Aeolus) befriended *me* for a full month and asked about everything,
> About Troy and the ships of the Argives and the homecomings of the Achaeans.
> And *I* told him everything in due order.
> But when *I* requested passage and asked to be sent off . . .
> He flayed a nine-year old ox and gave *me* the hide,
> In which he had bound up the pathways of the adverse winds.
> (*Od.* 10.14–20)

Odysseus' comrades look on Aeolus' gift of the sealed pouch in an inappropriate manner. As a gift from a host, this is their leader's personal property, to be enjoyed within the privacy of his own house. But the men view it as *geras:*

> Why, look at this! What a dear and valued friend Odysseus is
> To everyone, no matter what city or land he comes to!
> From Troy, he is carrying off for himself many fine heirlooms
> From the plunder. But we who have made the same journey
> Are returning home with empty hands.
> And now Aeolus has also given him these gifts of friendship.
> (*Od.* 10.38–43)

This is a pivotal moment in the poem. It is the first step in a sequence of events that, within the next one hundred lines, will end in catastrophe: the sinking of eleven ships and the slaughter of their entire crews—more than five hundred men—by the Laestrygonians. As in *Iliad* 6, the poet marks the pivotal moment with a conflation, combining warfare and hospitality and playing on the audience's expectations as raised by the syntax of each genre. The sailors know the pouch is a guest gift, since Odysseus has just returned from a long stay with a host. Assuming it to contain silver and gold (*Od.* 10.44–45), they correctly liken it to a typical *xeineion:* guest gifts often consist of precious metals. But in plotting to distribute its contents, they are treating it as *geras.* Their grumbling over Odysseus' accumulated winnings, while they themselves remain empty-handed, sounds curiously like Achilles' resentment toward the *geras-*

grabbing Agamemnon in *Il.* 1.161–68. *Geras,* we observed, engenders jealousy.[31] That jealousy is now transferred to Odysseus' mysterious guest gift as the crewmen publicize an item of intimately personal and undisclosed value.[32] Their presumptuous plot to steal it matches Agamemnon's outrage in the *Iliad:* they claim a token of honor that does not belong to them and, in the process, violate the gift itself and disgrace its owner. For the seizing of *geras,* or a *geras* equivalent, is tantamount to a stripping of honor. In terms of the narrative, the audience may therefore wonder whether the crewmen are activating the sequence of "wronged hero seeks revenge in the death of his colleagues."

As we examine the combined poetics and heroics of this narrative, it is interesting to note that, just as Diomedes introduces the hospitality theme into *Iliad* 6 in direct speech, Odysseus' crewmen themselves conflate the currencies of *geras* and *xeineia.* The poet draws our attention to the sailors' ignoble initiative by having Odysseus report—inexplicably—a speech delivered while he was asleep. Diomedes likewise takes it upon himself, in direct speech, to transform Glaukos into a guest with a question that would have intrigued the audience. Just as Diomedes deserves the credit for broadening his heroic arena with his expanded discourse, furthermore, Odysseus' crewmen must bear the blame for the disaster about to befall them. They are the ones who unabashedly treat a guest gift as a war prize. Indeed, if their complaint of empty-handedness is true, they are so unaccomplished in battle that they have no *geras* to call their own after ten years at Troy. Their clever conflation of *geras* and guest gifts may well end in failure, as have their previous endeavors. In *Iliad* 6, the same conflation introduces narrative patterns from two genres that the poet intertwines as he plays on audience expectations. That juxtaposition ends in the overtaking of the one genre by the other: weapons are dropped and lasting friendship is proclaimed as a battle-narrative gives way to a hospitality story. Now in the *Odyssey,* a similar tension in audience expectations is engendered. In the juxtaposition of a gift-seeking *nostos* and a battlefield dispute over *geras* (now occurring on a ship!), will the one pattern overtake the other? Will the story line of the *Odyssey,* with its contextual goal of homecoming, be derailed by a narrative pattern from war?

Driven back to Aeolus, Odysseus again seeks hospitality and punctiliously follows protocol: he arrives at the house, finds the host banqueting with his family, and sits at the threshold, waiting to be received (*Od.* 10.60–63). These gestures would normally be met with a welcome, a meal, a bath, and a bed—just as before. For their amplified description suggests to the audience that they will indeed be answered.[33] But the narrative pattern from a hospitality scene is not fulfilled. Aeolus does *not* rise from his throne to lift his guest by the hand. Odysseus, noticing the unfulfilled ritual sequence, tries to salvage the situation by "accosting [literally, "attaching himself to," *kathaptomenos*] Aeolus with soothing words" (*Od.* 10.70) with all the urgency of a lowly suppliant.[34] He intensifies his request for hospitality with a supplication gesture—but to no avail.[35] Aeolus replies with a denunciation that Odysseus and the poem's audience would have found equally shocking,

> Off of this island at once, you most contemptible of living creatures!
> For it is not right to receive or give passage to
> A man detested (*apechthomenos*) by the gods of Olympus.
> Off with you, since you have come here loathed by the immortals!
> (*Od.* 10.72–75)

In terms of narrative expectations, this is a rich moment. For the traditional hospitality syntax in which a welcoming host may reflect on a visitor's divinity is now abandoned. Aeolus knows that Odysseus, no god at all, is divinely loathed. The King of the Winds can therefore ignore protocol and deny his suppliant guest. Indeed, these are the harshest words Odysseus has ever heard from a host. Karl Reinhardt (1996, 88) comments: "The worst of it is not the storm caused by the winds rushing out of the sack, nor the uselessness of all of Odysseus' efforts. . . . Rather, the worst of it is what all this means: that Odysseus is hated and cursed by the gods." To suffer such a loss of status in divine eyes is the worst possible disgrace for a king "dear to Zeus."

Instead of receiving the welcome that a narrative *nostos* pattern would lead us to expect, Odysseus hears, in a variant from a war narrative that takes both him and us by surprise, the very abuse that Agamemnon heaps on Achilles:

> Go ahead and leave, if your heart is set on it. I, for one,
> Do not entreat you to stay on my behalf. I have others
> Who will show me respect, most of all counsellor Zeus
> But you are, in my eyes, the most detested (*echthistos*) of the kings dear to Zeus. . . .
> Go home now in your ships, and take your comrades with you.
> Lord it over your Myrmidons, since I care not a jot for you.
> (*Il.* 1.173–76, 179–80)

Aeolus' chastisement is parallel to Agamemnon's harangue in both content and structure. As is Achilles, Odysseus is told to leave on the spot and take his men with him. Both heroes are shamed as "detested" in their revilers' spewed contempt. Just as the dismissal by Agamemnon devastates Achilles, Aeolus' rejection crushes Odysseus. If indeed he is loathed by the gods and can rightfully be denied Zeus-sanctioned hospitality, he stands no chance of securing the protection or prizes of future hospitality. Both homecoming and honor are lost. On the narrative level, we may wonder whether the lost homecoming will be accompanied by an aborted poem. Odysseus' comrades altered the discourse when they conflated the story of their own *nostos:* transforming a guest gift into a war prize, they activated an ominous sequence from a war narrative. When Odysseus returns to Aeolus, the *Odyssey* poet has the option of proceeding with a hospitality scene and keeping the *nostos* narrative on track. Instead, he takes the detour initiated by the sailors themselves. The illegitimate seizure of *geras* will lead to the loss of heroes' souls.

At the parallel point in the Iliadic sequence, Achilles seeks isolation along the shore. His physical separation from the Achaeans is indicative of disgust with them. He prays for Zeus to send a horrendous death by pinning the men in by the ships, where the Trojans will pick them off. The ensuing events in the *Odyssey* fulfill the audience's expectations arising from this pattern—but on a horrific level and at a breakneck pace. On approaching the Laestrygonians, Odysseus allows eleven ships to enter the bottleneck cove and does nothing to steer them from the deadly trap. Odysseus' actions have been variously interpreted. Alfred Heubeck (1989, 49) posits that Odysseus keeps the flagship in a safe spot "out of a sense of responsibility proper in a commander." But this commander does not muster the fleet upon attack. Jonathan Shay (2002, 60–64) faults Odysseus for placing his self-protection ahead of protection of the others. S. Douglas Olson (1995, 55) explains that the men "ignore his lead" as they fall victim to their own disobedience. But Odysseus describes the men as sailing ahead on their own, while "I alone kept my black ship outside" (*Od.* 10.95). He is not leading at this juncture, and he issues no unheeded order. On the poetic level, Jenny Strauss Clay (2002, 83) suggests that Homer, in a "neither credible nor verifiable" manner, is ridding himself of the extraneous ships he has inherited from the *Iliad:* Odysseus' *nostos* requires only one ship, and the Laestrygonians, however implausibly, do the job.[36]

When we read the passage as a conflated narrative, however, Odysseus' actions make sense. For he is doing the same thing as Achilles in response to his shaming: he voluntarily separates himself from his comrades out of contempt for them. The scholiast may therefore have the best answer: this maneuver "makes preliminary arrangements for *Odysseus'* means of escape."[37] The leader leaves his men to their own devices, expecting them to do themselves serious harm —as happens everytime he parts. As Achilles does at the narratively parallel moment, Odysseus now wills the death of his comrades. As if in answer to Achilles' prayer, the Ithacan sailors are trapped in a harbor ("pinned alongside their ships") with no escape as they are ignominiously picked off, "harpooned like so many fish" (*Od.* 10.124). Odysseus gives no explanation for his decision to steer clear of the cove because Homer's audience, conversant in the syntax of narrative patterns, would have found it redundant. Indeed, an explanation would break the suspense.[38] The audience would also have found the poet's silence extremely engaging: Achilles only prayed for the death of his friends, and Zeus answered the prayer over the course of several books. Odysseus, by contrast, engineers the disaster himself and executes it on the spot.

The poet protracts our horror and suspense by invoking yet another narrative pattern. As Odysseus beats his retreat, he invokes a formula, "At that point, drawing my sharp sword from the side of my thigh" (*Od.* 10.126). These words present a glimmer of hope, for they traditionally appear as prelude to a hero's "deliberation between alternatives."[39] The formula appears in *Il.* 1.190 as Achilles impetuously "draws his sword from the side of his thigh" to slay Agamemnon. But Athena grabs him by the hair, and he replaces the weapon in order to hold out for a long-term, more profitable plan. Likewise in *Od.* 9.300 Odysseus "draws his sword from the side of his thigh" to slay the Cyclops. But when it dawns on him that acting on impulse would preclude escape from the cave, he resheaths it. As we hear Odysseus invoke the same formula on fleeing from the Laestrygonians, therefore, it occurs to us that he will surely rethink his rashness and put his weapon back as he invokes his distinctive talent for solutions that are both impromptu and strategic. But this expectation is precisely what the *Odyssey* poet now thwarts as he proceeds precipitously "contrary to audience expectations." To our dismay, neither does a god descend to pull Odysseus's hair nor does he change his mind on his own. Instead, he follows through with appalling swiftness. Not taking time even to untie the hawsers, he uses his drawn weapon in an unbroken motion to cut the cables and run.

As we listen, we are disappointed, horrified, and perplexed. For the poet has invoked a narrative pattern—the unsheathing of a sword by a subsequently reflecting hero—to lift our hopes that Odysseus will go to his men's rescue, just as he did among the Lotus-Eaters, and just as he did in the Cyclops' cave. Even if, in fulfillment of the war-narrative pattern invoked by the mutinous crewmen, we anticipate the wronged hero's rage to bring death to his companions, the Iliadic syntax leads us to expect that the deaths will occur long in the future—certainly not now. But these hopes are dashed as we hear of the inhuman harpooning of men whose *nostos* is irrevocably lost. On the narrative level, we are led to wonder what will become of the hero's homecoming. The comrades have lost Ithaca. Will Odysseus? Without Odysseus' reaching home, the *Odyssey* cannot continue as a poem.[40]

Conclusion

Zeus's declaration in *Od.* 5.36–40, equating guest gifts and *geras,* opens a fertile field for interpreting the actions of Odysseus throughout his *nostos.* The hero of the *Odyssey* is not a petty materialist who fails to meet the standards of other epic figures. Rather, as he strives for homecoming, he pursues the glory that is part and parcel of the identity of every Homeric hero. In this respect, he is analogous to Achilles in the *Iliad.* The heroes of both poems are motivated by the honorable pursuit of the recognition their societies confer. This recognition takes the form of *geras* in the one poem, of guest gifts in the other. The *Odyssey* presents not only homecoming as a heroic goal in itself but also the pursuit of hospitality along the way. The accumulation of goods by a *nostos*-seeking hero is on a par with an Iliadic warrior's pursuit of prizes won in battles that culminate in the taking of Troy. But, however prestigious these tokens may be, epic glory is no simple matter. Achilles' glory comes at the price of countless Achaean lives, just as Odysseus's comes with the loss of his comrades. For all their differences in content, therefore, both the *Iliad* and the *Odyssey* present a poignant examination of the price of glory. In both epics, a hero's honor is paid for by human death.

The analogy of *geras* and guest gifts is embedded in the oral tradition. This analogy allows the poet compositional flexibility as he constructs his epics. The equation of *geras* and guest gifts enables a particularly skilled poet to invoke the narrative contexts of these prizes—the oral traditions of warfare and hospitality—in innovative ways that make his poems stand out in the audience's mind. For each subgenre in the tradition engenders audience expectations that the poet manipulates for heightened effect. The conflation of a battle scene with a hospitality scene in *Iliad* 6 results in a highly amusing and exceptionally memorable conclusion of Diomedes' *aristeia,* leaving the audience admiring both the Achaean warrior and the poet himself. In *Odyssey* 10, the presentation of Odysseus as a seeker of guest gifts, combined with the narrative pattern of a dishonored warrior stripped of *geras,* results in an unforgettably horrific account of the destruction of the fleet that leaves the audience wondering whether the *Odyssey* will be completed as a poem. But Odysseus will reach Ithaca, and the *Odyssey will* be fulfilled: for, as we observed in the Glaukos-Diomedes scene, the hero's mission and that of the poet are symbiotic. In both poems, the poet matches conflated textual content with a conflated poetics that assures that his listeners will remember and admire him every bit as much as they remember and admire the heroes whose memory he perpetuates.[41]

Notes

1. For the purposes of this paper, the transliteration *xeineion* (plural *xeineia)* refers to "guest gift(s)"; the transliteration *xeneia* refers to "the ritual of hospitality and the host-guest relationship."

2. For the most focused study of the sequence of steps observed in Homeric scenes of *xeneia,* see Reece (1993).

3. Kirk (1990, 173).

4. Edwards (1987, 202).

5. As recently as *Il.* 5.601–06, for example, Diomedes discerns Ares fighting alongside Hector. Athena's optical tricks are also in effect in *Il.* 5.844–45, when she dons the helmet of death to make herself invisible to Ares.

6. The poet is thinking in terms of large compositional units and narrative patterns, within which he includes shorter formulas of noun-epithet phrases, half-lines, full lines, and line clusters. See Foley (1999, 201–37) and Edwards (1986; 1988; 1992). See also Fenik (1968, 229): "The poet's inherited diction and his inherited motifs and type scenes are two closely related aspects of a single traditional poetic style."

7. On the propensity for a hospitality scene to prove to be a theoxeny in disguise, see Reece (1993, 47–57, 181–87). On the intricacies of Odysseus' delayed revelation of his identity among the Phaeacians, see Fenik (1974, 5–60).

8. For an analysis of Diomedes' speech act, see Martin (1989, 124–30). Diomedes' verbal accosting of Glaukos occurs at a point in a battle scene where the

audience may expect one of the fighters to issue a threat, boast, or taunt: see Fenik (1968, 21)S.

9. Reece (1993, 26–28).

10. Diomedes' opening comment on Glaukos' drawing so near may therefore be based on the first step of a hospitality scene: "arrival at the destination." See Reece (1993, 13). Typically, a guest declares his own arrival. In announcing that Glaukos has "come forward" (using a compound of the verb *bainein*), Diomedes usurps his guest's prerogative from the outset.

11. See Martin (1989, 128): "We should not assume that Glaukus is naïve. Indeed, the long genealogical defense he gives confirms that he knows precisely what conventions Diomedes is using in this verbal assault."

12. Reece (1993, 28–29).

13. See also Calder (1984), who surveys the scholarship and posits that the scene concludes with a "geometric intrusion."

14. Edwards (1987, 79) observes that Diomedes' *aristeia* includes no initial arming scene. The hero is fully armed when he springs into battle in 4.419. In its place, the poet provides an elaborate description of the sunlike radiance of the armor (5.1–9). The conclusion of the *aristeia* with its emphasis on the same brilliant armor suggests that the poet conceives of the entire *aristeia* as a ring composition, coming full circle in the armor exchange. I posit this reading in contrast to that of Kirk (1990, 171), who finds "the whole episode [of the armor-exchange] . . . inorganic."

15. Cf. *Il.* 3.134–35: "the fighting has stopped . . . and their long spears stand plunged into the ground."

16. Reece (1993, 55); Finley (1982, 99–100).

17. Aristotle (*Eth. Nic.* 1136b9–14) defends Diomedes from charges of injustice on the grounds that Glaukos gives his less-valuable armor of his own volition.

18. Reece (1993, 89–90); Finley (1982, 57).

19. Kirk (1990,189).

20. Reece (1993, 35–36, 55–57); Finley (1982, 57–63).

21. For a study of the conflated poetics in *Od.* 14.526–33, where Eumaeus "arms himself" for his night watch at the sties, see Newton (1998, 149–50).

22. For a discussion of the dramatic technique of reversals occurring "contrary to the expectations" of the audience (rather than the expectations of the characters), see Else (1967, 348).

23. Stanford (1968, 66–80), Stanford (1965) comments on Odysseus' "inquisitiveness and acquisitiveness" (1.356) as well his "cupidity" (1.395). For Odysseus' appetites, see Pucci (1987, 157–65). Some of these negative assessments of Odysseus' materialistic priorities may be attributable, at least in part, to a class bias harbored by critics who look on one's open concern with wealth as a sign of social inferiority. See, for example, Finley (1982, 125): "The heroes had a streak of the peasant in them, and with it went a peasant's love of possessions, a calculating, almost niggardly hoarding and measuring and counting." See also the references to "shameful gain," "crass materialism," and "peasant shrewdness" in the various studies of *Il.* 6.232–36 surveyed by Calder (1984, 31–33). Indeed, one line of criticism of the armor exchange maintains that Glaukos, in knowingly accepting a lesser gift, exhibits a nobility of character lacking in the shrewdly avaricious Diomedes. It is unlikely, however, that Homer's audience—and his subsequent listeners/readers—would have attributed a moral victory to the Lycian. When, in the classical pe-

riod, the unmercenary Socrates invokes the episode (Pl. *Symp.* 219a), he cites Glaukos as no moral victor but, to the contrary, as a proverbial fool who strikes poor bargains.

24. Shay (2002, 41–62).

25. For this narrative pattern, cf. *Il.* 1.33–42, where Chryses, dishonored by Agamemnon, seeks the solitude of the shore and prays for the death of the Danaans, which quickly ensues; in *Il.* 9.524–99, the enraged Meleagros withdraws from battle until the Kouretes set fire to the city, allowing comrades to fall victim to his wrath. Likewise, in *Od.* 2.260–95, Telemachus is dishonored by the suitors in the Ithacan assembly and walks along the shore to pray to Athena for vengeance: in a variation on the narrative pattern, Athena orders him to man a ship and not fret over the future of the suitors, who have already condemned themselves with their own actions.

26. In *Il.* 11.20 Agamemnon dons the cobalt vest he received as a guest gift from Kinyras of Cyprus: *xeineia* are so personal in nature that they can be worn as articles of clothing.

27. Clay (1982, 116–17) suggests that Odysseus intends the sack of Ismarian wine as a gift for the host who dwells in the cave. Although the Glaukos-Diomedes episode clearly indicates that both host and guest give a gift in *xeneia,* throughout the *Odyssey* the gift exchange is not reciprocal. See Reece (1993, 35): "Gifts are offered by a host to a guest, never vice-versa." Telemachus takes no gifts for his hosts when he sets out to visit Nestor and Menelaus; Athena-Mentes brings no gift for Telemachus in book 1; Odysseus takes nothing to Circe and, necessarily after his raft wreck, has nothing for the Phaeacians; when Menelaus urges Telemachus to tour the Peloponnese and collect gifts from new hosts, he does not mention the traveler's need for host gifts (*Od.* 15.67–85). Space does not allow for a discussion of this intriguing difference between Iliadic and Odyssean hospitality. I suggest, here only briefly, that the *Odyssey* poet alters the ritual for specific purposes that enhance his poem. Having no need to part with any of his gifts, Odysseus can amass his presents as if they were *geras* and thereby achieve maximal status: Iliadic warriors do not part with their *geras,* and Odyssean wanderers do not part with their presents. In *Od.* 4.31–36 Menelaus announces that a person who has received hospitality is obligated to extend it to any and all strangers who may, in turn, appear at his door. The *Odyssey* poet thus places the obligation to reciprocate on future generations that lie even outside the family lines of former hosts and guests: unlike the Iliadic Diomedes, the Odyssean Menelaus does not restrict hospitality to the relatives or descendants of his former hosts. The *Odyssey* poet thereby universalizes the bond of *xeneia,* which, in this poem, transcends the confines of the clan: divinely mandated by Zeus Xenios, it must be offered to any and all strangers, regardless of any past relationship with the host. The *Odyssey* poet thereby establishes hospitality as a bond between men and the gods themselves. Thus, the poem "normalizes" the humble hospitality of Eumaeus the swineherd and—most significantly—makes the suitors' outrageous treatment of the beggar all the more egregious. The suitors' crime transcends the house of Odysseus and the clan of Laertes. These scoundrels, offensive to Zeus himself, are duly punished without mercy.

28. Prodded by Athena, Telemachus cuts short his visit with Menelaus and explains in *Od* 15.88–91: "I left no one in charge of my property when I came here. I fear that, during this search for my father, I myself may be killed or that some valu-

able heirloom be taken from my halls." Thus, the delaying traveler jeopardizes also the very homestead he wishes to embellish: an unguarded house is vulnerable to thieves and even murderers. In *Od.* 4.94–99 Menelaus laments that he overdrew his *nostos* in order to amass riches: had he returned sooner, he might have been able to save Agamemnon from murder at the hands of Aegisthus. The quest for guest gifts thus poses a threat to the hero's comrades on the way and to his dear ones back home. Particularly sensitive to Menelaus's zealousness as a clinging host is Reece (1993, 71–99). Edwards (1975, 56–59) observes the oddity of Menelaus's sending Telemachus off with a greeting, instead of a farewell, and with a libation that typically occurs when a guest is welcomed, not released. It appears that Menelaus is so reluctant to let his guest go that he attempts to resume his hospitality at the very point he is expected to dispatch the visitor.

29. For a study of "Homeric misdirection" in the *Odyssey* (based on Morrison's 1992 examination of the same device in the *Iliad*), see Richardson (2006).

30. See Newton (2005, 138–42).

31. In terms of narrative patterns, it is interesting to note that Achilles' grumbling over Agamemnon's getting better prizes is followed by his threat, "Now I will go to Phthia" (*Il.*1.169). Likewise, the sailors' complaint about Odysseus's accumulation of plunder and presents occurs within the context of a nearly completed *nostos:* in *Od.*10.30 the men are close enough to Ithaca to see men tending their fires. In each case, homecoming is not realized: Achilles never returns to Phthia, and Odysseus' sailors never again see Ithaca.

32. Only after the distribution of *geras* can the recipient look on it as personal, private, and even intimate. The owner's fondness may deepen over time: Achilles claims profound feelings for Briseis, just as Agamemnon claims to prefer Chryseis to his own wife (*Il.* 1.113–15, 9.341–43).

33. For the effect of "amplified descriptions" in heightening the importance of a scene and raising audience expectations of appropriate fulfillment of a sequential narrative, see Austin (1966). Indeed, there is nothing to prevent Aeolus from receiving Odysseus a second time. When Athena-Mentes leaves Odysseus' palace in *Od.* 1.315–18, she announces her intention to return; Odysseus himself is received twice by Circe (*Od.* 12.21–27); both Nestor and Menelaus expect to entertain Telemachus on his return trip (*Od.* 15.49–85, 195–214). In *Il.* 3.229–33 Helen tells Antenor that Menelaus extended hospitality several times to Idomeneus. Aeolus, having once extended hospitality to Odysseus, is indeed obligated to receive him again, since the guest-host bond unites clans permanently. Aeolus' rejection of his guest thus shocks not only Odysseus but also his Phaeacian audience, as well as the poem's external audience.

34. Cf. *Il.* 1.503–16. Thetis follows the protocol of ritual supplication when she grasps Zeus' knees and begs for his assistance. At the moment when Zeus would normally receive the suppliant by raising her from her knees, he sits motionless in somber silence. The *Iliad* poet thereby protracts this pivotal moment in his narrative: as the will of Zeus is about to be activated, the audience listens in suspense. Zeus' silence is pregnant. Thetis manages to salvage her supplication by "attaching herself to his knees and implanting" herself as she issues a second request, to which the god finally responds with a thunderous nod. For the poet's innovation in this supplication scene, see Newton (1984, 6–7). The *Odyssey* poet seems to be employing a similar technique in Odysseus's request to Aeolus: the hospitality seeker pres-

ents himself as a clinging suppliant, thereby rendering his request for shelter all the more urgent.

35. For Homer's "mingling" of hospitality scenes with similar activities, such as messenger scenes, visit scenes, and supplication scenes, see Edwards (1975).

36. Clay (2002, 82) also suggests that the Laestrygonian episode may be based on an older tale of the Argonauts' encounter with the Gegeneis, as preserved in Apollonius Rhodius, *Argonautica* 1.989–1010. In that adventure, the men escape safely. Clay comments, "If the poet indeed alludes to this incident from an old Argonautica, the audience would have expectations of a successful outcome. They would be seriously disappointed." It does indeed seem, from other aspects of this rapidly narrated adventure, that the *Odyssey* poet builds audience expectations only to thwart them.

37. Dindorfius (1855, 454).

38. For the rapid pace of the narrative, see Reinhardt (1996, 89–90).

39. Heubeck (1989, 30). See also Fenik (1968, 67–68). Stewart (1976, 53) reads Odysseus' sword-clenching reflection in the Cyclops' cave as a "significant milestone in the history of social thought, the answer of mere nature to the elaborate artificialities of the heroic code."

40. Cf. Slatkin (1996, 228): "The *Odyssey* incorporates an explicit awareness of the creative tension of composition, an awareness of the existence of possibilities that could have become other songs." These tensions, I suggest, are not restricted to other versions of "rival homecomings," although such versions are alluded to in the poem (and identified in Ahl and Roisman [1996, 27–42]). Besides the possibility that this particular *Odyssey* may be taken over by any number of other travel tales regarding the same hero, there also exists the possibility—which the poet introduces with his "poetics of conflation"—that, on a more generic level, this poem in the *nostos* tradition may be derailed by patterns from the war epic. Homer's Odysseus is therefore "in competition" with other Odysseuses, and the poem as a whole is in competition with war poetry. Even if Homer's original audience was not as conversant in the variant details of one hero's adventures as modern scholars would like to assume (see Scodel [1999]), it is perhaps reasonable to suppose that they were sufficiently sensitive to distinguish between the *narrative patterns* of war songs and those of homecoming poems.

41. A preliminary version of this paper was presented at the 103rd Annual Meeting of the Classical Association of the Middle West and South in Cincinnati, Ohio, April 11–14, 2007.

Works Cited

Ahl, Frederick, and Hanna M. Roisman. *The* Odyssey *Re-Formed.* Ithaca, NY: Cornell University Press, 1996.

Austin, Norman. "The Function of Digressions in the *Iliad.*" *Greek, Roman and Byzantine Studies* 7 (1966):295–312.

Calder, William M. III. "Gold for Bronze: *Iliad* 6.232–6." In *Studies Presented to Sterling Dow on his Eightieth Birthday. Greek, Roman and Byzantine Studies Monograph* no. 10 (1984): 31–36.

Clay, Jenny Strauss. 1982. *The Wrath of Athena: Gods and Men in the* Odyssey. Princeton, NJ: Princeton University Press, 1982.

———. "Odyssean Animadversions." In *Omero: Tremila Anni Dopo: Atti del Congresso di Genova, 6–8 Luglio 2000,* edited by Franco Montanari. Roma: Edizioni di Storia e Letteratura, 2002.

Dindorfius, Gulielmus. *Scholia Graeca in Homeri* Odysseam, *Tomus II.* Oxford, 1855.

Edwards, Mark W. "Type-Scenes and Homeric Hospitality." *Transactions of the American Philological Association.* 105 (1975):51–72.

———. "Homer and Oral Tradition: The Formula, Part I." *Oral Tradition* 1/2 (1986):171–230.

———. *Homer: Poet of the* Iliad. Baltimore and London: Johns Hopkins University Press, 1987.

———. "Homer and Oral Tradition: The Formula, Part II." *Oral Tradition* 3, nos. 1–2 (1988): 11–60.

———. "Homer and Oral Tradition: The Type-Scene." *Oral Tradition* 7, no. 2 (1992):284–330.

Else, Gerald F. *Aristotle's* Poetics: *The Argument.* Cambridge, MA: Harvard University Press.

Fenik, Bernard. *Typical Battle Scenes in the* Iliad: *Studies in the Narrative Techniques of Homeric Battle Description. Hermes Einzelschrift, Heft 21.* Wiesbaden: Franz Steiner Verlag, 1968.

———. *Studies in the* Odyssey: *Hermes Einzelschrift, Heft 30.* Wiesbaden: Franz Steiner Verlag, 1974.

Finley, Moses I. *The World of Odysseus.* New York: New York Review Books, 1982.

Foley, John Miles. *Homer's Traditional Art.* University Park: Pennsylvania State University Press, 1999.

Heubeck, Alfred, and Arie Hoekstra. *A Commentary on Homer's* Odyssey. *Vol. 2, Books IX XVI.* Oxford: Clarendon Press, 1989.

Kirk, G. S. *The* Iliad: *A Commentary. Vol. 2, Books 5–8.* Cambridge: Cambridge University Press, 1990.

Martin, Richard P. *The Language of Heroes: Speech and Performance in the* Iliad. Ithaca, NY: Cornell University Press, 1989.

Morrison, James V. *Homeric Misdirection: False Predictions in the* Iliad. Ann Arbor: University of Michigan Press, 1992.

Newton, Rick M. "The Rebirth of Odysseus." *Greek, Roman and Byzantine Studies* 25 (1984): 5–20.

———. "Cloak and Shield in *Odyssey* 14." *Classical Journal.* 93 (1998):143–56.

———. "The Ciconians, Revisited (Homer, *Odyssey* 9.39–66)." In *Approaches to Homer: Ancient and Modern,* edited by Robert J. Rabel. Swansea: Classical Press of Wales, 2005.

Olson, S. Douglas. *Blood and Iron: Stories and Storytelling in Homer's* Odyssey. Leiden: E. J. Brill, 1995.

Pucci, Pietro. *Odysseus* Polytropos*: Intertextual Readings in the* Odyssey *and the* Iliad. Ithaca, NY: Cornell University Press, 1987.

Reece, Steve. *The Stranger's Welcome: Oral Theory and the Aesthetics of the Hospitality-Scene.* Ann Arbor: University of Michigan Press, 1993.

Reinhardt, Karl. "The Adventures in the *Odyssey.*" Translated by Harriet Flower. In *Reading the* Odyssey*: Selected Interpretive Essays,* edited by Seth L. Schein. Princeton, NJ: Princeton University Press.

Richardson, Scott. "The Devious Narrator of the *Odyssey.*" *Classical Journal* 101 (2006):337–59.

Scodel, Ruth. 1999. "Odysseus' Evasiveness and the Audience of the *Odyssey.*" In *Signs of Orality: The Oral Tradition and its Influence in the Greek and Roman World,* edited by E. Anne Mackay. Leiden: E. J. Brill, 1999.

Shay, Jonathan. *Odysseus in America: Combat Trauma and the Trials of Homecoming.* New York: Scribner, 2002.

Slatkin. Laura M. "Composition by Theme and the *Mêtis* of the *Odyssey.*" In *Reading the Odyssey: Selected Interpretive Essays,* edited by Seth L. Schein. Princeton, NJ: Princeton University Press, 1996.

Stanford, William B. *The* Odyssey *of Homer, Edited, with General and Grammatical Introduction, Commentary, and Indexes.* Vols. 1 and 2. London: MacMillan, 1965.

———. *The Ulysses Theme: A Study in the Adaptability of a Traditional Hero.* 2nd ed. Ann Arbor: University of Michigan Press, 1968.

Stewart, Douglas J. 1976. *The Disguised Guest: Rank, Role, and Identity in the* Odyssey. Lewisburg, PA: Bucknell University Press, 1976.

Homer's *Odyssey*, Books 19 and 23: Early Recognition; A Solution to the Enigmas of Ivory and Horns, and the Test of the Bed

John B. Vlahos

Interpreting certain aspects of Homer's *Odyssey* has created problems for scholars for centuries. For example, in *Od.* 19, why does Penelope ask the stranger to interpret a dream she supposedly had when the dream is self-interpreting? What does she mean when she speaks of gates of ivory and horns? Why does she decide to hold a contest with the bow, with her as the prize, at a time when she has been told that Odysseus is near? And finally, what is the true purpose of the so-called test of the bed in *Od.* 23? This essay suggests that a plausible answer to these questions can be found only if we acknowledge that beginning in *Od.* 19 Penelope knows that she is speaking not to a stranger but to her husband, disguised as a beggar, and that their conversations therein are cryptic and discreet in order to prevent alerting the unfaithful serving maids.

THE MEANING OF PENELOPE'S REMARKS TO ODYSSEUS, DISGUISED AS A stranger, that dreams that pass through the gate of ivory are false and without fulfillment while those that pass through the gate of horns are true and will lead to achievement (*Od.*19.560–67) has eluded Homeric scholars for over a thousand years. In the eleventh century the classical scholar John Italus was taken before the emperor in Constantinople to explain their meaning and was frustrated by his inability to do so (Eustathius 1826, 219). In the twelfth century Eustathius, in his commentaries on the *Odyssey*, refers to them as inexplicable—an enigma (218–19). Joseph Russo recently pointed out that many generations of scholars have puzzled over the reasons for associating horn with truth and ivory with deception (2000, 103). The puzzlement continues to this day. The so-called test of the bed in book 23 has also confounded scholars for centuries.

An acceptable explanation to these enigmas can be found if we acknowledge that, beginning in book 19, Penelope knows that she is speaking not to a stranger, but to Odysseus, and that their conversation is cryptic and discreet in order to protect the secret of Odysseus' return.

The "standard" interpretation is that Penelope does not recognize the stranger to be Odysseus until the so-called test of the bed in book 23; their conversation in book 19 is regarded as being between queen and beggar, nothing more. This standard interpretation can be traced back to the scholia, notes written in the margins of the Homeric texts, possibly in the tenth or eleventh century, by scholars in Byzantium.

The belief that Penelope recognized the beggar to be Odysseus prior to the test of the bed is generally referred to as "early recognition." As will be described, early recognition shows Penelope to be more clever and astute than the standard interpretation allows, and it portrays her as being as cunning and resourceful as Odysseus. It also helps clarify some issues raised in book 19: the purpose for her supposed dream (*Od.* 19.535–50), an explanation of ivory and horns (19.560–67), and the reason for her announcing the contest with the bow (19.572–81). In addition, it clarifies the issue of the "test of the bed" in book 23.

It appears that no exegesis survived from Greco-Roman times that addresses the question of when Penelope first recognizes Odysseus. Robert Lamberton, in *Homer's Ancient Readers,* states, "There are surprisingly few readings of Homer preserved from antiquity . . . (n)or, despite all the comment on Homer from Roman poets and critics, do we find in that area any serious assault on the problem of interpreting the poems" (Lamberton 1992, ix, xxi).

Fragments of comments on the *Odyssey* from ancient scholars such as Crates and Aristarchus have survived, but they do not address the issue. Others, such as Porphyry, wrote extensive allegorical works, but they do not help us analyze the plot. Yet, early recognition seems to have been an issue in antiquity. Seneca (4 BCE–65 CE), in one of his letters, tantalizes us with the statement "Why inquire whether Penelope . . . suspected the man she saw was Ulysses before she was sure of it?" (1988, 73–75).

Although we are not yet certain, it may be that the standard interpretation was adopted in Byzantium in the ninth or tenth century, during a resurgence of interest in classical learning, and was later expounded upon in the twelfth century by Eustathius in his *Com-*

mentarii ad Homeri Odysseam. Eustathius, the most influencial of all Homeric scholars, was a twelfth-century scholar in Constantinople and a dedicated student of Homer. Later in life he was made archbishop of Thessalonica and subsequently a minor saint in the Orthodox Church. He wrote a four-volume commentary on the *Iliad* and two volumes on the *Odyssey*. His *Commentarii* were passed on to Western Europe in the fourteenth century together with copies of Homer's Greek text and were printed in Rome in the period from 1542 to 1550. These six volumes dominated Homeric studies for centuries. Later, Eustathius was criticized by Wolf in his 1795 *Prolegomena* to Homer, and the *Commentarii* on the *Odyssey* was last printed in 1825–26. Today his books are rarely read[1] and have yet to be translated into English. I believe that our standard interpretation, that recognition does not occur until book 23, can be traced back through the years in an unbroken line to Eustathius' *Commentarii.*

In 1950 Professor Philip Whaley Harsh of Stanford University challenged the standard interpretation by suggesting that Penelope recognizes the beggar to be Odysseus during the interview at the beginning of book 19 (1950, 11). I agree.

Harsh suggests a sequence of four steps to explain early recognition: (1) Penelope suspects in books 17 and 18 that the beggar may be Odysseus; (2) she confirms her suspicions during the interview in book 19; (3) the activities in books 17 and 18 and the interview in book 19 were held in the presence of serving maids, some of whom were spying for the suitors; and therefore, (4) the communication between Penelope and the beggar/Odysseus had to be cryptic and discreet to prevent alerting them (1950, 10). I suggest that Harsh's analysis is correct and I will attempt to show that applying his theory of early recognition to the text in book 19 leads to a plausible explanation of the meaning of the gate of ivory and gate of horns and leads to a feisty reunion in book 23.

Recognition

The stated purpose of the interview at the beginning of book 19 was for Penelope to question the stranger about Odysseus. When she berates Melantho, her disloyal serving maid, for trying to drive the stranger away before he could be questioned, she states, "Full well didst thou know, for thou hast heard it from my own lips, that I was minded to question the stranger in my halls concerning my husband" (*Od.* 19.93–95).[2] Yet, when the questioning begins (in the presence of her servants) she does not ask the stranger anything about Odysseus' whereabouts. Instead, she asks him questions directed toward proving his identity: "Who are you among men and from where" (19.105), "Tell me of thy stock . . . for thou art not sprung from an oak . . . or a stone" (19.162–63). When he tells her that he is from Crete and that he entertained Odysseus twenty years before, she asks him to describe his clothes, his manner, and his comrades (19.218–19).

Harsh believes that as a result of the beggar's answers, recognition occurs at 19.221–48. He bases this solely on his belief that the beggar's accurate and detailed description of Odysseus' jewelry and clothing, twenty years after the fact, convinces Penelope that the stranger before her is her husband. However, Harsh overlooked a number of additional facts that add strength to his argument. For example, at *Odyssey* 19.235, the stranger, in describing the clothes Odysseus wore on his supposed trip to Crete, states, "Indeed many women admired it," referring to his *chiton* (an undergarment), "shining like onion skin," worn "close to his body" (19.232–35). This is a lie and a tease: it is a lie because Homer tells us that Odysseus' story about his trip to Crete is not true (19.203), so women could not have admired him there; it is a tease, for no ordinary beggar, having to rely on the goodwill of his hostess, would have the audacity to make such a cruel statement to a grieving wife regarding an absent husband's sex appeal to other women. Scholars universally ignore this point. Yet, as Donald Lateiner states, "Everything he chooses to mention means something—or else why did he mention it?" (1998, 281). Her response to the affront, offering to make him an honored guest and then attempting to end the interview, without asking about Odysseus' whereabouts, tells us that Penelope recognizes it for what it is, a tease from her husband. At this point she is certain that the beggar is Odysseus.

With the knowledge that her husband is standing before her, she states that Odysseus is never going to return (19.258). This is intended to prevent the spying serving maids from suspecting the beggar's true identity. At this point (as at so many others) Homer plays with his audience. Odysseus does not immediately understand Penelope's motives and finds it necessary to contradict her by *voluntarily* informing her, in great detail, of Odysseus' purported whereabouts; he tells her that Odysseus is about to return with treasure, either openly or in secret (19.261–307).

Penelope does not want the disloyal servants to relay any of the beggar's pronouncements of Odysseus' return to the suitors. It is crucial to any hope they have of destroying the suitors that they maintain the element of surprise. She responds emphatically to the beggar's pronouncements by repeating that Odysseus shall not return (19.313). However she realizes the necessity of reassuring Odysseus that she recognizes him. When she subsequently tells Eurycleia to wash the beggar's feet, she says, "Come now, wise Eurycleia, arise and wash the feet of one of like age with thy master. Even as such as his are now haply the feet of Odysseus, and such his hands" (*Od.* 19.357–59). This was evidently a common means of identification. Menelaus recognizes Telemachos to be the son of Odysseus in part by the similarity in their feet and hands (4.147–50). Here, Penelope, by pointing out the similarity, is cryptically telling Odysseus that she sees the likeness, in order to reassure him.

Homer does not specifically tell his audience that she knows the beggar is Odysseus in disguise. Rather, he shows us by her demeanor; recognition produces a shift in her attitude. For example, in books 17, 18, and the beginning of 19 Penelope consistently voices hope for her husband's return, particularly at 17.44–45, 17.510, 17.529, 17.539–40, 18.254, and 19.127. From the moment Penelope is certain that the beggar is in fact Odysseus, she emphatically denies that Odysseus is going to return, in order to protect his disguise: 19.257–58, 19.313, 19.524–29, 19.568, 19.579–80, and 23.62–68. From this point on, until the reunion in book 23, Penelope is careful to reject any suggestion that Odysseus may return.

Homer then uses the foot-washing scenes (19.353–93 and 19.467–507) to give Penelope time to collect her thoughts and develop a plan of action. He also uses the interlude to create drama and suspense. When Eurycleia recognizes Odysseus' scar she tries to inform Penelope but fails to get her attention, as she is deep in thought. Odysseus throttles Eurycleia to prevent her from speaking (19.479–82). The impression that Homer creates for the unobservant is that Odysseus does not want Penelope to know the beggar's identity. In reality, Odysseus does not want the spying serving maids to know. Homer, too, can be devious.

Up to this point in the interview, the information Penelope shares with the beggar is general knowledge, such as her weaving and unweaving of the shroud for Laertes. From this point forward she carefully informs Odysseus of her inner fears and hopes—thoughts that circumspect Penelope would never have shared with a stranger, no matter how desperate she became. Speaking simultaneously to two audiences, Odysseus and the serving women, she has to convey her thoughts to him without informing them. Her thoughts are crafted and stated in such a manner as to be readily understood by Odysseus, but not by others. By repeatedly denying that Odysseus will return, she is endeavoring to prevent arousing the women's suspicions.

After his feet have been washed, Penelope warns the beggar, cryptically, of her primary concern, her fear of Telemachus' being harmed (as the son of Pandareus' daughter was) if they make a careless move (19.518–23). She then proceeds to inquire of Odysseus whether he plans to confront the suitors. She does this by means of a dream she concocted during the foot-washing interval. If he answers in the affirmative, she will advise him not to rely on the sword but to use instead the bow that she will make available to him by means of a contest.

The Dream

Choosing her words carefully, she proceeds with a request that the beggar interpret a dream she supposedly had.[3]

> But come now, hear this dream of mine, and interpret it for me. Twenty geese I have in the house that come forth from the water and eat wheat, and my heart warms with joy when I watch them. But forth from the mountain there came a great eagle with crooked beak and broke all their necks and killed them; and they lay strewn in a heap in the halls, while he was borne aloft to the bright sky. Now for my part I wept and wailed, in a dream though it was, and round me thronged the fair-tressed Achaean women, as I grieved piteously because the eagle had slain my geese. Then back he came and perched upon a projecting roof-beam, and with the voice of a mortal man checked my weeping, and said: "Be of good cheer, daughter of far-famed Icarius; this is no dream, but a true vision of good which shall verily find fulfillment. The geese are the wooers, and I, that before was the eagle, am now again come back as thy husband, who will let loose a cruel doom upon all the wooers." (*Od.* 19.535–50)

As all others since Eustathius, Murray's translation of the first line above varies from the literal meaning of Homer's text. Murray has Penelope ask the beggar to listen, then interpret. However, in the

Greek text Penelope tells Odysseus, *"All' age moi ton oneiron hypokrinai kai akouson"* (19.535), which translates literally as "but come, this dream of mine interpret *then* listen." The preceding anomaly was first noted in the twelfth century by Eustathius, who commented, *"o de prothysteron esti. Proton gar tis hypakousas eita hypokrinetai"* (1826, 217): "Which is the wrong way about, *prothysteron.* For first someone listens and then interprets."[4] The term used by Eustathius, *prothysteron,* was commonly used in antiquity, while the term "*hysteron-proteron*" (which means that words are out of their logical order, backward), has become commonly used in modern times (Bassett 1920, 39). Though *hysteron-proteron* may occasionally apply to phrases in Homer's text, I suggest it should not be applied here. The text as written makes sense without the necessity of alteration if Penelope knows that she is speaking to Odysseus. Because Eustathius does not consider the possibility that Penelope is speaking to Odysseus, cryptically or otherwise, he finds Homer's text backward, that is, in need of reversal. As a result of his application of *hysteron-proteron,* countless translators reverse the wording of the text, as Murray does, to mean, "listen, then interpret." They do so without informing their readers of the change in meaning.

I suggest that Homer says what he means, and means what he says. When Penelope says, "interpret *then* listen," she intends a succession of acts involving first the supposed dream, then a cryptic message regarding the gates of ivory and horns, culminating with the announcement of the contest with the bow. The fact that the meaning of the dream, as it unfolds, is quite clear and needs no interpretation supports the belief that she is not interested in an interpretation; she wants to know, "Do you plan to confront the suitors?"

But there is another possible meaning to the word *hypokrinai* (which generally means "interpret"), which supports this hypothesis. Eustathius goes on to say, "*Hypokrinasthai* in the *Iliad* means 'to simply reply,' [this would be at *Il.* 7.407, but not at *Il.* 12.228] thus he will be free to set forth a reply to the dream" (Eustathius 1826, 217). If Eustathius is correct that *hypokrinasthai* (*hypokrinai* as used by Homer in the *Odyssey*) could also mean "reply," then he unwittingly strengthens the argument that Penelope is knowingly speaking to her husband because, as the plot unfolds, Odysseus does not interpret the dream: he replies to it. However we translate *hypokrinai,* as "interpret," or "reply," what Penelope is asking Odysseus to do is "answer my question in the guise of a dream, *then* listen to my plan."

As she continues to describe her dream Penelope displays some feistiness. Before she gets into the substance, she attends to some unfinished business; she does not let Odysseus get away with his tease at 19.232–35. In her remarks about the geese (the suitors), she is retaliating for his tease about many women admiring her husband in his travels. Her words, seemingly sympathetic to the suitors, "my heart warms with joy when I watch them" and "I wept and wailed," at the slaughter of the geese, are in fact retaliatory barbs. But she softens the impact with *en per oneiro* (19.541), "only a dream," that is, "just kidding."

Penelope, at 19.548–50, then proceeds in one sentence to shift from the present to the past to the future in a subtle discurse that informs him that she knows that he is back and suggests that he plans to destroy the suitors. When in the supposed dream she has the eagle/Odysseus say, "The geese are your suitors—I was once the eagle but now I am your husband, back again at last, about to let loose a cruel doom upon them all," Penelope for the first time verbally is able to assure Odysseus that she knows he is back and gives him an opportunity to reply, in the guise of an analysis, that he plans to confront the suitors. Odysseus responds most emphatically. He ignores the superfluous portions of the dream and goes to the heart of the matter. He agrees with her that his goal is to destroy all the suitors, stating in effect, "Odysseus told you so" (19.555–58). Without arousing the suspiciaon of the serving maids, he confirms the one bit of information she needs in order to proceed to the next phase of her plan, the part that requires Odysseus to listen.

Gates of Ivory and Horns

Choosing her words carefully, Penelope continues:

> Stranger, dreams verily are baffling and unclear of meaning, and in no wise do they find fulfillment in all things for men. For two are the gates of shadowy dreams, and one is fashioned of horn[s] and one of ivory. Those dreams that pass through the gate of sawn ivory deceive men, bringing words that find no fulfillment. But those that come forth through the gate of polished horn[s] bring true issues to pass, when any mortal sees them. But in my case it was not from thence, methinks, that my strange dream came. Ah, truly it would have been welcome to me and to my son. (*Od.* 19.560–69)

When Euryalos, in book 8, wants to make amends to Odysseus, he gives him a sword, pointing out that the scabbard around it is of newly carved ivory, *neopristou elephantos* (8.404–05). Evidently, it was not unusual for swords to be carried in ivory sheaths. Quintus of Smyrna, in the third century C.E., describes Penthesileia's sword enclosed in a scabbard of ivory and silver (1996, 28). When Penelope rejects dreams that pass through carved ivory, saying that they will not lead to fulfillment of her dream (19.564–65), she is advising him that destruction of the suitors will not be accomplished by use of the sword. As mistress of the household she was aware that there were weapons on the walls of the *megaron* earlier in the day (16.295). Penelope must have noticed that the swords and other weapons had been removed (19.4–5, 31–33), because the walls are bare when she walks down that evening for the interview. As a result she is able to infer (1) that on the same day the stranger appears in the palace all the weapons are surreptitiously removed, (2) that this may have been done to keep them out of the reach of the suitors, and (3) that a confrontation may be imminent.

I further suggest that when Penelope states that dreams that pass through the gate of polished horns will "bring true issues to pass" (19.566–67), she is saying that he will fulfill her dream to destroy the suitors through use of the bow. The bow was made of polished, horns (at 21.281 the bow is "polished" and at 21.395 it is made of horns). In the *Iliad* Homer describes Pandarus's polished bow, made from a wild goat (4.105–10). That the bow was made of the horns of the goat is made explicit a few lines late. The Greek word for "bow" is *toxon,* which Autenreith defines as "bow . . . consisting of two pieces of horn (of the wild goat)" (2000, 305). In the Greek text Homer uses the plural of the word for horns, *keraessi* (19.563) and *keraon* (19.565), but uses the singular for ivory, *elephanti* (19.563) and *elephantos* (19.564).[5] The plural is emphasized because, as shown previously, it takes two horns to make one bow, and Odysseus will more readily associate horns with the bow.

Anne Amory, in an exhaustive article, had the answer in her hands but let it slip through her fingers. In her article she notes the possible connection of ivory with the sword and horn with the bow, but because she does not believe that Penelope recognizes the beggar to be Odysseus, she fails to understand how they relate to the passages in Homer's text (1966, 42–49). Significantly, the bow was stored in a locked storeroom in the palace (21.8–12), out of Odysseus' reach, but where Penelope had access to it. For the benefit of the spying servants, and perhaps because of the enormity of the task, Penelope proceeds to state that she doubts that her dream will come true, as much as she and her son would love to have it so (19.569). She is telling Odysseus that he can count on support from Telemachus while stating that she has misgivings about his chances for success. Her doubts will become fears that will haunt her at the beginning of book 20 and move her to tears as she procures the bow at the beginning of book 21.

EUSTATHIUS, IVORY, AND HORNS

Book 19 seems to have perplexed Eustathius in particular and the Byzantine scholars in general. Eustathius' writings indicate that he was baffled by Penelope's dream and her reference to gates of ivory and horns. In his attempt to explain their meaning, Eustathius shows his frustration, and that of his contemporary scholars, as follows: "One should know that many of the wise men [*polloi ton sophon*], have thoroughly examined [*exetripsan,* literally "worn down"] these gates of dreams, some treading through them one way, others the other way. And some scholars following the Poet and taking their starting point from him cautiously open such gates to those who wish to behold things about them, saying, this passage is an enigma [*ainigma ton logon einai*]" (Eustathius 1826, 218).

Since Eustathius makes no reference to ancient sources or scholia on this issue we can assume that the wise men that he is referring to are Byzantine scholars. For example, he twice refers to John Italus, an eleventh-century scholar in Constantinople, who, as mentioned, was unable to explain to the emperor the meaning of ivory and horns (*Commentarii* 219). Eustathius shows total bewilderment when he goes on to say, "Then these inexplicable dreams are those for which it is impossible to devise a specific judgment, to explain or to explicate. Therefore they are also hard to interpret" (1826, 218).

Later, in the brief opening synopsis to book 23 of his *Commentarii,* he specifically states that recognition will occur in book 23. It begins, *Anagnorismos Odysseos pros tin gynaika* (recognition of Odysseus by his wife). Again, it is not clear whether this is Eustathius's own interpretation or was the standard in Byzantium. Though he may have taken this from the scholia (Dindorf 1962, 715), we do not know, because he does not reveal his sources. If Harsh is correct, then Eustathius and his contemporaries must have missed the cryptic communications between Penelope and Odysseus and interpreted the activities in Books 17 through 23 through the eyes of the less observant suitors and serving maids.

Penelope Announces a Contest with the Bow

At this point, after advising Odysseus to use the bow and without waiting for a response, Penelope immediately proceeds to announce a means by which she can put the bow in his hands. Speaking as if she had finally decided to marry one of the suitors—again, so as not to arouse the suspicions of the servants—she suddenly and unexpectedly announces her intent to hold a contest with Odysseus' bow the next day (19.570–80). She declares that the man who can string the bow and shoot an arrow through all twelve ax heads is the man she will marry, leaving her house behind (19.577–80). This announcement has puzzled scholars for centuries. Joseph Russo asks, "Why does the queen decide at this point to set the contest of the bow for the very next day and stake her entire future on its outcome? This question remains one of the fundamental problems for any interpretation of xix and the consistency of Homer's portrait of Penelope" (Russo 2000, 104).

If Penelope does not recognize the beggar to be Odysseus, then Russo's point is well taken: to hold the contest at this time is totally irrational. If she truly was tired of putting them off, she could have picked the most desirable man in looks, wealth, character, and so on, to marry. But with the contest she will be taking a chance that an undesirable suitor will somehow string the bow, shoot an arrow through the ax heads, and take her home as his bride. This seems quite out of character for a woman of Penelope's circumspection. The answer is that she wants to create an opportunity to get the bow into Odysseus' hands. Interestingly, Russo states that this is a possible explanation but finds it "unattractive, . . . [it] assumes that an event of the utmost significance [recognition] has transpired in xix but has been kept out of sight by the poet, which is hardly Homer's manner" (2000, 104). Russo evidently requires direct verbal confirmation from Homer on this point. However, I suggest that Homer does not always tell us what is transpiring, he often shows us through the acts of the participants. This is of critical importance in helping us interpret Homer's poems. In his introduction to Fagles's translation of the *Iliad,* Bernard Knox states the point succinctly: "Homer shows us character and motivation not by editorial explanation but through speech and action. . . . We are not told what is going on in the mind of his characters; we are shown" (1998, 47).

I suggest that Homer's style is curvilinear rather than direct: he does not tell us things straight out but scatters clues about his opaque lines as a mystery novelist does. His audience has to detect the actors' motives by sleuthing. Penelope's announcement of the contest with the bow is a good example.

The contest is a brilliant idea. Odysseus is an expert with the bow (8.215–20) so Penelope is confident that if he can get his hands on it, he will use it with deadly effect. According to Telemachus, there are over one hundred suitors in the *megaron* eager to marry Penelope (16.245–51). With the bow Odysseus can cut them down rapidly from a safe distance. The powerful bow is extremely difficult to bend, and it requires extraordinary skill to shoot an arrow through twelve ax heads. She anticipates that the suitors will fail in their efforts and that Odysseus will be there to get his hands on it. Odysseus immediately realizes the benefit of the bow and he enthusiastically urges her not to delay the contest, stating that before the suitors can "handle and hook it," Odysseus will be home with her (19.582–87). With the contest agreed upon, the queen goes up to her well-lit room. Homer tells us, "not alone, for with her went her handmaids as well" (19.601). She goes to bed believing that the beggar is Odysseus and is intent on keeping his identity a secret. She does not know that both Telemachus and Eurycleia are aware of the beggar's true identity.

Penelope's Tantalizing Craving

Immediately after announcing the contest and just prior to retiring in Book 19, Penelope makes what has to be one of the most sensual and inspirational statements in all of Homer's works. She addresses the beggar as follows: "If thou couldest but wish, stranger, to sit here in my halls and give me joy, sleep should never be shed over my eyelids. But it is in no wise possible that men should forever be sleepless, for the immortals have appointed a proper time for each thing upon the earth, the giver of grain" (*Od.* 19.589–93).

She is subtly telling him that she loves him and is eager to be with him but that everything has its proper time, implying that their time together will come. Virtuous Penelope cannot be saying this to a stranger.[6] Nor is this her intuition or subconscious mind speaking.

Her thoughts are carefully crafted and discreetly stated. This is a promise to her husband of a warm, loving reception at the proper time and place after he has destroyed the suitors. What could be more inspiring to a man about to confront his enemies? The beauty of the pronouncement is that it is prophetic. The next night they do in fact stay up all night reveling in all the longed-for joys of love (23.300–01).

Ctesippus

Penelope's efforts in keeping the beggar's identity a secret are rewarded the next morning when the suitors arrive to feast at the palace. One of them, Ctesippus by name, taunts the beggar and throws an ox hoof at him, saying, "Nay, come, I too will give him a stranger's gift, that he in turn may give a present either to the bath-woman or to some other of the slaves who are in the house of godlike Odysseus" (*Od.* 20.296–98).

How did Ctesippus know that the bath woman, Eurycleia, washed the beggar's feet? None of the suitors was present; they all left at the end of book 18 (18.427–28). Only Odysseus, disguised as a beggar; Penelope; Eurycleia; and the serving maids were present! Evidently, one of the disloyal serving-maids told Ctesippus, and possibly others,[7] of what transpired during the interview, including the bathing of the beggar's feet. But as a result of Penelope's caution in repeatedly insisting that Odysseus is not returning, the serving maids do not suspect the beggar's true identity.

The Contest

The next day Penelope announces the contest of the bow to the suitors, offering herself as the prize. All the suitors have to do is to string the bow and shoot an arrow through the holes in twelve ax heads (21.68–79). As it turns out, none can even string the bow. When the beggar asks to try his strength to string the bow, Antinous, one of the leaders of the suitors, objects and threatens to harm him. Penelope, eager to get the bow in Odysseus's hands, tells him not to show disrespect to Telemachus's guest and reassures him that the beggar surely does not expect to marry her if he succeeds. Telemachus then takes over; sends his mother up to her room, out of harm's way; and has the bow placed into Odysseus's hands, with a quiver full of arrows. Odysseus, assisted by his son and two loyal servants, is able to stand back and use the bow with deadly effect. In book 22 they slay all the suitors.

Probing Eurycleia

Book 23 begins with Eurycleia's scrambling upstairs to tell Penelope the news that Odysseus is home and that he has killed all the suitors. Penelope, ever cautious, is still intent upon keeping the beggar's identity secret until she is certain that disclosure is safe. She proceeds to probe and obtain information out of Eurycleia by ridiculing her and accusing her of having been driven mad by the gods (23.10–14). The nurse repeats that Odysseus is home and adds that Telemachus knew it all along (23.25–31). Penelope leaps from her bed, and with her eyes streaming tears, hugs Eurycleia while asking her whether truly he has come home and how, alone, he destroyed the suitors (23.35–38). Eurycleia responds that she did not see it and did not ask. She goes on to describe what she saw, after the fact, Odysseus splattered with blood and bodies scattered about (23.40–46). Perhaps as a result of Eurycleia's lack of firsthand knowledge of how the suitors were killed, or perhaps because she wants to keep her options open, Penelope tempers her enthusiasm and resumes the fiction that Odysseus will never return. She regains her composure and, ever careful, probes further: "But this is no true tale, as thou tellest it; nay, some one of the immortals has slain the lordly wooers in wrath at their insolence and their evil deeds. . . . But Odysseus far away has lost his return to the land of Achaea, and is lost himself" (*Od.* 23.59–68).

Eurycleia responds by accusing her of being ever distrustful and goes on to describe the scar she saw on Odysseus's leg, proof positive that this is Odysseus (23.73–75). But Penelope shows no concern about the scar. This is significant. In matters of importance cautious Penelope always presses for more information. For example, she insists that Telemachus tell her all he heard on his travels (17.101–06). She insists that the beggar give details in describing Odysseus (19.215–19). In book 23, earlier, she probes Eurycleia to get information on the slaying of the suitors. And finally, she makes Odysseus tell her about the troubles they still have to face in the future (23.256–62). Her failure to inquire about the scar is further indication that, to her, identity is not an issue. Just as Odysseus is able to coax information from an unwary Eumaeus in book 14, here like-minded Penelope (cf. *Od.* 6.180, 184)[8] pries the information she needs from an unsuspecting Eurycleia while maintaining the pretense that Odysseus will never return.

Her Dear Husband

Having wheedled from Eurycleia all she knows about the slaughter, Penelope invites her to go down to see the dead suitors and the one who killed them. In depicting Penelope's thoughts as she descends the stairs, Homer leaves no doubt about her knowledge of the stranger's identity: "She went down from the upper chamber, and much her heart pondered whether she should stand aloof and question her dear husband, or whether she should go up to him, and clasp and kiss his head and hands" (*Od.* 23.85–87).

In the Greek text Homer uses the words *philon posin,* "beloved husband," in describing the object of Penelope's thoughts. Murray, Lattimore, Fitzgerald, Cook, Mandlebaum, Fagles, and Lombardo, together with innumerable others, all translate *posin* to mean "husband." This is clear and unambiguous. It has been suggested that Penelope is indecisive and confused as she tries to decide how to greet her "dear husband."[9] However, the opposite seems more appropriate. She has stated two alternatives, to rush forward and embrace him, or to stand back and question him. She ultimately chooses the latter. Her thinking is clear, logical, and rational, not indecisive or confused. Her subsequent actions are consistent with her prior thoughts.

Interestingly, Eustathius, in commenting on this passage, does not attempt to explain Penelope's thoughts and options. He glosses them over, saying, "And thus on the one hand she will do neither thing immediately, for the decision is made on the spur of the moment, and the woman did not at all know what must be done. But on the other hand the poet proceeding onwards will indeed set this all in order persuasively" (Eustathius 1826, 296). Most Homeric scholars either ignore this passage or, as does Eustathius, attempt to minimize its significance. To accept it at face value places them on the horns of a dilemma. If she knows at this point that the beggar is Odysseus, then she must have known earlier, and, furthermore, she will not have to test his identity later in the so-called test of the bed.

Just as Odysseus ponders in book 6 on the proper manner to approach Nausicaa in order to seek her help (6.141–44), and just as in book 24 he ponders on whether or not to test his father (24.235–40), so here like-minded Penelope ponders on the most appropriate manner to approach her dear husband.

Test What?

If she knows that this is Odysseus, then what is left to test? It is natural that when a husband returns after an absence of twenty years, a wife will want to know whether he has changed and whether he still cares for her. These are important, fundamental questions. Simply asking him will not do. She needs a sign, a symbol, perhaps remembrance of something with special significance to them both, to show her that he still cares.

Up to the beginning of book 23 Odysseus has been careful not to show affection for his wife, obviously because of the need to protect his disguise. At the same time, he is aware that Penelope has been resisting the suitors' advances; he has observed her tears of longing (19.204–09), agreed with her plan to use the bow (19.583–87), heard her fond anticipation of their being together (19.589–90), and heard her cries of grief at the beginning of book 20 when she anticipates that he will be killed. Through her words and acts she has made it abundantly clear that she still cares for him. But he, on the other hand, has yet to give any indication that he still cares for her. Penelope finds herself faced with the choices that Juliet faces in Shakespeare's *Romeo and Juliet.* Recall that Juliet goes out on her balcony and declares her love to what she thought was an empty garden. When she discovers that Romeo has heard her pronouncements of love, she, being young and naïve, trusts him not to take advantage of her. Under similar circumstances, Penelope, being older and wiser, chooses to test Odysseus's love. She has to know: Does he still care, where is his heart, is he still the same warm, loving, and considerate husband who left for Troy twenty years before? These issues need to be addressed before they can resume their marriage.

Domestic One-Upmanship

Penelope walks down to the *megaron* and sits in the glow of the fire, opposite her husband. Odysseus is sitting by a tall pillar, waiting.

He says nothing; she says nothing. He offers no explanation for his ten-year delay in returning from the war. He does not thank her for rearing such a worthy son. Nor does he thank her for putting the bow in his hands. In fact, he does not even speak to her. He sits there, the universally acclaimed hero of Troy and, now, the great avenger. In his mind his fame has reached the skies (9.19–20). He awaits her obeisance. Instinctively, she hesitates.

The first person to speak is Telemachus. He is oblivious to the undertones of the drama unfolding before him. Homer uses him beautifully here—his words make it possible for both parents to speak to him, not each other, as they jockey for position. He may be setting the tone for Odysseus when he says: "My mother, cruel mother, that hast an unyielding heart, why dost thou thus hold aloof from my father, and dost not sit by his side and ask and question him? . . . Thy heart is ever harder than stone" (*Od.* 23.97–103). Telemachus has been verbally sparring with his mother as early as book 1 as he tries to extricate himself from her protective domination (1.345–59). Labeling his mother as "hard hearted" may have put the thought in Odysseus' mind at this point and at 23.166–70. To Telemachus' meddling reproach she responds that she is lost in wonder and cannot speak, nor look him in the face, "But if in truth he is Odysseus, and has come home, we two shall surely know one another more certainly; for we have signs which we two alone know, signs hidden from others" (*Od.* 23.107–10). Penelope's mention of "signs hidden from others" is the first indication that there are symbols that they have cherished during the years of separation that, as we will see, kept alive the embers of their love.

Heubeck, in commenting on the Greek text of 23.108–10, admits to some form of recognition by Penelope at this point. He believes that her use of *we* (*noi;* 23.108, 1100, and *emin;* 23.109) indicates that Penelope has, as he says, "subconsciously," abandoned many of her doubts and reservations (Russo 2000, 323).

Odysseus is patient with her, and a bit condescending. He seems to be aware of her strategy, he tells his son: "Telemachus, suffer now thy mother to test me in the halls; presently shall she win more certain knowledge. But now because I am foul, and am clad about my body in mean clothing, she scorns me, and will not yet admit that I am he" (*Od.* 23.113–16).

Without giving Penelope an opportunity to respond, Odysseus proceeds to have a long discourse with Telemachus, man to man, on how to hide the slaughter from the town folks (23.117–40). He does not include Penelope in the discussion. She has managed the kingdom and their estate without him for twenty years, and in his desperate hour of need she provided him with the means to destroy the suitors. Now, with further business at hand, he is excluding her. A domestic standoff is in the making.

What's Gotten into You?

Without yet speaking to her, Odysseus leaves to bathe and wash off the blood and gore. Then, handsome and godlike, he returns to the seat that he had left and once seated speaks to Penelope, directly, for the first time. He knows that she recognizes him. He makes no attempt to prove his identity. Instead, without giving her a chance to speak, he echoes—somewhat impatiently and with annoyance in his voice—what Telemachus said earlier, and says: "Strange lady! To thee beyond all women have the dwellers on Olympus given a heart that cannot be softened. No other woman would harden her heart as thou dost, and stand aloof from her husband who after many grievous toils had come to her in the twentieth year to his native land. Nay come, nurse, strew me a couch, that all alone I may lay me down, for verily the heart in her breast is of iron" (*Od.* 23.166–72). In the Greek text the word for Murray's "strange lady" is *daimonie.* According to Cunliffe, it can mean "under superhuman influence, possessed, [one] whose actions are unaccountable or ill-omened" (1963, 82). The word can also be affectionate or sarcastic, depending on how it is applied. Hector, for example, uses it in tenderly addressing Andromache as he hands their child back to her (*Il.* 6.486). Here, Odysseus seems to be using it somewhat disparagingly to convey his annoyance at Penelope's failure to approach and greet him. Russo, in another context, points out that Homer's characters often use the word in a state of heightened emotion to address someone familiar who is behaving unexpectedly, a form of rebuke (2000, 78). Russo goes on to suggest that a good colloquial translation might be "what's gotten into you?" I agree. Russo proceeds to point out that the word is always used in a somewhat intimate manner. It would not be used in reference to strangers. He goes on to say, "The constant element of meaning is an intensity on the speaker's part meant to create an atmosphere of intimacy that might oblige the addressee to co-operate." In the preceding context Russo's analysis fits perfectly: Odysseus shows annoyance at his wife's inexplicable refusal to approach and greet him and is trying to coax her into abandoning her reserve.

It is noteworthy that Odysseus makes no effort to prove his identity. To him it is a nonissue. In the statement "and stand aloof from her husband" (23.169), Odysseus implies that she knows who he is, and that she is consciously withholding her greetings. Before she has a chance to reply to his rebuff, he tries to force her hand by ordering Eurycleia, the nurse, to prepare him a couch out in the hall (23.171–72). This is a power play of great significance; he threatens to sleep alone in the hall and not in their bridal chamber, which, as we shall see, is their special haven. Needless to say, Penelope is not intimidated by Odysseus's blustering. Although he threatens to sleep alone, she knows that after being away twenty years he did not return home to sleep in a separate bed.

Penelope Responds

Her terse response to his blustering is one of the most poignant moments in the *Odyssey;* in it she demurs to his accusations, states her concern, and calls his bluff. Her response can be broken down into two parts. First, feisty as ever, she throws back at Odysseus, disparagingly, the word *daimoni* and states her case. A careful reading of the Greek text is important at this point, particularly at 23.175:

> "daimoni', out' ar ti megalizomai out' atherizo
> oute lien agamai, mala d' eu oid oios eestha
> ex Ithakis epi neos ion doliheretmoio.
>
> (*Od.* 23.174–76)

As will be discussed later, these lines have created problems for scholars for centuries. Fagles translates them loosely, as follows:

> "Strange man,"
> wary Penelope said. "I'm not so proud, so scornful,
> nor am I overwhelmed by your quick change. . . .
> *You look—how well I know—the way he looked,*
> setting sail from Ithaca years ago
> aboard the long-oared ship."
>
> (Fagles 1995, 461; my italics)

Fagles gives us what has recently become the "standard" translation of her response. His phrase in line 175, "*You look . . . the way he looked,*" is not in the Greek text; it was added (with good but misguided intentions) to bolster the theory that the stranger/beggar's identity is still at issue.

A. T. Murray, on the other hand, in the 1919 Loeb translation of the *Odyssey* translates the phrase literally: "Strange sir, I am neither in any wise proud, nor do I scorn thee, nor yet am I greatly amazed, but right well do I know what manner of man thou wast, when thou wentest forth from Ithaca on thy long-oared ship" (1919, 23.173–75). Line 23.175, *mala d' eu oid oios eestha,* translates literally as "moreover, I know what manner of person you were." The key word *eestha,* second person, singular, past imperfect of the verb *to be,* translates literally "you were." Fagles's phrase, "the way *he* looked," refers to a third party and raises the issue of recognition, while the Greek text indicates that her comments are directed, not at a third party, but at Odysseus himself.

The tendency of translators to modify Homer's text at 23.175 (which my research shows began in the second half of the twentieth century) may be the result of their following the suggestion of the noted scholar W. B. Stanford. In 1948 Stanford published his highly acclaimed two-volume commentary on the *Odyssey.* In his discussion of 23.175 he suggests that Homer's "what manner of person you were" is an abridgment that needs modification. He suggests changes to the Homeric text to add support to the issue of identity (1973, 397–98). Subsequently, translators such as Fagles, together with Fitzgerald, Lattimore, Mandelbaum, Lombardo and Dimock (in the 1995 2nd edition of Murray's Loeb translation), change the meaning of 23.175 to incorporate a question of identity.

Penelope's Concerns

This then takes us to the question of what Penelope is referring to when she raises the issue of what manner of person Odysseus was before he left for Troy. I suggest that she is telling him her concern that though he is her husband, she does not see in him the same person who left for Troy. She is referring to his character and apparent lack of affection.

A determination of Odysseus's character prior to his departure for Troy requires a careful reading of the poem (the lack of affection has briefly been referred to). If we piece together various comments, we can get an idea to what Penelope is referring. Homer has him described by Mentor as a kind king, mild as a father (2.230–34); by Penelope as a just and considerate ruler (4.687–93); by Athena as a kind and righteous king (5.8–12); by Eumaeus as loyal and protective of his friends (16.428–30); and by Eurymachus as kind and generous to children (16.442–44). In the underworld his mother tells Odysseus that she ended her life because she missed his counsel and his gentle ways (11.202–03). Most importantly, Penelope's description of his parting words, at 18.259–70, portrays a thoughtful, loving, and trusting husband; a father concerned about his infant son's future; and a son considerate of his aging parents' comfort and welfare.

Scholars have noted Odysseus's humanity in the past. W. B. Stanford, for example, comments on the fact that Odysseus has two supreme qualities, intelligence and gentleness. He points out that Athena has a special liking for him because of his gentleness, courtesy, and compassion (1954, 39–40). Penelope is telling Odysseus that she is standoffish because she remembers and wants back the same considerate, gentle, and loving husband who left for Troy twenty years earlier.

Douglas J. Stewart's View

The preceding observations on early recognition are not entirely unique. Douglas J. Stewart agrees with Harsh that Penelope recognizes the beggar to be Odysseus in book 19 (though at 19.357–59, not at 19.231–35). He, too, does not believe that she is testing the beggar's identity in book 23:

> This is a test of sorts, as the poet himself says, indulging in perhaps the only piece of frank literary explanation in the Homeric corpus (23.181: "She did this to test her husband"). But criticism has been a bit dull about what kind of test, I suggest. Does she need to test his identity, by having him declare a piece of evidence that only she and Odysseus knew? That seems unlikely. . . . If Penelope is testing Odysseus for something here, I think that it is not for redundant evidence of his minimal and technical identity, but for plausible evidence of his humanity. . . . Above all, having won through to the security of his home and his rightful place in society once again, will he relax his guard to the degree that

> is natural in one's familiar and proper place, or will he remain distrustful and unnaturally canny to the end? (Stewart 1976, 138–39)

She needs to see the spontaneous act, the unpremeditated expression, or the ultimate surd of the arbitrary self before she is ready to conclude that he is, has become, one might say, himself again (Stewart 1976, 137).

Which He Made Himself

After stating her concerns, Penelope proceeds to the second part of her response, by seeming to oblige Odysseus's wishes for separate sleeping accommodations. She instructs Eurycleia to move their bed out of the bridal chamber so he can sleep in the hall alone.[10] Here again, the Greek text is of primary importance. Penelope's words are

> "all' age oi storeson pykinon lechos Eurycleia,
> ektos eustatheos thalamou, ton r' autos epoiei."
>
> (*Od.* 23.177–78)

> ("Yet come, Eurycleia, strew for him the stout bedstead
> outside the well-built bridal chamber which he made himself.")

The key words, *ton r' autos epoiei,* "which he made himself," can only refer to Odysseus, the man standing before her, not a third party. This has bothered scholars for centuries. In 1948 Stanford suggested changing the meaning by translating the words into "the Master himself made" (1973, 398). This refers to a third person and avoids giving the impression that Penelope recognizes the man standing before her to be her husband. As do many others, Fagles translates the passage as follows:

> Come, Eurycleia,
> Move the sturdy bedstead out of our bridal chamber—
> That room that the master built with his own hands.
>
> (Fagles 1997, 461)

The word *master,* is not in the Greek text. Fagles's well-intended insertion reflects further attempts of scholars, who are not cognizant of early recognition, to give what they consider consistency to Homer's text.

William Henry Melmoth and Eustathius

The meaning of Homer's text at 23.174–78 has puzzled scholars for centuries. This is reflected, for example, in William Henry Melmoth's 1799 translation of Homer's poems wherein his notes include comments on the *Commentarii* of Eustathius. Melmoth states, with obvious pride, on the title page of his book, that his translation closely follows the interpretations of Eustathius and other scholars, particularly Alexander Pope. Melmoth's note regarding this passage is enlightening,

> It must be allowed that this is a very artful turn of thought in Penelope. Ulysses commands a bed be prepared, Penelope catches the word, and seeming to consent, orders Eurycleia to carry the bed out of the bridal apartment, and prepare it. Now this bed was of such a nature as to be inwrought into the substance of the apartment itself, and could not be removed: if therefore Ulysses had acquiesced in the injunction given by Penelope, and not discovered the impossibility of it, she might have very justly concluded him to be an impostor, being manifestly ignorant of the secret of his own marriage bed.
>
> But Eustathius states an objection against this whole process of the discovery, which he calls insolvible [*sic*]; the difficulty is as follows: Penelope imagines that the person who pretends to be her husband, is not really Ulysses, but a God, who not only assumes his form, but, to favour the imposture, the resemblance of the wound received from the boar: now if he be a God, how is it possible she should conceive him to be ignorant of the secret of the marriage-bed, and consequently how can she be convinced of the reality of Ulysses from his knowledge of it, when it must necessarily be known to a God, as well as to the real Ulysses? All that she ought to gather from it is, that the person with whom she speaks is Ulysses, or a God. Eustathius replies, that Penelope upon the discovery of the secret makes no scruple to yield; because whether it be Ulysses, or a God, her case is happy; if he prove to be Ulysses, she has her wishes; if a God, it is no small piece of good fortune. (Melmoth 1799, 619)

Eight hundred years after Eustathius, Stanford concedes that knowledge of the bed does not necessarily prove the stranger's identity and that the matter is insoluble. He states, "As Eustathius, Bishop of Thessalonica (to whose compilation of ancient commentaries these chapters owe much), remarks, Penelope's problem about the stranger was really insoluble: for if the stranger was (as she feared) a god in the guise of her husband, what was to prevent him in his omniscience from knowing even the Secret of the Bed?"

(Stanford 1954, 58–59). Modern scholars seem to ignore this observation. Their efforts to bolster the issue of identity in book 23 by manipulating Homer's text misdirect its interpretation and add confusion to the development of the plot.

The Bridal Bed as the Symbol of Their Love

The bridal chamber and the bed therein have special significance for Odysseus and Penelope. For the twenty years that Odysseus is away Penelope does not sleep in it; she sleeps in another room, upstairs (17.101–04, 19.600, 21.356, 23.1–2, 23.85). The bridal chamber is located on the ground floor. Odysseus states that one leg of the bed was formed from an olive tree planted in the ground and that he trimmed the trunk and fashioned it into a bedpost (23.190–98). Evidently, only Odysseus, Penelope, and Aktoris, a servant woman, had ever been in the chamber (23.225–28). Homer does not tell us the current whereabouts of Aktoris, so that leaves only Penelope and Odysseus with knowledge of the special significance of the chamber and the bed therein. Penelope's reference to it as the "bridal" chamber (23.178, 229) indicates that they consummated their marriage on the bed in that room. This would give it special significance.

The fact that Penelope does not sleep in the bridal chamber in Odysseus's absence implies that they considered it their special haven, to be occupied either together or not at all. As long as the bed remains immobile, anchored in the ground, so shall their love be unwavering. Thus, the immovable bed in their bridal chamber is the symbol of their steadfast love, their secret sign.

Odysseus's Anguish

When Odysseus tries to force the issue by insisting on sleeping out in the hall, Penelope ups the ante. Her response is that not only can he sleep in the hall, he can sleep there in their nuptial bed, outside their special haven. Odysseus is devastated (23.181–83). For twenty years he has struggled to return to what he believed to be his loyal wife only to be told that their bed is now movable, an indication that her love may no longer be steadfast. In grief and anger he proceeds to recall, in exquisite, loving detail, how he built and fashioned, first the bed, and then the room around it (23.183–201). He then states with dismay, "Thus do I declare to thee this token: but I know not, woman, whether my bedstead is fast in its place, or whether by now some man has cut from beneath the olive stump, and set the bedstead elsewhere" (*Od.* 23.202–4). His fervent description of the symbol of their love, his passionate concern that some man might have moved it, and, by implication, taken his place, loosens her knees and melts her heart (23.205–6). His fond recollection tells her that he still remembers with affection the items that are special to them; his grief shows that he is not cold and aloof, but vulnerable and human; together, they prove to her his love.

Reunion

Tearfully, Penelope rushes toward him, wraps her arms about his neck, and kisses his head (23.207–08). She quickly devises an excuse to calm his anger and soothe his wounded feelings. She admits she failed to greet him (23.213–14; not that she failed to recognize him). She implies that her caution in not immediately greeting him was for his benefit. Cleverly, she compares herself to Helen, who, as we know, unleashed her passions on another man while her husband was away, while she, Penelope, during her husband's absence, kept her passions in check (23.213–24). She then tells him, "But now, since thou hast told the clear tokens of our bed . . . thou dost convince my heart, unbending as it is" (23.225–30). Her "convinced heart" (23.230) has to do with love, not recognition. Relief flows over him as he bursts into tears and holds tightly to his loving, truehearted wife (23.232). Athena obligingly holds back the dawn so that they will have more time to enjoy their long awaited reunion (23.241–46).

But Penelope is not through. On their way to bed and the joys of lovemaking, Odysseus casually mentions that their troubles are not over (23.248–53). She tells him, "Thy bed shall be ready for thee whensoever thy heart shall desire it. . . . But since thou hast bethought thee of this . . . tell me of this trial, for in time to come, methinks, I shall learn of it, and to know it at once is no whit worse" (*Od.* 23.257–62).

This is the statement of an intelligent, rational woman with an agenda. Here, while she still has leverage, she further establishes her status in their marriage by asserting her right to share in the knowledge of the troubles they will have to face together in the future. Only after Odysseus explains to her the trials Tiresias predicted (23.265–84) do they revel in the longed-for joys of love (23.300–01).

Penelope's initial denial of Odysseus's return when awakened by Eurycleia is to protect his disguise and probe for information. Her subsequent refusal to greet him is a ploy to buy time in order to assess the situation, be sure of his affection, insist on his respect, and strengthen her position as a partner in their marriage. She breaks down the emotional wall he has built around himself, determines that he still cares for her, and emphasizes her loyalty. This is the crafty, resourceful woman Odysseus left in charge of his vast estate twenty years earlier. Calypso, with all her gifts, is no match for her.

Conclusion

The importance of early recognition is that it offers a solution to many problems and answers many questions that have plagued scholars for centuries. In addition, it allows Homer to portray Penelope as being every bit as wily, resourceful, and, when necessary, devious as Odysseus, qualities that she needs to survive the twenty years of her husband's absence, particularly the three years that the suitors are camped in the palace. Specifically, early recognition leads to an explanation of the meaning of ivory and horns and clarifies what would otherwise be inconsistencies in the bed trick in book 23.

Notes

I am indebted to Richard P. Martin, Mark W. Edwards, and Barbara Clayton at Stanford University, and Donald Lateiner at Ohio Wesleyan University for reading this paper during various stages of its development and offering valuable comments and suggestions. Needless to say, I remain entirely responsible for any remaining errors and omissions.

1. There are significant exceptions. Stanford, in the *Ulysses Theme* at 58, states that he owes much to Eustathius and refers to him repeatedly in his notes, as does Russo in *Commentary,* vol. 3 (1992).

2. All translations of Homer's text are by A. T. Murray, 1919, Loeb Classical Library (1st ed.), unless otherwise indicated. Literal translations are the author's. Translations of Eustathius's text are by Amelia Robertson Brown.

3. "Though Penelope does have dreams in the *Odyssey,* I see no reason to believe that she actually had this dream. It can be better seen in its context of covert and guarded negotiation as her attempt to convey a message to the beggar, whom

she now has good reason to think may very well be Odysseus himself" (Winkler 1990, 153). Winkler goes on to state, at 160, that he is 99 percent convinced that she was aware of the beggar's true identity.

4. Eustathius (1826, 217).

5. E. L. Highbarger takes *keraessi* as "horns" in the plural and connects them with the Gates of Heaven in Egyptian and Mesopotamian mythology. He states, "It is highly important for the interpretation of the Vergilian passage that Homer, Plato, and other writers describe the Gate of Horn(s) in the plural, while the Gate of Ivory is presented in the singular. So far as I am aware, no writer has ever observed this distinction, because in the Roman poets the plural noun has disappeared and an adjective in the singular (*cornea*) is substituted" (1940, 2).

6. "There is nothing suggestive in this. Penelope is confirming that Odysseus has been as entertaining a story-teller as Eumaeus had prophesied (17.513–21). But, it is ironical, in that Penelope is using language that would be appropriate between husband and wife—only she does not know that the beggar is her husband" (Jones 1988, 184). Though Jones does not believe that Penelope recognizes the beggar to be Odysseus, he perceives that the tone of Penelope's longing seems to be directed toward her spouse.

7. In book 24 (167–68) Amphimedon states that Odysseus told Penelope to arrange the contest with the bow. Though he is mistaken (it was Penelope's idea), Amphimedon's knowledge of the fact that Penelope and Odysseus communicated must have been information given to him by one of the serving maids, who had slipped out to rendezvous with the suitors the night before (20.6–7).

8. Odysseus is describing what he considers the ideal marriage when he wishes *homophrosyne,* like-mindedness, on Nausicaa and any future husband at 6.181–84. I believe that Homer portrays Odysseus and Penelope as having a unique understanding of one another, a like-mindedness, that allows them to speak cryptically in the presence of others. Both are portrayed as clever, observant, and, when necessary, devious. Eustathius missed the connection between Odysseus-Penelope and likemindedness. J. B. Hainsworth in volume 1 of "A Commentary on Homer's Odyssey" in the 1988 English translation also fails to apply *homophrosyne* to Odysseus and Penelope (Heubeck 1990, 305). However, four years later, in volume 3 of the Commentaries, Russo, in explaining Odysseus's enthusiasm for Penelope's wheedling gifts from the suitors, comments on what he calls "instinctive *homophrosyne,*" which he claims "shows that such mental harmony is an important part of Odysseus's conception of the ideal marriage" (Russo 2000, 67).

9. See Russo (2000, 321), where Alfred Heubeck attempts to find an explanation to negate the literal meaning of Homer's text. With regard to her two options he states, "The poet is concerned here not so much with the act of decision, as with the heroine's mood, her indecision and confused emotions."

10. The potential irony in this attains mythical proportions. After twenty years of wandering, Odysseus returns home and his wife makes him sleep in their bridal bed alone, out in the hall.

Works Cited

Amory, Anne. "The Gates of Ivory and Horn." *Yale Classical Studies* 20 (1966): 1–57.

Autenrieth, G. *Homeric Dictionary*. Translated by Robert Keep. 1984. Reprint. London: Duckworth, 2000.

Bassett, Samuel B. "*Hysteron Proteron Homerikos* (Cicero, Att. 1,16,1)." *Harvard Studies in Classical Philology* 31 (1920) :39–62.

Cunliffe, R. J. *A Lexicon of the Homeric Dialect.* 1924. Reprint. Norman: University of Oklahoma Press, 1963.

Dindorf, W. *Scholia Graeca in Homeri Odysseam.* 1855. Reprint. Amsterdam: A. M. Hakkert, 1962.

Eustathius of Thessalonica. *Eustathii Commentarii ad Homeri Odysseam.* Vol. 2. Edited by J. G. Stallbaum. Leipzig: Weigel, 1826.

Fagles, R. *The Odyssey,* 1995. Reprint. New York: Penguin Books. 1997.

Harsh, P.W. "Penelope and Odysseus in *Odyssey* XIX." *AJP* 71 (1950): 1–20.

Heubeck, Alfred, Stephanie West, and J. B. Hainsworth *A Commentary on Homer's Odyssey. Vol. 1.* 1988. Reprint, Oxford: Clarendon, 1990.

Highbarger, E. L. *The Gates of Dreams.* Baltimore: The Johns Hopkins University Press, 1940.

Jones, P. V. *Homer's Odyssey, a Companion to the Translation of Richmond Lattimore.* Carbondale and Edwardsville: Southern Illinois University Press, 1988.

Knox, Bernard. "Introduction to *The Iliad.*" In *Homer, The Iliad.* Translated by Robert Fagles. 1990. Reprint. New York: Penguin Books, 1998.

Lamberton, Robert. "Introduction." In *Homer's Ancient Readers.* Princeton: Princeton University Press, 1992.

Lateiner, Donald, *Sardonic Smile, Nonverbal Behavior in Homeric Epic,* 1995. Reprint. Ann Arbor: University of Michigan Press, 1998.

Melmoth, W. H. *The Works of Homer the Celebrated Grecian Poet: The* Iliad *and the* Odyssey. London: Alex. Hogg, 1799.

Murray, A. T. *Homer the Odyssey.* Vol. 2. 1919. Reprint. Cambridge, MA: Harvard University Press, 1972.

Quintus of Smyrna. *The War at Troy, What Homer Didn't Tell.* Translated by Fredrick M. Combellack. 1968. Reprint. New York: Barnes & Noble. 1996.

Russo, Joseph, Manuel Fernandez-Galiano, and Alfred Heubeck. *A Commentary on Homer's* Odyssey. Vol. 3. 1992. Reprint. Oxford: Clarendon Press, 2000.

Seneca. 1988. *Seneca, 17 Letters.* Translated by C. D. N. Costa. Wiltshire, England: Aris and Philips, 1988.

Stanford, W. B. *Ulysses Theme.* Oxford: Basil Blackwell, 1954.

——— *The Odyssey of Homer, Edited with General and Grammatical Introductions, Commentary and Indexes.* 2nd ed. 1948. Reprint, Edinburgh: R. & R. Clark, 1973.

Stewart, D. J. *The Disguised Guest: Rank Role and Identity in the* Odyssey. Lewisburg, PA: Bucknell University Press 1976

Winkler, J. J. *The Constraints of Desire.* New York: Routledge, 1990.

Conversation in the *Odyssey*

Scott Richardson

Characters in the *Odyssey* do not as a rule say what they mean. Dialogue tends toward obfuscation rather than illumination, and conversation in this epic is a game at which some people are better players than others. Playing the game properly requires a keen ability to use words to convey meaning indirectly and a sensitive awareness of what has been said despite what has been said. Homer's attitude toward language extends to a generally suspicious view of the world, in which the characters' success in life, even their survival, owes a great deal to both using and recognizing speech as a means of disguising thoughts and intent. Human communication is smoke and mirrors, and the world of the *Odyssey* is characterized by distrust and uncertainty.

The epigrammatic saying that speech has been given to us for the purpose of concealing our thoughts came into his mind. (Joseph Conrad, *Under Western Eyes*)

WHEN IT OCCURS TO NAUSICAA THAT SHE HAD BETTER DO LAUNDRY IN preparation for her own wedding day, which will surely occur soon, she delays her father's workday with a request for the proper equipment, explaining, with a façade of ingenuity that might have fooled anyone else, that she must look out for her family's hygiene:

> "It is proper for you yourself to plan plans
> with the chiefs wearing clean clothes on your skin.
> But you have five sons in your house,
> two married, but three red-blooded bachelors;
> they always want to go to dances wearing
> freshly cleaned clothes; I have to think about all these things."
>
> (*Od.* 6.60–65)[1]

Alcinous has no trouble decoding his daughter's appeal and grants it without betraying his understanding of her true intention:

> Thus she spoke, for she was ashamed to name her youthful marriage
> to her dear father. And he understood everything and replied:
> "I do not begrudge you mules, child, nor anything else.
> Go! The slaves will prepare for you a wagon
> lofty and well-wheeled, fitted with a wagon cover."
>
> (*Od.* 6.66–70)

We have just heard a conversation in which the communication takes place beneath the surface of the words: what is spoken by both parties is not what is truly conveyed by Nausicaa nor meant by Alcinous. This indirect interchange is a paradigm of the distinctive mode of conversation in the *Odyssey.*

I like to think of language as a medium for the clear disclosure of what people want to express. In conversation, words transmit information, requests, and the thoughts of my interlocutor. It is a straightforward process: say what you mean, use language to convey what you are thinking, and then I will understand. But I can see the author of the *Odyssey* rolling his eyes in disgust at my banal literalness and naively unimaginative attitude toward language. In this poet's hands language tends toward obfuscation rather than illumination. His characters do not as a rule say what they mean, and conversation in his epic is something of a game at which some people are better players than others. Playing the game properly requires a keen ability to use words to convey meaning indirectly and a sensitive awareness of what has been said despite what has been said. The first speaker in this Henry James dialogue does not stand a chance in the world of the *Odyssey:*

> "Why is it so necessary for you to go to the theatre tonight, if Miss Rooth doesn't want you to?"
>
> "My dear child, she does. But that has nothing to do with it."
>
> "Why then did she say that she doesn't?"
>
> "Oh, because she meant just the contrary."
>
> "Is she so false then—is she so vulgar?"
>
> "She speaks a special language; practically it isn't false, because it renders her thought, and those who know her understand it." (James 1948, 437)

Likewise, conversation in the *Odyssey* is a cryptic puzzle, intelligible and rewarding to those who know how to solve it, baffling to those who take it at face value.

Homer's attitude toward language extends to a generally suspicious view of the way the world works.[2] Dialogue in the *Odyssey* is founded on indirection, and the characters' success in life, even their survival, owes a great deal to both using and recognizing speech as a means of disguising thoughts and intent. This view of language as smoke and mirrors not only comments on the nature of human communication[3] but also supports a worldview at the heart of the *Odyssey* as a whole, one characterized by distrust and uncertainty.

Apart from instructions, gestures of hospitality, laments, prayers, and requests (and even some of these are not only what they appear), the preponderance of dialogue that is straightforward and honest is from the mouths of characters who prove in other ways artless: Zeus, Nestor, the servants, the suitors other than Eurymachus, Telemachus early on, and Alcinous most of the time. Zeus and Nestor, the divine and human voices of social and narrative order, stand above the game; the others either do not realize there even is such a game or have not yet learned to play it very well. The great majority of conversations in the *Odyssey*,[4] however, feature one or more of these techniques: indirect address, implication, hidden or coded meaning, lying, feigned ignorance, injunction to secrecy, concealment of facts, expressions of disbelief, evasion, disguised sentiments, testing, indirect steering or goading, presentation of false reasons, or performances in character.

Odysseus, of course, an eminently suspicious man, is the champion of all these kinds of indirection and concealment, the consummate manipulator of language to suit his advantage. It might be instructive, however, to return first to our apprentice conversationalist, who shows promise but has not yet developed the finesse that gives Odysseus his edge. Nausicaa has the proper Odyssean instinct when she manipulates her father into giving her mules and a wagon, but it seems to escape her notice that Alcinous has seen through her coded request. She also fails to acknowledge that she did not think of the laundry idea on her own. Athena, who wants a warm reception for her hero, cold-bloodedly misleads her with the cock-and-bull expectation of an impending marriage (6.25–40), and the girl innocently takes Athena's words at face value and pays for it in subsequent disappointment. Unaware of the divine machinations and relishing her apparent success at concealing her meaning and still getting her way, she goes on to ply her novice talent on the master deceiver by the stream. After Odysseus delivers a masterful speech in which his hints and flattery impart all the characteristics of a potential husband without disclosing his identity or his true intentions toward her, Nausicaa offers herself to him with what she thinks to be a cleverly disguised proposition through indirection. She worries that if they are seen together, people will talk:

> "And then some worthless fellow would meet us and say,
> 'Who is this tall and handsome stranger walking with
> Nausicaa? Where did she find him? He's going to be her husband.'"
> (*Od.* 6.275–77)

A great part of the girl's adolescent charm is her delight in participating in conversational indirection without recognizing its transparency in her hands and without realizing that others are engaged in the same gambit with her. Her obviousness highlights by contrast the techniques of the *Odyssey*'s seasoned conversationalists, and her natural impulse to speak obliquely suggests that an attitude toward language as a power to use judiciously and to one's advantage is innate to the characters in the world of the *Odyssey.*

Though some years her senior, Telemachus is only now beginning to fathom the game of language, which for him, as for his father, can mean survival. The ability to conceal, lie, and feign innocence with words is a hallmark of Telemachus's education in the *Odyssey.*[5] By the end he is still rather immature in this respect but a far cry from the blunt-speaking youth we see at the beginning. After Athena's visit rouses him from inaction, he asserts himself before the suitors in no uncertain terms, calling them insolent, claiming dominion over his father's house, telling them that he will order them out at the assembly he himself will call the next day, and calling on Zeus to destroy them (*Od.* 1.367–80, 389–98). A bit of Athena, goddess of deception, does cling to him, however, after she leaves: when asked about his mysterious visitor, Telemachus dissembles and gives Athena's prepared legend, though he now realizes, as Homer tells us, that his guest was a deity (*Od.* 1.417–20). His virgin address to the assembly in book 2 takes him back to the fumbling stage of the concealment game: he announces forthrightly his disgust with the suitors (*Od.* 2.50–58, 63–67), his wish that they would leave his household alone and even that they would be slaughtered (*Od.* 2.58–62, 68–79, 138–45), his intention to leave Ithaca in search of news of his father (*Od.* 2.212–17), and his plans thereafter (*Od.* 2.218–23)—no subtlety here, nothing but straightforward communication to his mortal enemies of his thought and intent.

By the time he returns home, however, he has learned the value of telling less than he knows and saying something other than what he means. An ally of his new-found father, Telemachus can now tell bald-faced lies even to his mother, give no sign that the new beggar is anyone special, and play his role in Odysseus' subterfuge convincingly. He has learned the way of the world, and the survival of father and son depends on this particular education. He can give his father a knowing glance and remain silent when Eumaeus worries about the suitors' violence (*Od.* 16.476–77). He holds his tongue when first an object is thrown at his father (*Od.* 17.489–91) and speaks cunningly at the second throw (*Od.* 18.406–09). Nevertheless, he is still a beginner. He cannot control his temper after the third assault but lashes out with a torrent of heartfelt abuse first toward the culprit and then toward the suitors as a whole (*Od.* 20.304–19).[6] A more telling sign of immaturity appears in the recognition scene between Odysseus and Penelope, when the boy reverts to his naive view of language and scolds his mother for not believing the simple truth that has been uttered clearly in plain Greek, that the man before her is her husband (*Od.* 23.97–103). Her reply shows her to be one of the elite:

> "If truly indeed
> this is Odysseus and he has come home, we two would
> certainly know each other best of all; for there are between us
> signs which we know, hidden from everyone else."
> (*Od.* 23.107–10)

Of course, the true addressee of this retort is not her son at all but the man she is about to test with the fiendishly clever bed trick, and the indirectness itself of this challenge testifies to her high level of play. Her son, however, still has a lot to learn about the game of communication.

Penelope's indirect address to the man claiming to be her husband by way of an apparently direct statement to her son and the implication in her bed trick that she has been a faithful wife represent the two most prevalent forms of indirect communication in the *Odyssey*.[7] Addressing someone other than the one intended to listen is a tactic that arises early in life when, as small children, we tell visitors about ourselves by directing our words toward our parents. Even the suitors can manage that. Deliberate implication shows more skill and greater awareness of conversation as a game.

Penelope's entry in book 1 marks the first instance of indirect address, which will become almost the norm in conversation with more than two people present. When she berates the bard Phemios for his song about misadventure on the return from Troy (*Od.* 1.337–44), her real targets are the hateful suitors who relish the topic. Telemachus, possibly another indirect addressee, responds to his mother with a harsh reprimand (*Od.* 1.346–59) that is actually meant, though clumsy in execution, as an attempt to impress upon the suitors that he is now an adult, a man among men. In book 18, mother and son again indirectly confront the suitors in the guise of a conversation with each other (*Od.* 18.215–25, 227–42). At the assembly in book 2 Telemachus and the suitors insult each other by means of addresses to the Ithacan people (*Od.* 2.40–79, 178–207). Speaking to one party while formally addressing another early on becomes a typical strategy of communication in this epic that scorns the direct approach.

To convey information or sentiments by implication asks for cooperation between interlocutors, so the one who pursues this method and expects to be met halfway by the other indicates a certain amount of respect for the other's ability to participate. Gauging that ability is part of the game. Odysseus's brilliantly controlled speech to Nausicaa (*Od.* 6.149–85) flatters her by treating her as an adult, since she is asked to read between the lines, and at the same time he makes sure that the adolescent gets very broad hints of his implications: that he has been a leader of men, that he finds her marriageable, that he is a great man brought low, that she has no reason to be afraid. Perhaps he is rather obvious in our eyes, but, since he has left it for her to pick up on the unstated, the inexperienced girl gratefully and eagerly falls for the stranger's lure, especially his disingenuous suggestion of an imminent marriage. Her response implies a worldly awareness of suffering (*Od.* 6.187–90), and her indirect address to him via her friends about the Phaeacians' close relationship to the gods implies that he will be treated well but he had better behave himself (*Od.* 6.199–210). His refusal of help with a bath implies that he is no sexual threat (*Od.* 6.218–22). Her next indirect address awkwardly implies that he would be an ideal husband (*Od.* 6.239–46), a suggestion she elaborates soon with transparent indirection (*Od.* 6.273–90). This conversation has won Nausicaa over to the stranger's cause more firmly than a straightforward exchange possibly could: the demands of implications have created a bond of mutual participation, an intimacy that Odysseus is careful, for his benefit, that she misunderstand.

The conversations between Odysseus and the Phaeacians in books 7 and 8 involve a great amount of implication at a somewhat more subtle level than with Nausicaa. After Odysseus' direct supplication of Arete (*Od.* 7.146–52), we follow a series of implied questions concerning the visitor's identity, background, and abilities; a veiled discussion of the relationship between the stranger and Nausicaa, culminating in an outright proposal by Alcinous that the man marry his daughter, which must then be smoothed over as a blunder; indirect self-characterizations by Odysseus without revealing his identity, suggesting the quantity and seriousness of his woes, his piety, his fame, his participation in the Trojan War, and, after the open offer of marriage, his lack of interest in wedding the girl; indirect insults and reconciliation; and implied plans for an escort home. At the end Alcinous finally straight forwardly asks in a long speech for the stranger to tell his story (*Od.* 8.536–86), launching the Apologue of books 9–12. Their badinage until this point has been largely conducted at the level of hints and inference with reasonable accuracy of mutual comprehension, typical of the conversations throughout the *Odyssey*. When characters can make themselves understood with suggestion or insinuation, they tend to avoid straightforward statements. Outright assertions or questions expose the speakers; indirect speaking keeps them more securely hidden and protected.

Early in his apprenticeship Telemachus finds himself the middleman, with no apparent awareness of the subtext, in a married couple's indirect conversation rich in implications that amount to hidden meanings. The uneasy reconciliation of Helen and Menelaus finds expression in an encoded swapping of tales ostensibly meant to give their young visitor a picture of his father in Trojan War days, but their discourse is actually directed toward each other. Helen, claiming to be repentant now of her folly years before, tells of once rescuing the disguised Odysseus within the Trojan walls (*Od.* 4.240–64), an anecdote really meant for her husband, who is to understand that she was working for the Greek cause from the inside and deserves to be thought well of now. Menelaus responds in kind with a tale of her treachery at the very end of the war when Helen tried, by mimicry of their wives' voices, to lure the warriors out of the Trojan Horse (*Od.* 4.271–89). Telemachus hears two fine stories about his father and gives no sign that he is following the exchange below the surface. The married couple, however, who speak each other's language, are engaged in what must have been a common metaconversation: "I was really on your side." "No, you were not, you shameless liar."

The Spartan couple understands each other's coded messages as Alcinous deciphers Nausicaa's more simply encrypted request. We see other instances in which the words spoken mask a message understood only by the initiated. When Antinous calls on the suitors to obey Telemachus, he is very close to making an open admission of their plot to kill the boy, but not quite: it is clear to those in the know, not to anyone else (*Od.* 20.271–74). Odysseus asks for a turn at the bow contest in a way that gives a clear signal of his murderous intention to Telemachus and the herdsmen but goes right by the suitors and Penelope (*Od.* 22.275–84). Once Odysseus has figured out that Penelope's bed ruse (*Od.* 23.174–80) was her test of his identity, he can go further and interpret her choice of this sign as a clear message, not stated openly by either of them, that there is no one else who could have known their secret: the test itself was an encoded implication of her faithfulness. Such exchanges that exclude bystanders without access to the conversation below the surface reflect the nature of dialogue in the *Odyssey* generally: we cannot trust the face value of the words to convey what is in the speaker's mind.

In some instances of hidden meaning, however, we cannot be certain who understands what or even whether there is a hidden meaning at all, and a good part of our narrative enjoyment results from the ambiguity. The recognitions and self-disclosures of Odysseus have spurred some scholarly controversy. Many take Homer at his word that no one recognizes the hero until he says so, whereas others have presented various forms of the argument that Penelope and even Eumaeus have some awareness, ranging from a vague notion to absolute certainty, well before the formal self-declaration.[8] The encounters between husband and wife in books 18 and 19, no matter how one gauges their level of knowledge, are indeed characterized by speeches that, at least in one direction, convey information indirectly or can be interpreted by the listener as a coded message.

The first "conversation" between husband and wife after a twenty-year separation can serve, at least in Odysseus' mind, as a model for successful indirect communication such as we saw, in a rather spiteful form, with Helen and Menelaus. Athena prompts Penelope to make her first appearance to her husband without telling her the real reason for going downstairs (*Od.* 18.158–68). Typically, there is a discrepancy between Athena's purpose and Penelope's stated reason for this unaccustomed move: they have in common that the queen is to show herself before the suitors (though Penelope does not understand why), but Athena wants her to excite the admiration of her husband and son (*Od.* 18.161–62), whereas Penelope, who does not know that her husband is in the hall, says she will warn her son to beware of the suitors (166–68). In fact, she makes no such warning but rather scolds Telemachus for negligence as a host to the beleaguered stranger, a shortcoming he is in fact feigning to conceal Odysseus's identity (*Od.* 18.215–25). She goes on to address the suitors with a narrative whose truth value is uncertain (except to Odysseus, and he tells us nothing) and then with an admonition that suggests an intention whose sincerity is ambiguous even to the external audience.[9] She says that her husband upon his departure instructed her to marry another if he had not returned from the war by the time of their son's emergence into adulthood (that is, now), virtually announcing her impending decision to choose from among them, hateful though such a marriage would be (*Od.* 18.257–73).[10] She follows up this mixed message of enticement and repulsion with a plea for a proper courtship with gifts, the effectiveness of which perhaps owes something to its being stated indirectly (an implied negative comparison to proper suitors of the past) rather than with a direct request (*Od.* 18.274–80).

The suitors accept her words as both a true account of the past and a promise of her intention to marry soon. Odysseus, on the other hand, receives with joy what another might regard as a direful announcement from the wife he sees and hears now for the first time in twenty years:

> Thus she spoke, and much-suffering godlike Odysseus rejoiced,
> because she was wheedling gifts from them and was charming their
> hearts
> with soothing words, but her mind was intending other things.
> (*Od.* 18.281–83)

We cannot be certain whether Odysseus is correct that his wife has other intentions nor why he could be confident in his interpretation nor even what he assumes those other intentions to be. In this situation he is in much the same position as the narrative audience trying to analyze the text of this ambiguous speech. He feels certain of his exegesis, but we cannot share his certainty. What we can tell is that, in the spirit of their famous like-mindedness, the hero of indirect communication is imputing some of his craft to his wife and assumes that her words mean something other than what they appear to mean.[11] In his mind she is, as it were, directing her speech over the heads of the suitors toward the stranger in the back, who readily decodes her message as a clever subterfuge that works in his favor.

We can agree that the fireside interview between beggar and queen in book 19 is a treasure house of indirect communication even if we differ widely about which statements are meant to be taken, by us or by either of the interlocutors, at face value and which as encrypted messages. Her tale of the shroud trick and pressure to remarry (*Od.* 19.137–61), his false autobiography (*Od.* 19.172–202), her test question (*Od.* 19.215–19), his detailed reply (*Od.* 19.221–48), her assertion of her husband's death (*Od.* 19.257–60), his counter-assertion of his imminent return (*Od.* 19.268–307),[12] the byplay about washing his feet and his resemblance to Odysseus (*Od.* 19.317–60), her self-interpreting dream (*Od.* 19.535–53), his confirmation of the obvious interpretation (*Od.* 19.555–58), her sudden and bizarre announcement of the bow contest to settle the marriage question (*Od.* 19.571–81), his approval of this contest and prediction of the winner (*Od.* 19.583–87)—the entire conversation, which the maids in the room can safely hear with a literal ear, gives us the distinct sense that the real communication is carried on well below the surface of the words, though we cannot be sure exactly what is meant and what is picked up by whom. The only blatant statement in this interview is Penelope's direct quote of the victorious eagle in the dream she claims to have had, who tells her in plain words what the dream signifies (*Od.* 19.546–53), an interpretation she quickly dismisses as a false prophecy (*Od.* 19.560–69).

We would like to know what Odysseus and Penelope each understand to be going on during their conversation and to what extent they are attuned to each other's mind, but we must resign ourselves to informed speculation and intuition. Our imperfect knowledge leads us to the recognition that the characters of the *Odyssey* are not the only practitioners of indirect communication. I would attribute the notorious ambiguity of book 19 to the ethos of obfuscation in the epic and place our narrator among those who practice indirection with no compunction.[13] Another author, Tolstoy for example, who regularly interprets signs the reader might not catch and conveys his characters' actual thoughts, would be happy to clarify the situation and leave us in no doubt that Penelope knows or does not know, that Odysseus knows she knows or does not know whether she knows, and so on. Homer, however, is not always interested in the direct communication of the characters' true knowledge or conjectures.[14] Rather, he delights in giving us hints.

The second half of the *Odyssey* is essentially a grand performance, with Odysseus as director as well as lead actor, guiding the rest of the cast in what they might or might not realize to be roles in his show. His false autobiographies form the most salient contribution to this atmosphere,[15] and they are joined by the techniques of indirection already discussed as well as close relatives of lies that create a false presentation of reality designed to attain victory and reunion: feigned ignorance, concealment of facts, false reasons, evasion, secrecy, disguised feelings, indirect direction of the plot, and words to preserve a false persona.

We have seen such performances throughout the *Odyssey*, and not only by its hero. Athena sets the tone even before her impersonation of Mentes when she steers the Olympian conversation away from Zeus's topic to the family that matters to her and pretends to believe that her favorite is hated by Zeus, thereby getting the plot of the *Odyssey* under way. This goddess serves as the divine embodiment of the very set of attributes we have been talking about—trickery, lies, deception, communication by indirection. She then visits Telemachus in disguise and gives him advice in an underhanded fashion. She sends him off to Pylos and Sparta for, as she tells him and has already told Zeus, the purpose of learning about his father (*Od.* 1.93–95, 280–92), but she later confesses to his father that her true mission was to make a man of him (Od. 13.421–24). She could tell the boy directly and fully all he wants to know about Odysseus, but the indirect nature of communication she helps to promote in this narrative serves her purpose here whereas a straightforward message would ruin the plan. The point is not for Telemachus to know the facts but rather for him to advance toward adulthood so that he will rise to the demands of his conspiratorial role on his return. Secrecy is vital to attain this end. The false reason for his journey and the concealment of the facts lead to the maturity and self-confidence she needs him to gain to be of practical help to his father upon their reunion.

A similar and more important instance of divine misleading arises when Odysseus asks Circe permission to depart. She gives him the bad news that he must first enter the kingdom of Hades to consult the prophet Teiresias, for, she says,

> "He will tell you the road and measures of the path
> and how you will make the return on the fishy sea."
> (*Od.* 10.539–40)

Teiresias does no such thing. He barely mentions the sea voyage and tells Odysseus nothing on that score that Circe does not already know. Later, the goddess herself gives detailed instructions for the journey (*Od.* 12.25–27, 37–110). The trip to the underworld has been superfluous, a pointless agony, if we are to believe Circe, and some erudite readers have taken Circe at her word and have worked out explanations, defenses, and solutions as drastic as excising all of book 11.[16] But the underworld adventure does belong here. It is central to the development of Odysseus' character and to the themes of identity, family, and mortality. It is telling that Odysseus himself does not think the journey superfluous at all. Unlike many scholars, he is not upset with Circe for sending him on a wild goose chase when she had the information all along. As with Telemachus' voyage, this journey has had as its object something more profound than the specious reason given by the dispatching goddess. After two or three years of listless wandering and malingering with no particular sense of urgency, Odysseus has reached an ambivalence that must turn into determination if he is to make Ithaca the priority and the Trojan War an episode of the past. His conversations with Anticleia, Agamemnon, and Achilles about fathers, wives, and sons encourage him not to dwell on his previous persona and push him toward reaffirming his Ithacan identity as son, husband, and father.[17] If we believe Circe's actual words, we have missed the point. Odysseus, in this case, is a better reader than most of us. He knows the idiom. He knows how language can be used to conceal the true message. He can read between the lines.

Hermes gives a splendid cameo performance in his scene with Calypso. When he arrives to order Odysseus off the island, the goddess's reception of her visitor (5.87–91) betrays the suspicion the perceptive characters properly maintain toward friendly overtures, and she is treated to what Hermes calls a truthful account of his mission, a sure sign of disingenuousness (*Od.* 5.97–115). He feigns reluctance to take on this duty, implying that she too must accede though reluctant, and pretends to know little about this person she has on the island or what he means to her; he implies that Athena has nothing to do with it, that fate is to blame. Calypso is no less talented an actress. When Hermes leaves, she approaches Odysseus with the new plan as though it were her idea, and she tries to steer him away from accepting the offer by falsely implying that she is eager for his departure but is not so sure about the gods' willingness; she feigns compassion and invents troubles ahead that Hermes said nothing of (*Od.* 5.160–70, 182–91, 203–13). Odysseus does not fall for her performance, convincing though it might have been. Master actor that he is, the hero has learned to be as suspicious of others' words as others should be of his. Only after a thorough examination will he decide which lines to believe and which to dismiss as false.

He carries that attitude with him to Ithaca. It would be out of keeping with the ethos of the *Odyssey* for Odysseus to make a direct approach to regaining his position on Ithaca, practical problems aside. In fact, I suspect we generally overemphasize the practical in considering his behavior. Despite the urge to insist that Odysseus must keep his secret from Penelope and Eumaeus so that they do not blow his cover or so that he can test their loyalty, the essential reason Odysseus maintains the pretense before even his eminently and obviously loyal wife and swineherd till the last possible moment is that in his world the straightforward must on principle be avoided.

That practicality is not necessarily the main point can be seen in the fascinating encounter with Laertes after the slaughter of the suitors. With nothing to gain by it, Odysseus treats his father to a false tale that causes him needless grief.[18] This apparently absurd behavior makes sense only by considering the nature of conversation in the *Odyssey* as a whole. Forthright speaking implies either naïveté or trust. A winner, a survivor, in this world does not walk straight toward the destination but approaches it obliquely. The goal is to come out a winner, even if that means needless pain or prolongation of uncertainty along the way. Odysseus, the most successful player of this game, has great respect for the power of indirection, and he maintains this course until directness is absolutely necessary. He keeps all his loved ones on a need-to-know basis, and he follows faithfully his strategy of keeping everyone in the dark until the last possible moment in order for his plot to succeed.

As a director who cannot afford to be seen as such, Odysseus enjoins secrecy on those who know his identity and must use indirect methods to steer the course of events and the thoughts and decisions of those unaware. For a while those in on the secret do not know who else is in that club. Telemachus, the first and, as far as he knows, the only one to join the plot, stays in character when, alone with Eurycleia, he asks about "the stranger" and speaks badly of Penelope's treatment of him (*Od.* 20.129–33); she, also in character after threat of death if she slips (*Od.* 19.482–90), defends her mistress without letting on that the man is no stranger (*Od.* 20.135–43). Neither knows that they are both part of the same conspiracy until he fails to astound her after the battle with the revelation that she is summoned by his "father" (*Od.* 22.397). When Odysseus orders Eumaeus to have Eurycleia lock up the women before the battle, the swineherd, new to the deception game after his clumsy but successful delivery of the bow to his master, keeps the secret by telling the maid falsely that Telemachus gave the order (*Od.* 21.381–85), ignorant of her participation in the plot. From the outset, keeping facts and plans concealed from opponents and friends alike has been an important feature of Odyssean conversation: when the gods make their plans secretly in Poseidon's absence (*Od.* 1.19–95), Athena holds a secret conversation with Telemachus (*Od.* 1.123–318), Telemachus demands that Eurycleia stay mum about his departure (*Od.* 2.349–76), and the suitors plot an ambush against Telemachus (*Od.* 4.632–72, 770–77). The concealment of Odysseus' identity and plot on Ithaca through lies, misleading speeches in character, suppression of true feelings, and evasions of direct answers is the grand, sustained culmination of a pattern that characterizes conversation throughout.

If Odysseus is going to control the plot from a position of secrecy, he will not have much opportunity to guide the other characters' actions in a straightforward manner. Athena, as so often, shows at the beginning the technique her favorite will employ masterfully. Her opening speech is a model of indirect goading (*Od.* 1.45–62): she reaffirms Zeus' sentiments about Aegisthus, about whom she cares nothing at this point; pretends that Zeus is hard-hearted toward Odysseus after describing his plight; and asks a suggestive question. Without making an open request, she maneuvers Zeus into taking steps to get her hero back home. Her initial strategy, as Mentes, with Telemachus includes feigned surprise at the presence and outrageous behavior of the suitors (*Od.* 1.224–29), a detailed account of the sorry condition of Laertes (*Od.* 1.188–93), the pointed question whether he is his father's son (*Od.* 1.206–12), a tale (possibly false) suggesting Odysseus' vicious streak and vengeful nature (*Od.* 1.253–66), and an indirect comparison between Telemachus and Orestes (*Od.* 1.296–302). In this context of indirect goading, her explicit advice (*Od.* 1.269–85) sinks in readily.

Odysseus reprises Athena's role upon meeting his son in Eumaeus's hut. At first Odysseus stays quiet while the other two speak to him indirectly. Telemachus almost phrases his question of the stranger's identity so as to address Odysseus but technically puts it to Eumaeus (*Od.* 16.57–59); after summarizing the visitor's false tale, Eumaeus, though formally addressing Telemachus, informs the stranger that he is handing him over to the young man (*Od.* 16.61–67); Telemachus recaps his situation at home for the stranger by telling Eumaeus about his inability to offer proper hospitality (*Od.* 16.69–89). When Odysseus breaks into the conversation (*Od.* 16.91–111), he feigns ignorance of the boy's plight with the suitors and goads him indirectly with his question,

> "Tell me, do you willingly subject yourself, or do the people
> throughout the land hate you, following the voice of a god,
> or do you put any blame on your brothers, whom a man
> trusts when they're fighting if a great quarrel arises?"
> (*Od.* 16.95–98)

He wishes he were young again and able to combat their outrage, since he would rather die than see it perpetrated in his house. At great length he, as Athena, offers his son an outsider's view of the anomalous situation with the implication that there is no reason to tolerate it. Telemachus' shame could not be more skillfully aroused by a direct assault, and he now stands ready to meet his father and join in his plot. Odysseus performs a similar ploy to get a rise out of Laertes (*Od.* 24.244–79), and he encourages Penelope at the interview to ask him further questions and excites her curiosity by pretending to be coy and unwilling to talk about himself (*Od.* 19.107–22). Odysseus' manner of directing the scenes consists to a great extent in putting others in a state of mind or inducing them to take an action without actually telling them what to think or do.

When the point of one's words is to manipulate the situation to suit one's interests rather than to reveal and communicate, conversation is game and performance. The game of language in the *Odyssey* can be playful at times, but essentially the obfuscatory use of speech reflects a treacherous and precarious world in which survival and happiness depend on assuming that appearance is deceiving and the straightforward is masking a reality that must be deciphered. Those who play the game well listen carefully to what is not stated outright and express what they mean by not saying what they mean.

Notes

1. All translations of the *Odyssey* are my own, meant to be literal rather than literary.

2. As Walcot (1977, 14) observes, "No one can permit himself the luxury of trusting anyone else in Homer's world." For an analysis of this world in terms of the spy novel, see Richardson (2006b).

3. Tannen (1986) bases her sociolinguistic analysis of conversation on the premise that indirect communication is the norm in human interaction.

4. The *Odyssey* is a very talk-oriented epic. According to my count, of the 12,110 lines of the *Odyssey,* 8,219 are in direct speech (67.9 percent). If we discount books 9–12, almost entirely Odysseus's first-person tales of his adventures, 5,996 lines of 9,877 are in direct speech (60.7 percent).

5. Todorov (1971, 70) suggests that speaking is the principal sign of the boy's growing up: "Le passage de Télémaque de l'adolescence à la virilité est marqué presque uniquement par le fait qu'il commence à parler." I would add that to begin to speak is, for the son of Odysseus, to begin to conceal through speaking; to be an adult in his world is to know how to use language to undermine or to distract from the truth.

6. De Jong (1994, 38–39) discusses these passages in the context of a study of unspoken thoughts.

7. In her commentary de Jong (2001) notes each instance of indirect address, which she calls "indirect dialogue" and defines in the glossary: "A talks to B about character C or about things which concern C (and which he intends C to hear) without addressing C" (xiv). I count sixty-nine speeches in which a person not addressed is the principal intended recipient of the message and eighty-six speeches in which important information (sometimes false) is not stated outright but must be inferred by someone listening carefully. Not included are instances of possibly encoded messages or statements with a hidden meaning that an uninformed listener would not be able to infer.

8. Since Harsh's controversial proposal (1950) of Penelope's early recognition of her husband, many have weighed in on the question of how much Penelope knows or suspects before her overt recognition in book 23. See especially Whitman (1958, 303–04), Amory (1963), Austin (1975, 200–38), Russo (1982), Emlyn-Jones (1984), Winkler (1990), and Katz (1991). Roisman (1990) argues for an early recognition of his master by Eumaeus.

9. Various recent interpretations of Penelope's motivation and speech and of Odysseus' amused reaction can be found in Austin (1975, 208–10), Van Nortwick (1979), Emlyn-Jones (1984, 9–12), Byre (1988), Winkler (1990, 146–47), Katz (1991, 78–93), Russo (1992, 58–67), and de Jong (1994, 40–42).

10. De Jong (2001, 467) observes that in the interview of book 19 Penelope fails to mention to the beggar these instructions of Odysseus that she remarry when giving him an apparently thorough account of her predicament; "this suggests that the instructions were her invention."

11. De Jong (1994) brings out their like-mindedness in her analysis of the couple's unspoken thoughts (47) and concludes, "Their capacity to control their emotions, to remain silent, or to say something other than what they feel, marks

Penelope and especially Odysseus as the typical heroes of the *Odyssey,* poem of disguise and dissimulation" (48).

12. Odysseus introduces this lie with the telltale avowal of truth: "For I will tell you truly and I will not conceal" (19.269). As Todorov (1971, 73) perceptively observes, "L'invocation de la vérité est un signe de mensonge."

13. For a discussion of the various ways in which this narrator proves to be a participant in the game of indirection, see Richardson (2006a).

14. Winkler (1990, 143) admonishes us not "to assume that Homer is an utterly transparent narrator, always telling us all that can be known. As the characters he describes are normally devious and cautious about their words, so we should not deny to Homer too the possibility that he will avail himself of a certain cunning in setting out the cross-purposes of his plot." In speaking of the plurality and complexity of narratives in the *Odyssey,* Slatkin (1996, 229) says "it is clear that it is not easy for an audience to get a straight story, to discriminate among stories, or even to know what a straight story is." In preparation for an analysis of two narrative problems in the *Odyssey,* Scodel (1998, 1) asserts "a common narrative technique: the narrator seeks to generate both suspense and significance by misdirecting the audience about the role the gods are to play in the action." Parry (1994), on the other hand, who sees the poet as "the most important recorder of the truthful past" (12), champions the view that Homer is to be trusted.

15. The literature on lies and disguise in the *Odyssey* is extensive. Some of the more helpful discussions can be found in Stanford (1950), Trahman (1952), Todorov (1971), Heatherington (1976), Stewart (1976), Walcot (1977), Haft (1984), Emlyn-Jones (1986), Murnaghan (1987), Roisman (1990), Bowie (1993), Pratt (1993), Parry (1994), Reece (1994), Richardson (1996), and King (1999). Lateiner (1995) shows how facial gestures, body language, and other nonverbal behavior can convey the truth behind concealing words or, when manipulated with talent, enhance the liar's performance; on Odysseus' exploitation of the nonverbal in his lies and disguises, see especially chapters 5 (83–92) and 9 (167–202).

16. Page (1955) is typical of the analyst's inclination to excise all or much of book 11.

17. It is interesting that the conversations in the underworld scene seem themselves straightforward and honest, with no undercurrent of hidden messages or innuendo. The characters mean what they say.

18. See Scodel (1998) for a recent discussion of Odysseus' motivation in lying to Laertes and an assessment of previous interpretations. Winkler (1990, 134–36) discusses this scene in the context of the contemporary practice in Mediterranean villages to lie and conceal even to family members as a matter of course. See also Friedl (1962), Walcot (1977, 18–19), and Most (1989) on the Mediterranean penchant for lying on principle, which would account for the lie to Laertes (18–19).

Works Cited

Amory, Anne. "The Reunion of Odysseus and Penelope." In *Essays on the* Odyssey, ed. C. H. Taylor. Bloomington: Indiana University Press, 1963.

Austin, Norman. *Archery at the Dark of the Moon: Poetic Problems in Homer's* Odyssey. Berkeley: University of California, 1975.

Bowie, E. "Lies, Fiction and Slander in Early Greek Poetry." In *Lies and Fiction in the Ancient World,* edited by Christopher Gill and T. P. Wiseman. Austin: University of Texas Press,1993.

Byre, Calvin S. "Penelope and the Suitors before Odysseus: *Odyssey* 18.158–303." *American Journal of Philology* 109 (1988): 159–73.

Conrad, Joseph. *Under Western Eyes.* 1911. Reprint. New York: Random House, 2001.

De Jong, Irene J. F. "Between Words and Deeds: Hidden Thoughts in the *Odyssey.*" In *Modern Critical Theory and Classical Literature,* edited by Irene J. F. de Jong and J. P. Sullivan. Leiden: Brill, 1994.

———. *A Narratological Commentary on the* Odyssey. Cambridge: Cambridge University Press, 2001.

Emlyn-Jones, C. "The Reunion of Penelope and Odysseus." *Greece & Rome* 31 1984: 1–18.

———. "True and Lying Tales in the *Odyssey.*" *Greece & Rome* 33 (1986): 1–10.

Friedl, Ernestine. *Vasilika: A Village in Modern Greece.* New York: Holt, Rinehart & Winston, 1962.

Haft, Adele J. "Odysseus, Idomeneus and Meriones: The Cretan Lies of *Odyssey* 13–19." *Classical Journal* 79 (1984): 289–306.

Harsh, P. W. "Penelope and Odysseus in *Odyssey* XIX." *American Journal of Philology* 71 (1950): 1–21.

Heatherington, M. E. "Chaos, Order, and Cunning in the *Odyssey.*" *Studies in Philology* 73 (1976): 225–38.

James, Henry. *The Tragic Muse.* 1890. Reprint. London: Penguin, 1948.

Katz, Marilyn A. *Penelope's Renown: Meaning and Indeterminacy in the* Odyssey. Princeton: Princeton University Press, 1991.

King, Ben. "The Rhetoric of the Victim: Odysseus in the Swineherd's Hut." *Classical Antiquity* 18 (1999): 74–93.

Lateiner, Donald. *Sardonic Smile: Nonverbal Behavior in Homeric Epic.* Ann Arbor: University of Michigan Press, 1995.

Most, Glenn W. "The Stranger's Stratagem: Self-Disclosure and Self-Sufficiency in Greek Culture." *Journal of Hellenic Studies* 109 (1989): 114–33.

Murnaghan, Sheila. *Disguise and Recognition in the* Odyssey. Princeton: Princeton University Press, 1987.

Page, Denys. *The Homeric* Odyssey. Oxford: Oxford University Press, 1955.

Parry, Hugh. "The *Apologos* of Odysseus: Lies, All Lies?" *Phoenix* 48 (1994): 1–20.

Pratt, Louise H. *Lying and Poetry from Homer to Pindar: Falsehood and Deception in Archaic Greek Poetics.* Ann Arbor: University of Michigan Press, 1993.

Reece, Steve. "The Cretan *Odyssey:* A Lie Truer than Truth." *American Journal of Philology* 115 (1994): 157–73.

Richardson, Scott. "Truth in the Tales of the *Odyssey.*" *Mnemosyne* 49 (1996): 393–402.

———. "The Devious Narrator of the *Odyssey.*" *Classical Journal* 101 (2006a): 337–59.

———. "The *Odyssey* and the Spy Novel." *Classical and Modern Literature* 26 (2006b): 110–40.

Roisman, Hannah M. "Eumaeus and Odysseus—Covert Recognition and Self-Revelation?" *Illinois Classical Studies* 15 (1990): 215–38.

Russo, Joseph. "Interview and Aftermath: Dream, Fantasy, and Intuition in *Odyssey* 19 and 20." *American Journal of Philology* 103 (1982): 4–18.

———. "Books XVII–XX." In *A Commentary on Homer's* Odyssey, by Joseph Russo, Manuel Fernández-Galiano, and Alfred Heubeck. Vol. 3. Oxford: Oxford University Press, 1992.

Scodel, Ruth. "The Removal of the Arms, the Recognition with Laertes, and Narrative Tension in the *Odyssey.*" *Classical Philology* 93 (1998): 1–17.

Slatkin, Laura M. "Composition by Theme and the *Mêtis* of the *Odyssey.*" In *Reading the* Odyssey*: Selected Interpretive Essays,* edited by Seth L. Schein. Princeton: Princeton University Press, 1996.

Stanford, W. B. "Studies in the Characterization of Ulysses—III: The Lies of Odysseus." *Hermathena* 75 (1950): 35–48.

Stewart, Douglas J. *The Disguised Guest: Rank, Role, and Identity in the* Odyssey. Lewisburg, PA: Bucknell University Press, 1976.

Tannen, Deborah. 1986. *That's Not What I Meant! How Conversational Style Makes or Breaks Relationships.* New York: Ballantine, 1986.

Todorov, Tzvetan. "Le récit primitif." In *Poétique de la Prose.* Paris: Éditions du Seuil, 1971.

Trahman, C. R. "Odysseus' Lies (*Odyssey,* Books 13–19)." *Phoenix* 6 (1952): 31–43.

Van Nortwick, Thomas. "Penelope and Nausicaa." *Transactions of the American Philological Association* 109 (1979): 269–76.

Walcot, P. "Odysseus and the Art of Lying." *Ancient Society* 8: 1–19.

Whitman, Cedric H. 1958. "The Odyssey and Change." In *Homer and the Heroic Tradition.* New York: Norton, 1958.

Winkler, John J. "Penelope's Cunning and Homer's." In *The Constraints of Desire: The Anthropology of Sex and Gender in Ancient Greece.* New York: Routledge, 1990.

The End of Speeches and a Speech's End: Nestor, Diomedes, and the *telos muthôn*

Joel Christensen

This paper offers a close reading of Nestor's claim to Diomedes in *Il.* 9 that he "has not reached the *telos muthôn*" (9.56: *atar ou telos hikeo muthôn*). The argument evolves through several steps. First, it establishes the critical importance of the utterance itself by examining the "stakes" of the scene in which it occurs. Then, it turns to what should be expected of this combination syntactically and semantically according to archaic Greek parallels. Once these expectations have been discussed, it investigates the ways in which the phrase garners context-specific meaning in conjunction both with what Nestor says about the use of speech in *Il.* 9 and the way Nestor himself uses language in responding to Diomedes. The paper argues that Nestor's speech responds aptly to the nuances of a combustible political situation and that his use of the unique phrase *telos muthôn* nicely embodies his sophisticated approach. In short, the paper suggests that the phrase possesses an innate and integral ambiguity—or better, polysemy—that furnishes responses to complex rhetorical and political crises. The paper closes by reconsidering why these crises crystallize around Nestor and Diomedes—the former is a conventional paragon of language use and political authority and the latter may be seen as facilitating the dramatization both of a young man coming into his political own through the use of speech and of an evolution of political speech that occurs during the course of the epic itself.

SPEECH IS PARAMOUNT IN THE *ILIAD*. ALTHOUGH THE EPIC HAS BEEN CHARacterized as a poem of force—meaning physical violence—the extent to which the language of Homeric characters drives the plot and provides critical reflections on its development is remarkable. Because we are so far removed from the language and culture represented in the poem, we are often barred from the nuances of speech in Homer. While there have certainly been fine contributions to our understanding of Homeric speech from an analysis of individual speaking habits,[1] typologies of speech acts,[2] and the application of sociolinguistics to Iliadic speeches,[3] there are still leaps and bounds to be made in apprehending expectations for the use and style of speech from a Homeric perspective, that is, a perspective grounded in the ways in which the Homeric poems teach us about the promises and pitfalls of public language.[4]

Indeed, the *Iliad* and the *Odyssey* are replete with information about speech that, over time, informs careful readers about the conventional uses of and expectations for speech in the Homeric world. Speeches are colored by their narrative "framing," the matrix of assumptions developed by formulaic speech reactions, and the felicitous or infelicitous outcome of a speech itself.[5] Apart from these categories some remaining pieces for the puzzle are unique evaluations of speech—metaspeech—by Homeric speakers. Close analysis of the context of such passages constitutes an essential step in judging the aesthetics and dynamics of public speech according to non-anachronistic criteria.

As a part of this effort, this paper offers a close reading of Nestor's claim to Diomedes in *Iliad* 9 that he "has not reached the *telos muthôn*" (9.56: *atar ou telos hikeo muthôn*).[6] The meaning of this phrase, I suggest, has not been adequately understood from either a lexical or a thematic perspective. A clearer consideration of the phrase will enhance our understanding not only of this critical moment in the *Iliad* but also of the dynamics of Homeric speech in general.

The argument evolves through several steps. First, I establish the critical importance of the utterance itself by examining the "stakes" of the scene in which it occurs. Then, I turn to what should be expected of this combination syntactically and semantically according to archaic Greek parallels. Once these expectations have been discussed, I investigate the ways in which the phrase garners context-specific meaning in conjunction both with what Nestor says about the use of speech in book 9 and the way Nestor himself uses language in responding to Diomedes. I argue that Nestor's speech responds aptly to the nuances of a combustible political situation and that his use of the unique phrase *telos muthôn* nicely embodies his sophisticated approach. In short, I suggest that the phrase possesses an innate and integral ambiguity—or better, polysemy—that furnishes responses to complex rhetorical and political crises. I close the paper by reconsidering why these crises crystallize around Nestor and Diomedes—the former is a conventional paragon of language use and political authority, and the latter may be seen as facilitating the dramatization both of a young man coming into his political own through the use of speech and of an evolution of political speech that occurs during the course of the epic itself.

The Crisis of Book 9: The King, the Elderly Adviser, and the Young Man

In book 9 Nestor's declaration that Diomedes "has not reached the *telos muthôn*" (9.56: *atar ou telos hikeo muthôn*) is prompted by the younger hero's reaction to a speech from Agamemnon at a moment of crisis for the assembled Achaians. Their best warrior has withdrawn from the war over a quarrel with Agamemnon and recent Trojan success has pinned the Achaians on the shore behind recently constructed fortifications. Book 9's pattern of speech and response, when compared to a recent assembly from *Iliad* 7, serves to establish a moment of political crisis mediated through language in the form of Nestor's comments to Diomedes. Hence, it will be necessary to survey the situation briefly.

At the beginning of book 9, Agamemnon is troubled—he stands to address the assembly as he weeps and repeats much of his "test" from book 2—he calls for the Achaians to give up on taking Troy and to turn home.[7] Agamemnon's call is greeted with silence by the assembled Achaians, a reaction that in Homer, not surprisingly, often indicates either awe or, as in this instance, dread and uncertainty.[8] Indeed, the moment evokes a similar uncertainty from book 7 where Paris' offer to return Menelaos' possessions but not his wife (7.385–97) is also met by silence (7.398–99) only to be broken by Diomedes with a curt rejection of the Trojan proposal (7.400–02) which is followed in turn by the same narrative description of laudatory shouting (7.403–04 = 9.50–51). The similarity of the pattern, however, belies the difference in stakes. In book 7, the herald Idaios offers multiple plans to the Achaians: a truce for the burial of war dead (already suggested by Nestor, 7.327–43) and the cessation of hostilities secured by the return of stolen goods *sans la femme*.[9] In those circumstances, Diomedes interrupts a silence caused by incredulous speechlessness; his brief dismissal of the Trojan offer serves several purposes. First, he articulates the collective disdain of the Achaians for Paris' plan (and thereby emphasizes the sea change in political unity that has occurred between this moment and the chaos of book 2). By giving voice to this rejection, Diomedes bestows a unity upon the Achaian assembly that is distinct from the disunity of the Trojans as implied by the fragmented "plans" reported by their herald. And, finally, by disabusing the herald of his objectionable detail, Diomedes, consciously or not, allows Agamemnon to credit the rejection of one proposal to the Achaians en masse, on the one hand, but, on the other, to accept the proposal for the burial of the dead magnanimously.

The political unity implied by the assembly of book 7 and the close thematic and formulaic echoes between that assembly and the opening of book 9 should not be discounted. In the case of the former, the rupture between the Achaians at large and Agamemnon, initiated by his unwillingness to heed the shout of the Achaians and honor Chryses in *Iliad* 1,[10] is nearly erased from memory by the elaborate theatrics of book 7. Lest we miss the point, it is Agamemnon himself who responds to the Achaian acclamation of Diomedes by telling the herald Idaios, "Certainly you hear the response of the Achaians, how they judge this, yourself; it strikes me in the same way" (7.406–07: *êtoi muthon Akhaiôn autos akoueis / hôs toi hupokrinontai; emoi d' epiandanei*). Note the correlation in diction between the two passages. Agamemnon's disruptive displeasure over the loss of a girl from book 1 (1.24: *ouk Atreïdêi Agamemnoni* ***<u>hêndane</u>*** *thumôi*) is later replaced by his facile agreement with the Achaian assembly regarding the return of Helen (*emoi d' epi<u>andan</u>ei*).

As for the echoes between the assemblies of books 7 and 9 that help to develop the tension of the latter scene, I have already noted the structural similarity centered around Diomedes' speech. The proximity of the passages—separated by a single book—increases the effect of the contrast. In Book 9, Agamemnon is now the one eliciting silence from the Achaian assembly; Diomedes' ire, instead of being directed at an outsider, is now focused on the commander in chief. Here, however, unlike the politically disruptive dissent of Thersites in book 2, Diomedes does not reject "Agamemnon's war" but merely Agamemnon. Since details of this speech will be essential for the evaluation of Nestor's response, it will be useful to include the entire speech here,

> So he spoke and everyone became silent in the quiet, then the sons of the Achaians stayed silent for some time. After a while Diomedes, good at the war-cry, spoke among them. "Son of Atreus, I will fight with you first, which is right, lord, in the assembly, but don't you get angry. You

> criticized my courage first among the Danaans, when you said I was unwarlike and a coward. The young and the old Argives know all these things. But the child of crooked-minded Zeus bestowed upon you a split-thing: he granted that you be honored among all others because of the scepter, but he did not give you courage; and that is the greatest strength. Godly one, do you really expect that the sons of the Achaians are as unwarlike and as cowardly as you publicly proclaim? If your heart urges you to go, then go. There is the path, your ships stand near the sea, the many ships that followed you from Mykenai. But the rest of the long-haired Achaians will remain until we actually take Troy. But, even if you have the others flee to their dear paternal land with their ships, then we two, Sthenelos and I, will fight until we find the end of Troy." So he spoke and all the sons of the Achaians shouted out in response as they wondered at the *muthos* of horse-taming Diomedes. (*Il.* 9.29–49)[11]

Our first question might be why Diomedes' speech is so effective. As in book 7, it seems that he, far better than Agamemnon, has his finger on the collective Achaian pulse. His opening language sounds temporarily like a constitutional appeal or an invocation of parliamentary procedure.[12] What follows, however, are several distinct speech acts that add up to a strategy of isolating Agamemnon. First, by recalling earlier invective (Diomedes' claim that Agamemnon has questioned his bravery before) and flinging it back at Agamemnon, he casts Atreus' son as the worst kind of coward: one who impugns another's bravery but lacks in gumption himself. Diomedes ridicules this hypocrisy with a finely posed and hyperbolic rhetorical question followed by a bare imperative (*erkheo*).[13] The end of his speech is, essentially, a crescendo first promising that the war will go on without Agamemnon and then climaxing with the boast that Diomedes and Sthenelos will fight on until (not *if*) Troy falls.

It is the emotion behind and caused by Diomedes' speech that gives it its power. The Achaians respond so vocally to the disarming of Agamemnon partly because Diomedes' speech is well stated but also because it recapitulates the refrain common to Achilles' and Thersites' prior dissents (Agamemnon is not there for the war). Rather than propose an abandonment of the effort as the earlier speakers do, Diomedes takes "sticking his guns"—to use a wildly anachronistic metaphor—to an absurd degree. Typically willing to ride the emotional torrent, the Achaians prefer the youth's bluster to the king's despair.

That Diomedes' speech and its reception are somehow threatening is underscored by Nestor's immediate response. As the Achaians acclaim Diomedes' speech, Nestor rises to address him and Agamemnon in turn:

> "Son of Tydeus, you are strong in war and in counsel you are the best among all those your age. Surely no one will reproach this speech, however many Achaians there are, nor will anyone speak back, but you have not reached the fullness of speech (*telos muthôn*). Really, you are young, and you could even be my child, the youngest by birth, but you utter knowing things before the kings of the Argives, since you speak according to tradition (*kata moiran*). But come, I, who proclaim to be older than you, will speak out and go through everything, no one will dishonor my *muthos,* not even strong Agamemnon. Brotherless, lawless, and homeless is that man who longs for horrible civil war." (*Il.* 9.53–64)[14]

Nestor's speech reflects the danger imminent in Diomedes' words—his remarkably strong gnomic reflection on the dangers of civil strife ("Brotherless, lawless, and homeless is that man who longs for horrible civil war") amounts to an intrapoetic declaration on the danger of this scene.[15] The thematic pattern (problematically convened assembly followed by civil strife) that culminates in Diomedes' speech echoes two earlier civil disputes in the Achaian camp: the assembly called by Achilles in book 1 (leading to the quarrel between Agamemnon and Achilles) and the assembly following Agamemnon's false dream in book 2 (followed in turn by the dissolution of the ranks and Thersites' protests).[16] The expectation set up by this latter pattern, then, is that Diomedes' speech—essentially a challenge to Agamemnon's authority—will yield further strife.

Nestor's response is integral in preventing this from happening. The agility of his approach, moreover, is noteworthy—he endorses Diomedes' dissent while mitigating its effects. Throughout his address to Diomedes Nestor provides comments that can only enhance our understanding of the "rules" that govern speech in the Homeric world. While a portion of his comments emphasizes the age-based hierarchy of Achaian political authority, Nestor makes several points on the *content* of Diomedes' address that prove to be instructive.

Let us consider Nestor's endorsements first. Nestor authorizes Diomedes' comments with hyperbole—*no one* would criticize what he has said! Even though Diomedes is young, he utters "knowing things" among the kings.[17] Nestor, then, concedes that Diomedes has spoken *kata moiran* ("according to tradition").[18] My examination of the formulaic speech affirmation *kata moiran* in the *Iliad* has revealed that the phrase offers judgment on speech from the perspective of "traditional" or conventional values. The assertion that a speaker has spoken *kata moiran* is often followed by an *alla* ("but") that can be adversative or connective but is, in the *Iliad,* more often the former.[19] Speakers use this formula to assent to the traditionality of their interlocutors' comments even while questioning the applicability of the tradition to their current circumstances; the phrase points to the traditionality of its assertions but also communicates that such precedents may not apply.[20] That Nestor in no way contradicts Diomedes' claim that it is right (*themis*) to fight (*makhêsomai*) with a foolish leader (*aphradeonti*) in the assembly may imply theoretical approval of his contention.

In actuality, the right to criticize the king in the assembly entails the same responsibility as any other social right: it must be applied judiciously. Nestor's endorsements, accordingly, function as sugar to offset the coming medicine. The adversative *alla* that follows his affirmation points to none other than the speaker himself. He, Nestor claims, because he is older, is capable of touching upon "everything." Note the metaphor connecting Nestor's comments on his linguistic ability and Diomedes'. Diomedes has not "reached" the *telos muthôn* (*atar ou telos* ***hik****eo muthôn*), but Nestor claims that he will "touch upon everything" (*panta di****iks****omai*).[21] From Nestor's perspective, his speech will thoroughly and completely address the matter at hand while Diomedes', in contrast, is not even complete.[22] By offering both an affirmation of and a remonstration with Tydeus' son, he diminishes Diomedes' standing, appropriates his words, and amplifies his own position before he proceeds to advise.

The "End of Speeches": Possible Meanings

What it is that Nestor is actually criticizing is hard to understand. Apart from the implied criticism of *kata moiran,* Nestor hedges his compliments on Diomedes' language with an enigmatic reservation: Diomedes has not reached the *telos muthôn.*[23] What does this phrase mean? An ancient commentator glosses it as "you will not place a completion on your words."[24] Bryan Hainsworth translates it as "beside the point" (1993, 67). Hilary Mackie suggests that the phrase indicates "perfection in speaking" and points to Diomedes' speech at the end of book 9 (697–709) as proof of what he has learned (1996, 30). And Cedric Whitman suggests that Nestor criticizes Diomedes for stopping short: there is more to be said (1958, 167). Although Whitman is unclear as to what he means by this exactly, one implication is that Diomedes fails to do what Nestor does, namely, to dissolve the assembly and cope with the crisis in the council of elders, where Nestor proposes clear and pragmatic alternatives to Agamemnon's foolishness (9.65–78; 96–172).[25]

What is lacking in these suggestions is support based on Homeric philology. Since the phrase *telos muthôn* is "unique" insofar as it is not repeated elsewhere and does not appear to be heavily "formulaic," judicious methodology is required. Conventional philology instructs us to search for parallel constructions; from the perspective of orality, we similarly search for echoes or "resonance," iterations or reformations of similar linguistic units that create complex and interactive layers of meaning.[26] Insofar as Homeric language is exactly that, a language developed in concert with its meter and sharing a lexicon with Archaic poetry in general, the following methodology will probably appear rather conventional.[27] We, no matter how well read in Ancient Greek, often need lifetimes to appreciate the nuance and subtlety available to the long-gone ancient audience. Hence, as Oliver Taplin expresses it, Homeric philology becomes an archaeology of sorts (1992).

In order to apprehend more closely what this phrase means, there are several levels that need to be considered, including the etymological background, general semantic spheres for the words involved, and the syntactical operation of *telos* in archaic poetry. While there are a number of instructive examples in Homeric Greek that will also be considered, it will help to offer first a brief survey of the development and use of these words. In the next few sections, I will survey what might be expected from the phrase *telos muthôn* according to archaic poetry in general and Homeric usage in order to show the subtle differences in potential meanings activated by syntax and context.

Muthos and *Telos:* Backgrounds

Of the two words in the combination *telos muthôn, muthos* may be easier by far to pin down than *telos*. The noun *muthos* has a rather wide semantic range in Homer, denoting a speech, plan, thought, or story.[28] As Richard Martin has shown, however, *muthos* may denote a "plan" or strategy in Homeric poetry, but in referring to speech acts by Homeric heroes it can refer to either a command/proposal or a boast/threat.[29] In Book 9 and elsewhere, Homeric speakers use the word to denote forceful public speeches, including directives. Either understanding of *muthos,* or perhaps even both, makes sense for Nestor's phrase *atar ou telos hikeo muthôn.*

Similarly, in the absence of parallels from other languages or a clear Proto-Indo-European root, it is difficult to ascertain the historical semantic sphere of *telos.* Additional lexical items generated from the root complicate the issue further.[30] Pierre Chantraine provides as meanings for the original noun "achévement, terme, realization," each of which could alter our understanding of what Nestor actually means when he addresses Diomedes (1977, 1101).

Indeed, even in danger of making anachronistic generalizations, the semantic sphere of the word *end* in modern English is similar. For instance, we use a partitive expression to denote local termination as in the "end of the block"; similarly, we possess temporal partitive expressions such as "end of the hour." Other metaphors like "end of days" reveal the extent to which the lexical item lends itself to use in metaphors. From another perspective, the English *end* acquires a resultative aspect as in the phrase "the ends justify the means," a usage that renders the word synonymous with "outcomes" or even purpose as in the expression "to what end?"

Homeric Greek showcases a similar range of expressions complicated in turn by the accumulation of meanings from *telos*' verbal reflexes and semantic contamination caused by assumed etymological relationships with verbs such as *tellô* or *telomai,* "accomplish."[31] But, since Homeric poets and audiences, although sensitive to potential etymological relationships,[32] were probably prepared to disambiguate polysemy through an understanding of the context, it is helpful to examine some intersections of semantics and syntax for these words.

Syntax of *Telos*

Translations of the phrase *telos muthôn*[33] cited earlier are incomplete because they may not "square" with the data provided by the use of *telos* in archaic poetry in general. Upon reading the phrase for the first time, it is easy enough to translate as "end of speeches" but such a simple translation overlooks the ambiguity of the genitive in the Greek and the peculiarity of the word *telos* in the context of book 9.

From my examination of the linguistic data, the use of *telos* to refer to an actual end, an achievement, or the completion of a stated goal is often tied in part to the syntax parasitic upon it. While there are some examples of *telos* denoting a "state," "stage," or "outcome" with no subordinate syntax,[34] most instances of this noun include either a dependent genitive or dative construction. And the meaning seems to vary depending upon syntax. For instance, when used with the dative and the preposition *epi,* an agent brings fulfillment (*telos*) to or places completion (*telos*) *on* something, as when, in the example to be discussed later, Agamemnon tells a story in which Hera declares that Zeus is lying and will not bring completion to his plan: "you lie, you will not place completion (*telos*) on your plan (*muthos*) (19.107: *pseustêseis, oud' aute telos muthôi epithêseis*).[35] In other combinations with the dative, *telos* tends to retain a sense of completion or advantageous outcome.[36]

The genitive case provides the most productive syntax for *telos:* in partitive constructions, *telos* signifies the "end of life" (e.g., *thanatoio telos*)[37] with various periphrastic expressions or "the end of war" (*telos polemoio*).[38] In objective genitive usage, *telos* constructions can denote the completion of affairs (*Il.* 16.630: *en gar khersi telos polemou*);[39] the flipside of this is the interpretation of subjective genitive usages where the syntax may signify *how* or *whether* things reached their completion.[40]

Another meaningful intersection between semantics and syntax to consider for the assertion "you have not reached the *telos muthôn*" (*atar ou telos hikeo muthôn*) is the occurrence of *telos* with verbs of motion. Generally, *telos* is used with verbs of movement to denote arrival at the end of something, usually metaphorized from literal place arrival to the achievement of an end stage, as in the end of war (*Il.* 3.291: *telos polemoio kikheiô*) or the end of summer (Hes. *Op.* 664: *es telos elthontos thereos*).[41]

Of additional importance for Nestor's phrase is the use of *telos* by Euripides in his *Hecuba.* Before he announces his descent to the underworld, the ghost of Polydorus entreats his mother to "accept the end of my addresses" (413: *telos dekhêi dê tôn emôn prosphthegmatôn*). Here *telos* most clearly points to the termination of his conversation, the *end* of his addresses.

Iliadic Instances

These tendencies, drawn from Homer and other archaic poets, point to *telos muthôn* as denoting a *local* end to *muthoi*. Typical syntax points to a partitive connection between *telos* and the genitive *muthôn*, thereby implying that Nestor is complaining about the end point of *speeches* (or propositions) in general. In turn, one may infer that, from Nestor's perspective, Diomedes either ends his comments incorrectly or does not properly end his speech at all. Such an analysis, however, is itself incomplete without first examining whether or not these syntactic and semantic generalizations obtain under similar circumstances in Homer. The Homeric instances are limited—in both their number and their similarity—but they are sufficient to assist in a tentative evaluation.

Each of the Iliadic passages presents syntactical or numerical differences from Nestor's phrase. The dative construction discussed earlier occurs twice in the *Iliad.* In book 19 Agamemnon's Hera taunts Zeus by claiming that he will not place a *telos* on his *muthos,* using the *telos, epi* + dative construction (107: *oud' aute telos muthôi epithêseis*), which also signals a completion or fulfillment of the proposal/plan made in his speech (that a son, born that day, would reign among men). Again, in book 20, Hektor assures the Trojans that Achilles will not bring a completion to his *plans* or *threats* (369: *oud' Akhileus pantessi telos muthois epithêsei*).

There are several combinations of *telos* and the genitive, but in each case there are numerical or lexical obstacles to assuming the identity of semantics and syntax. Near the end of book 9 (9.625) Ajax tells Odysseus that the embassy should leave Achilles because there will not be a *muthoio teleutê,* a completion or fulfillment of the *muthos* (Nestor's *plan* to propitiate Achilles): that is, it will not achieve its intended perlocutionary effect.[42] This use of the objective genitive is dependent upon the relation between *teleutê* and its denominative verb *teletaô,* which tends to indicate "bringing something in the accusative to successful completion."[43] While there is some semantic overlap between *teleutê* and *telos,* the phrase *muthoio teleutê* should be put aside, temporarily.

A similar collocation of singular *muthos* and *telos* (rather than *teleutê*) occurs later in the epic with somewhat different meaning. In book 16, Achilles requests that Patroklos assent to his words and follow his plan completely (16.83: *peitheo d' hôs toi egô muthou telos en phresi theiô*). Achilles' slightly awkward phrase, which is, as best as I can describe it, a predicative genitive (or perhaps periphrasis for "a complete plan"),[44] prefaces very specific injunctions: do this, but do not do any of these things. What Achilles means to convey with the phrase *muthou telos* is that he will provide Patroklos with the *whole story,* not that he will provide Patroklos with a plan/boast that should be or has been achieved, but that his speech represents a complete plan, a *teleios muthos.*

The final example is the most problematic. In book 16, when Patroklos tells Meriones to stop taunting since "the *telos* of war is in hands, and the *telos* of words in council" (16.630: *en gar khersi telos polemou, epeôn d' eni boulêi*), it seems that words find their *telos* (in an Aristotelian sense) in council. Such a translation, however attractive, ignores the clearest understanding of *telos polemou* in Homer, which is locative: the first half of Patroklos' sentence may be simply "in hands [comes] war's end" if we preserve the partitive genitive. This, in turn, provided we follow the parallelism developed between the two parts, would render the second half as meaning "the end of words is in council," that is, that *outside* council words have no place. The parallelism is, however, probably more semantic than syntactic. Patroklos clarifies his meaning in the next line, where he declares, "so, it is not at all necessary to multiply *muthon,* but it is necessary to fight" (16.631: *tô ou ti khrê muthon ophellein, alla makhesthai*). Here, then, Patroklos reveals a semantic elision performed through the syntactic parallel: completion resides in the power of hand, whereas *epea*—the instruments of *muthoi*—reach their end point before battle.

Although there are some sticking points in these examples, these Iliadic phrases tell us a little about what might be understood from Nestor's comment in book 9. In the example from book 16 (*peitheo d' hôs toi egô muthou telos en phresi theiô*), Achilles implies that he will give Patroklos a complete plan, or the whole story. In books 19 and 22, the *telos* is something an agent gives to a plan or a threat; at the end of book 9 (625: *ou gar moi dokeei muthoio teleutê*) this same semantic idea is expressed with an objective genitive. This last phrase, Ajax's own *muthoio teleutê,* is semantically and contextually closest to Nestor's. Indeed, as David Elmer has suggested, there is an attractive parallelism in having Nestor declare an absence of a *telos* at the beginning of book 9 and ending the book with Ajax's confirmation of this (2006, 176–82).

Nestor's Phrase and Its Context

So far, I have surveyed the use of *telos* in archaic Greek in general and through close phrasal echoes in the *Iliad.* I have suggested that while the syntax "activated" by the noun can be helpful in determining which meanings are appropriate for a given usage in English translation, overlapping semantic spheres and thematic affinities can obscure this picture. Following the analogy of Polydorus' multiple addresses cited, Nestor's plural *muthoi* may indicate summary criticism of previous speeches or imply that Diomedes has provided multiple *muthoi* in his single performance, as he has in fact done by combining various speech acts in one speech. The resulting interpretation I propose falls somewhere between the final end of Polydorus' addresses and the "complete" end of the periphrastic expressions describing death (and marriage). Nestor's *telos muthôn* refers both to the absence of the terminal sequence that Nestor believes befits a mature speaker and, by implication, to the "perfection" or achievement of maturity in speaking that Nestor displays in subsequent scenes.

It is certainly attractive to imagine that Nestor's *telos muthôn* refers not to the terminal end of a speech, but rather to the completion of a plan embedded in the speech and that this echoes Ajax's declaration that there is no *teleutê* at the end of book 9. But there *is* an essential difference between these examples: Ajax refers to the completion of one specific *muthos;* Nestor refers to *muthoi.* The plurality of Nestor's *muthoi* implies a discussion about *muthoi* in general rather than one specific plan: the "end" of speeches in abstract rather than the concrete end of a single speech. Ajax's phrase looks to the fulfillment of a singular goal, whereas the generality of Nestor's implies a more synoptic commentary.

Clearly, Nestor declares that Diomedes' speech is somehow incomplete, but what he means remains to be seen. The D Scholia suggest that Diomedes' speech is lacking because it includes neither advice nor instructions for the sentries. This is another good starting point, but perhaps a little reductive in its specificity.[45] If we understand Nestor's comment in a concrete fashion, he may be claiming that Diomedes has not reached the "end" of speeches because he has left out an important element (or more). As discussed previously, the harmony of the Achaian acclamation produces a dissonance when compared to the assembly of book 7 in the presence of a realienated Agamemnon. Rather than reprimanding Diomedes for failing to set the sentry, I submit, Nestor's phrase is saturated with meaning—his primary implication is that Diomedes' speech does not solve a political problem.

Such a claim, of course, deserves additional support. Behind Nestor's objection is the understanding that the speech context is politically explosive: as in *Iliad* 1, a younger hero of impressive genealogy publicly challenges the commander in chief. This anxiety is expressed in Nestor's condemnation of civil strife: "Brotherless, lawless, and homeless is that man who longs for horrible civil war" (*aphrêtôr athemistios anestios estin ekeinos / hos polemou eratai epidêmiou okruentos*). Nestor's most strident criticism is not aimed at his addressee alone; rather, his message is for the assembled Achaians.

This message itself helps to explain the tenor of Nestor's complaint to Diomedes. As David Elmer (2006) has argued, the dynamics of public speech approbation throughout the *Iliad* and the *Odyssey* indicates that the public language most prized from the epic's perspective is that which preserves social unity instead of causing civil strife. From this perspective, the singular *muthos* in question in book 9—alluded to by Ajax's *muthoio teleutê*—is the reunification of the Achaian polity through the reconciliation of Agamemnon and Achilles. Diomedes, however, does not articulate this concern within his speech—even at the end of book 9 Diomedes is ready to war without Achilles. After Agamemnon's emotional plea for retreat, Diomedes successfully rallies the troops, but at a cost; he prevents the dissolution of the host but fails to restore its social unity.

Such a reading does some violence to the passage by not fully considering the consequences of Nestor's plural *muthoi.* I would like to supplement earlier readings of Nestor's comment by expanding its scope. The *telos muthôn,* as I have suggested, is polysemous in nature. The plurality of the *muthoi* allows Nestor's criticism to apply both to the particular moment and to the general exigencies of public speech. Within Nestor's phrase, then, is contained both the *goal* of public speech (social cohesion) and an implicit *methodology:* apprehending both aspects allows us to appreciate Nestor's words as a critique of not only the content of Diomedes' speech but also its execution (the rhetoric).

One implication of Nestor's critique, as I have framed it, is that Diomedes has chosen the wrong rhetorical strategy. The narrative calls Diomedes' speech a *muthos* (9.51) but its qualities have more in common with the language of invective—Martin's boast or threat—

than deliberation. Indeed, Diomedes' speech appropriates the diction of invective from Agamemnon's earlier rebukes and uses repetitious insults to question his valor (35: *aptolemon kai analkida;* 39: *alkên d' ou toi dôken;* 41: *aptolemous t'emenai kai analkidas*).[46] These repetitions build to the rhetorical climax of Diomedes' speech, which is, essentially, a boast that he and Sthenelos could take Troy alone (9.45–49). If Nestor means to criticize both Diomedes' end point and his plural *muthoi* (his declarations, insults, imperatives, and boast), then the ambiguity of the phrase *telos muthôn* is well suited to expressing concern both for what *is* in Diomedes' speech and what is *not.*

Nestor, then, is actually remonstrating with Diomedes in part for the illocutionary aspect of his speech. Diomedes aims to *shame* Agamemnon and create a united opinion against him in order to preserve the expedition against Troy and forestall the chaos ignited by similar sentiments in book 2. Therefore, Nestor criticizes Diomedes' rhetorical strategy *and* his choice of speech genre. This is not to imply, of course, that Diomedes' speech is ineffective. Indeed, the rhetorical ploy of his pledge counterbalances his valor against Agamemnon's cowardice to render the latter ridiculous. The problem is that Diomedes' speech creates a unity defined against Agamemnon, at its most stark, a unity that involves only him and Sthenelos: in short, a bitter splitting of the already embattled Achaian polity.

For Nestor the *telos muthôn* implies a recognition of traditional "rules" of critical speech, including identity of speaker, propriety of speech type, and accord with speech context, as well as an emphasis on the outcome of the speech, that a "full" *muthos* in the context of the assembly offers a plan in such a way that the speaker achieves his intended effect and contributes to social cohesion.

Nestor's subsequent words offer supporting details for these rules.[47] First, Nestor takes great pains to remind Diomedes of his youth. While declaring the unassailability of his own words, Nestor implies that Diomedes is "out of line" because of his age.[48] Second, Nestor's strong condemnation of civil strife evokes the destabilizing threat of Diomedes' dissent. The social context (in front of the whole assembly) of Diomedes' criticism represents a threat to the social order (but, surely, no less a threat than Agamemnon's cowardice represents to the safety of the army). Finally, Nestor's own words are instructive for what Diomedes should have done. In his speech he dissolves the assembly and calls for Agamemnon to hold a *boulê,* and it is there where *he* is critical of the king and formulates a course of *action*.[49]

Thus, I submit that the phrase *telos muthôn* conveys an array of meanings. On one level, Nestor may imply that Diomedes' "plan" to take Troy alone is untenable. On another, the phrase conveys traditional guidelines or limits on the use of speech. Such criticism of the commander-in-chief in the context of the assembly is dangerous for the Achaians and may be beyond the acceptable norm for the youngest of the "elders" (*gerontes*). Diomedes' challenge has the potential to confuse the assembly and further destabilize Achaian authority. Rather than allow another argument (e.g., Achilles and Agamemnon in book 1) or leaving space for a negative appraisal of the king (e.g., Thersites in book 2) Nestor, as neutrally as possible, ends the assembly and deals with Agamemnon in the more private context of the council.

Nestor and Diomedes

One remaining question is why Nestor is the one to make these comments. I have already noted that Nestor is often pictured as the *Iliad*'s public speaker par excellence. Indeed, my interest in the *telos muthôn* began with the realization that although Nestor appears to be positioned by the epic as an authoritative speaker, there is a jarring dissonance when he "fails" his first task (to mediate between Agamemnon and Achilles). I believe that this failure is not due to the insufficiency of his language, but the insufficiency of his political model for the strange world the *Iliad* depicts. Nestor's deployment points to a break with the epic past that he is supposed to represent. His failure emphasizes the distance between the past of myth and the political present of the *Iliad*'s combatants. During the civil strife it is Nestor who tries to resolve Achaian problems by plying the trade of public speech for which even the narrative grants him notice.[50] As the epic progresses, however, and after Achilles returns, Nestor and his words fade away.[51]

Nestor's prominence in the epic and his subsequent departure are both mirrored by the young Diomedes. This leads to a second question raised by my examination: why is Diomedes the focus of his efforts? One of the subplots of the *Iliad*'s ruminations on speech is how exactly a man might come to exhibit excellence in his execution of *muthoi*. Diomedes is the one character who most clearly develops as a speaker during the epic, and a strong reason for this may be his function as a "replacement Achilles" in the epic.[52] Prior to book 9, Diomedes rarely speaks in public political contexts; after Nestor's criticism his public speeches take on a different nature. The following is an outline that summarizes his story of speech:

1. Diomedes (implicitly) witnesses the actions and speeches of *Iliad* 1–3.
2. Diomedes shows he knows the appropriate parameters for political and martial speech (*Il.* 4).
3. Diomedes practices public speech and is acclaimed by all the Achaians in his refusal of Paris' offer to return the gifts but not Helen (7.400–02). Acclamation (7.403–04).
4. Diomedes practices public speech in criticizing Agamemnon and is acclaimed by all (9.50–51) but is criticized by Nestor for not reaching the *telos muthôn* (9.53–62).
5. Diomedes practices public speech in reaction to Achilles' rejection of the assembly (9.697–709) and is acclaimed by all the kings. Acclamation (9.710–11).
6. Diomedes volunteers to go on a nocturnal spying mission during the council of kings and is encouraged by Agamemnon to choose any companion he wants regardless of nobility (10.219–39).
7. Diomedes executes public critical speech and offers a plan (14.110–32). He is obeyed by all the kings and departs from the epic as a speaker. Acclamation (14.133).

Note the increasing political impact of his speeches and the corresponding development in who approves his oratory. Diomedes is deployed in the epic to illustrate the travails of a young man who tries to use speech in accord with traditional expectations; he functions as a parallel for Achilles in the *Iliad*.[53] There is a gap throughout most of the epic in the Achaian council that *should* have Achilles developing and completing *muthoi*. The political exigencies of the epic, however, make this impossible. Instead, speech conventions are subverted at the beginning of the epic and the Achaians' most effective speakers spend a great deal of time trying to reestablish order. In short, although Nestor looks for the fullness of *muthoi* in *Iliad* 9, perhaps his assertion that Diomedes has not achieved this fullness is tautological: *all* speech may be incomplete until Achilles returns.

* * *

In this paper I have argued from a lexical and thematic perspective that Nestor's declaration that Diomedes has not reached the *telos muthôn* conveys several messages concerning the propriety of Diomedes' speech and the goal(s) of public speech in general. Nestor's comments, furthermore, furnish significant information regarding the limits on and expectations for public speech from the perspective of the *Iliad*'s characters, that is, a perspective that prizes the internal dynamics of the epic's world over later developments. Appreciating Nestor's own understanding of the appropriate use of speech makes us as readers better able to apprehend alterations in rhetorical register throughout the epic and to understand that, while Nestor does indeed present conventional regulations for speech, these rules must be adapted during the course of the plot in response to changing political circumstances. The use of public language *evolves* during the epic, and understanding Nestor's stances—especially as they change—prepares us to appreciate more clearly what the *Iliad* has to say about speech.

Notes

A form of this paper was originally presented at the APA Annual Meeting in San Diego, 2007. Special thanks is due to that audience as well as to E. T. E. Barker for keen criticism and encouragement. Some of this work was developed during dissertation research under the guidance of David Sider, Leonard Muellner, and Michele Lowrie funded by New York University's MacCracken and Lane Cooper Fellowships.

1. For characterization through speech in Homer see Griffin (1986). For investigations into Achilles' language specifically, see Friedrich and Redfield (1978), Scully (1984), Martin (1989), and Mackie (1996).

2. The most thorough attempt to date to map out the structure of Homeric speeches is Lohmann (1970). For speeches analyzed as "type scenes," see Edwards (1992) and, more recently, Beck (2005). See also Graver (1995), de Jong (1987), Crotty (1995), and Lardinois (2000).

3. For the application of sociolinguistic theory to Homer see especially Minchin (2007) but also Minchin (1991), Clark (1992), Lloyd (2004), and Brown (2006).

4. Traditionally, there has been reluctance to attribute "rhetoric" to the Homeric epics. Generally, scholars reserve the identification of Rhetoric proper for works following the creation of prescriptive handbooks for the execution of persuasive speech (Schiappa 1999, 6; Kennedy 1980, 18–20). The paradoxical stance of historians of rhetoric is that rhetoric does not exist before the term *rhetorikê* is coined (fourth century B.C.E.). Thomas and Webb suggest that *rhetorikê* denotes a prose art that is dependent on literacy and tied to new understanding of speech, namely, that oratorical skill was no longer attributed to the Muses' inspiration but rather to the practical training of specialists (1994, 9). Definitions drawn from comparative studies in oral cultures can help to mitigate such problems. Recent studies (e.g., Kirby 1992 and Walker 1996) incorporate analogical evidence from social and

political anthropology in order to frame the function of language in the Hesiodic and Homeric poems more accurately.

5. For speech framing, see Beck (2005, 24). Cf. Dickson (1995, 127) and Bakker (1997, 163). For the terminology of "felicity" regarding "speech acts," see Austin (1975). For the application of speech-act theory to Homer, see Martin (1989), Roochnik (1990), and Clark (1997).

6. Nestor as an elder may be especially well suited for such authoritative commentary on language. He has often been characterized as a spokesman for "traditional values" among the Achaians. See Falkner (1995, 1–21), Martin (1989, 23–24), Whitman (1958, 166–67), and Segal (1971, 93). For Nestor as an epic singer, see Dickson (1995); for a recent reappraisal of Nestor's effectiveness as an adviser, see Roisman (2005). For Nestor as the epic's ideal speaker, see Martin (1989, 81), Falkner (1995, 15), and Mackie (1996, 132).

7. Agamemnon's "test," the *diapeira,* occurs in the *Il.* 2.1–440. Agamemnon receives a false dream from Zeus indicating that he will overcome the Trojans if he attacks the following day. Before he does this, he announces to his council of *basileis* that he will test the army; the council does not respond to this plan. The army flees in response to Agamemnon's call for retreat; only speeches by Odysseus and Nestor restore the order. For a careful examination of the complex messages "intended" by Agamemnon, see Thalmann (1988, 7–9). For the argument that Agamemnon's testing of the army is traditional and acceptable, see Knox and Russo (1989). Cf. McGlew (1989). In book 9, Agamemnon repeats much of the same speech in his call for flight (9.18–25 = 2.11–118; 8.26–8 = 2.139–41). For appraisals of Agamemnon's ineffective use of language see Martin (1989, 113–37) and Wilson (2002, 51); contra Griffin (1991).

8. As a reaction to speeches, collective silence can denote fear (as when the Achaians are too frightened to face Hektor in single combat [7.92]) or confusion/anxiety (as in the Achaian response to Odysseus' report on the embassy to Achilles [9.632]). For a discussion on the importance of silence in Homer in general, see Montiglio (1993). For specific discussions of silence in speech-reaction lines, see Foley (1995) and Person (1994). Diomedes may have a particular inability to abide silence: he breaks it at 7.400, 9.32, 9.698, and 10.221.

9. Idaios' reported speech is actually a composite of the "plans" presented by Paris and Priam during the Trojan assembly of book 7. Paris (7.354–64), reacting harshly to a proposal by Antenor (7.348–53), offers to return Helen's possessions but not her; Priam, avoiding comment on his son's offer, orders Idaios to present the Achaians with Paris' proposal alongside his own suggestion for a truce and the burial of the war dead.

10. "Then all the rest of the Achaians shouted out in praise both to respect the priest and to accept the shining ransom; but this was not pleasing to his heart, to Agamemnon, Atreus's son" (*Il.* 1.22–24).

11. All translations are my own.

12. With this I have in mind the phrase *Atreïdê, soi prôta makhêsomai aphradeonti' hê themis estin, anaks, agorêi.* Kirk (1985, 122–23) notes that assertions that an act is *themis* indicate "proper behavior" from a traditional perspective but may also be used by a character to claim that questionable conduct is in fact correct. For trends in interpreting *themis* in Homer see Hammer (2002, 115–21).

13. For contrasting hierarchical relationships as revealed by imperative type, see Minchin (2007, 189–221).

14. Universal acclamation is the strongest form of social approval available in the Homeric world, but it takes different, lexically marked forms. For the various levels of speech acclamation and their significance vis à vis social unity, see Elmer (2006, passim).

15. Gnomic expressions (*gnômai*) in Homer tend to be universalizing proverbial statements positioned by the poem to be "traditional" in origin. Nevertheless, there are some distinctions in the use of *gnômai* by individual speakers. For the operation of *gnômai* in Homer in general, see Lardinois (1997). Nestor's *gnômai:* 1.274, 278–79, 4.320, 8.143–44, 9.63–64, 11.793, 11.801, and 14.63, 23.315, 316–17, 318, 319–21 (Lardinois 2000, 649). I would add *Il.* 4.323. Hainsworth comments on the appropriateness of the proverb to Nestor—"The gnome suits Nestor's age"—and refers to Aristotle *Rhetorica* 1395a "for the appropriateness of proverbs to the elderly" (1993, 67).

16. Nestor plays an important role in both the conflict in book 1 and the chaos of book 2. In book 1, he attempts to mediate between Agamemnon and Achilles (1.254–84); in book 2, he speaks after Odysseus in an attempt to reunite the Achaians behind Agamemnon (2.337–68).

17. In the *Iliad* the verb *bazein* occurs three times and only in commentary on speech: 4.355, Odysseus to Agamemnon (*taut' anemôlia bazeis*), in book 9, and 14.92 (*artia bazein*). In Hesiod's *Works and Days bazein* is used to describe the fault-finding harsh speech of one who is disrespectful to his parents (186 and 788). *LfrgE* notes that this verb, onomatopoetic in origin, appears pejorative in many instances but has an uneven application in Homer. Generally it corresponds to rather dismissive descriptions of speech such as German *prappern* or English *to prate.* Furthermore, the designation of Diomedes' words as "prudent" (*pepnumena*) may also convey special meaning. Heralds receive this epithet four times (3.148, 7.276, 7.278, and 9.689). Before they speak, Antenor, Meriones, and Polydamas are described as "prudent" (3.203, 7.347, 13.254, 13.266, and 18.249). Cf. Dickson (1995, 18). Hainsworth, on the contrary, sees *pepnumenos* as an epithet for "subordinate or youthful characters who know their place" (1993, 67).

18. Commentators have debated whether the phrase *kata moiran* describes a speech's orderly arrangement or its "rightness." See Finkelberg (1987, 137) and Ford (1992, 123). Dickson (1995) suggests that the phrase often indicates what is correct from the perspective of traditional precedent (129–30), whereas Nagy argues that the phrase more aptly signifies "according to destiny" (1979, 40–41). For most of this paper I leave the term untranslated, but I believe that all the commentators are correct in pointing to what is correct from a "traditional" perspective. The difficulty resides in the range of use for this phrase. Keenan (1975) offers a nice parallel for the phrase *kata moiran* (when used in conjunction with speech) from Malagasy oratory. Speech criticism, she suggests, in a traditional system must be grounded in the tradition itself. Criticism of *kabary* (ceremonial speech) among the Malagasy entails alleging that words are not *ara-dalana* or "according to tradition" (96). A parallel for my translation ("according to tradition") from the Greek tradition is in a problematic line from Hesiod's *Works and Days* where the speaker appears to refer to "keeping watch well over the days from Zeus according to tradition" (765: *êmata d' ek Diothen pephulagmenos eu kata moiran*). In this context the phrase appears to denote precedent—that which has happened before—in the context of conventional wisdom as the *poet* presents it. Significant for this interpre-

tation, perhaps, is the use of the phrase *kata moiran* to denote properly performed sacrifices (e.g., *Od.* 3.457 and 8.54).

19. In the *Iliad* lines 1.286, 8.146, 9.59, and 10.169 are each followed by an *alla* that I read as adversative; 15.206 and 24.379 are followed by connectives. Line 23.626 does not appear to be followed by either type of *alla.* In the *Odyssey* the phrase occurs far more frequently, but only a few occurrences seem to be followed by an adversative statement (e.g., 3.331, 4.266, 20.37, and 22.486). In the *Odyssey,* the narrator declares that someone has spoken *kata moiran* twice (7.227 and 13.48). Unsurprisingly, the character praised on each occasion is Odysseus. A significant number of the occurrences of this phrase in the *Odyssey,* moreover, occur during Odysseus's tale to the Phaiakians whn he frequently asserts that sacrifices and other actions were *kata moiran* (9.245, 9.309, 9.342, 10.16, and 12.35).

20. Nestor has his speech declared *kata moiran* twice (2.186 and 8.146) and makes the same judgment on others' thrice (9.59, 10.169, and 23.626).

21. Both *hikeo* and *diiksomai* are forms of the verb of motion *hikneomai.*

22. Schol. BT *Il.* 9.61a *ex.* 1–2 glosses *panta diiksomai* as meaning "I will move through the matter from beginning to end." An interesting feature of this passage, however, is that Nestor does not actually address the matter at all—he waits to talk about Agamemnon's behavior until the council of elders. In another occurrence of this phrase (H. *Dem.* 416) Persephone makes the same announcement as Nestor (*panta diiksomai*) and then proceeds to narrate the full story of her kidnapping. The argument that Nestor's comment on his own language is about speech organization and thoroughness is supported by the only other occurrence of the compound *diikneomai* in the *Iliad.* In book 19, Agamemnon uses the same verb to praise Odysseus' attempt to persuade Achilles that the army needs to eat before going to war (19.186, *en moirêi panta diikeo kai kateleksas*). Agamemnon's comments are in approval of Odysseus' argument and his course of action.

23. On the significance of this passage in Diomedes' "education" as a speaker, see Martin (1989, 24–26).

24. Schol. A *Il.* 9.56 ex. 1–2.

25. The suggestion that Nestor's criticism points to his own subsequent actions is offered by the D Scholia. Schol. D *Il.* 9.56 ex. 3–8: "'*But you have not reached the end of speeches*': 'You will surely not bring a completion to your speech'—for [Nestor] means that the things which were spoken to the king are *in need of something* (*deóntôs*); that [Diomedes] omits matters of advice (*sumboulês*) and affairs concerning security, those very things which he [Nestor] supplements himself."

26. The language of "resonance" has been developed in the work of J. M. Foley (1988, 1991) and, recently, Graziosi and Haubold (2005) building on the oral-formulaic work of Milman Parry (1971) and Albert Lord (1960).

27. While Homeric scholarship spent a good deal of the twentieth century debating "formulae," I follow scholars such as Bakker (1997), who views the Homeric dialect as a poetic language.

28. According to the first entry in the *LSJ, muthos* can be "anything delivered by word of mouth." Chantraine is a little more explicit: "suite de paroles qui ont un sens, propos, discours" (1977, 718).

29. Martin (1989, 15ff.) sets out to clarify the semantic distinction in Homeric usage between *muthos* and *epos.*

30. The historical development of the noun is unclear. From the perspective of

onomastics, Mycenaean evidence may attest to the relative antiquity of the root (Chantraine 1977, 1102–03). As a neuter *s*-stem noun it yields a denominative verb, *teleiô* (*teleô;* "fulfull, accomplish"; cf. Sihler [1995, 521], which in turn yields a deverbative noun *teleutê* ["completion, accomplishment"], which forms an additional deverbative verb *teleutaô* ("complete, accomplish"). See Meissner (2007) for a very thorough examination of *s*-stem nouns in early Greek. Unfortunately, he does not discuss *telos.* Of some interest as well is the adjective *teleios,* which can denote "full-grown" (*Il.* 24.34; Theognis 1354). This adjective also seems to be able to point to the final part of a thing. See Emped. fr. 98.9.

31. Of course, in Homer, the most productive reflex of this verbal root is *epitellô* "to enjoin, command." Examples of semantic contamination in the case of *telos* include *Il.* 10.56 (*es phulakôn hieron telos*), where *telos* seems to refer to a military unit (perhaps taking its meaning from *epitellô*). Cf. Hes. *Op.* 637–38 or *Il.* 20.102, where *telos* appears to refer to the "balance" or even "state" of battle (Chantraine 1977, 1101–03). Unclear as well is the development of the meaning "dispersal of pay" (*Od.* 21.450: *misthoio telos*). *Telos* also refers to a state or outcome on several other occasions in archaic poetry (*Od.* 9.5; Pin. *O.* 13. 57; and Hes. *Op.* 669). These later meanings may have some connection with the understanding of *telos* as a fate or outcome contingent upon Zeus. See, for example, Arch. fr. 268.1–2 and Sol. fr. 13.17. Cf. Pin. *Nem.* 7.57: *tini touto moira telos empedon.*

32. Here I have in mind examples of folk-etymological wordplay such as in Hesiod's *Theogony* where the narrator explains that the Titans (207: *Titênas*) were named thus by Ouranos as an insult because they were always overreaching (209: *titainontas*) as a result of their ignorance and arrogance.

33. In order to generate these syntactical "rules," I have surveyed the archaic Greek poets (from Homer through Pindar), the canonical Athenian Tragedians (and Aristophanes), and the prose of Herodotus using the *Thesaurus Linguae Graecae* under an institutional license.

34. See, for example, *Il.* 18.378 (*hoi d' êtoi tosson men ekhon telos*) or *Od.* 9.5 (*ou gar egô ge ti phêmi telos khariesteron einai*), where *telos* means a "state" or "situation" (or in the former case, some degree of completion), or Hes. *Op.* 474, where *telos* refers to an outcome granted by Zeus. I will avoid comment on the fairly clear adverbial development of the phrase *es telos* in early prose and poetry.

35. Cf. *Il.* 20.369 (also discussed later); Sol. fr. 13.58 (*iêtroi· kai tois ouden epesti telos*) and Pin. *I.* 1.26–27 (*eph' hekastôi / ergmati keito telos*). For *telos* as a fulfillment of a prayer, see *Od.* 17.496 (*ei gar ep' arêisein telos hêmeterêisi êlthen*).

36. For advantage or outcome, see *Il.* 11.439 (*gnô d' Oduseus ho hoi ou ti telos katakairion êlthen*). Cf. Pin. *Nem.* 7.57. Possessing control over an outcome is sometimes expressed with *telos* plus *en* and the dative. See Hes. *Op.* 669 and Pin. *O.* 13.104. Interesting as well is Theog. 164 (*telos d' ergmasin hepetai*), where the dative is dependent on the verb.

37. This genitive use may also take a dative of reference as in *Il.* 3.309 (*hoppoterôi thanatoio telos peprômenon estin*). Cf. *Il.* 5.553 and Pin. *O.* 10.67.

38. Other than death, life events expressed periphrastically with *telos* in Archaic poetry include marriage (*Od.* 20.74: *telos gamoio*) or an expression for full growth (Hes. fr. 30.31: *hêbês poluêratou es telos êlthen*) or the end of a journey (*Od.* 22.323: *nostoio telos;* cf. Pin. *Nem.* 3.25). This construction may also be used temporally as in "the end of summer" (Hes. *Op.* 664: *es telos elthontos thereos*).

39. This problematic example is discussed further later. In Homer, it seems that an objective genitive use with *telos* is rather uncommon. Apart from *Il.* 16.630, the best examples for the objective use appear to occur with *teleutê* (e.g., *Il.* 9.625–26: *ou gar moi dokeei muthoio teleutê / têide g' hodôi kraneesthai*). For other possible objective genitive constructions with *telos* see Pin. *O.* 2.17, *Nem.* 8.45, and 10.29–30, and *I.* 1.6.

40. See, for example, Pin. *P.* 9.44, *Nem.* 8.45; and Sem. fr. 1.1–2.

41. Similar are expressions denoting the completion of full growth (Hes. fr. 30.31; Eur. *Alc.* 4.12–13 and *Med.* 920–1), the end of life (Pin. *Isth.* 3/4.22–23) and the achievement of a particular goal (Pin. *Isth.* 3/4.45). Bacchylides appears to use *telos* to refer to a literal end (5.45).

42. For the terminology of "perlocutionary" (the *actual* effect of a speech act) as opposed to "illocutionary" (the intended effect of the speaker), see Austin (1975).

43. Cf. *Il.* 8.9, 13.375, 14.280, and 15.74. For the verb *teletaô* and the completion of thoughts, plans, and desires, see *Il.* 18.328, *Od.* 2.171, 2.275, 3.56, and 21.200. Overlap in the semantic spheres of *telos* and *teleutê* can be seen especially in equivalent expressions such as in the example of *biotoio teleutê* (*Il.* 7.104) *thanatoio telos.* Note, though, how much clearer the objective usage of the former phrase is in English. Cf. Hes. *Sc.* 357 and Emp. fr. 8.5. Of significance for distinguishing *telos* from *teleutê* may be Hes. *Th.* 637–38 (*oude tis ên eridos khalepês lusis oude* **teleutê** / oudeterois, ison de **telos** tetato ptolemoio). Here *teleutê* most clearly means "completion" or "end" in an objective genitive construction. *Telos*'s meaning, however, is a little more difficult.

44. Cf. the periphrasis for death (*thanatoio telos*) discussed earlier, notes 38 and 43.

45. See note 25.

46. For an extensive analysis of blame expressions in Homer, see Vodoklys (1992). Cf. also Nagy (1979, 211–75) and Martin (1989, 30–35).

47. Martin (1989, 25) also sees Nestor's speech as something of an instructive demonstration of a *muthos.*

48. Nestor's insistence that not even Agamemnon will reproach *him* supports this. Fear of violent or threatening reproach from Agamemnon may be an underlying motif in the *Iliad.* Nestor's words recall Kalkhas' anxiety in book 1 (74–83).

49. The examination of Nestor's speech patterns throughout the *Iliad* reveals an important distinction in the uses of language before the Achaian assembly and the council of kings, the *boulê.* In the council, Homeric speakers speak more briefly, exhibit fewer "poetic" or rhetorical devices (*gnômai,* similes, examples drawn from the past (*paradeigmata*), etc.), and are more formal with addresses and imperative forms than in the more intimate context of the council. Such stylistic alternation, perhaps, is evidence of a consciousness of performance contexts. In large part this difference is configured by the different purposes of each political context. The council, as Barker (2004, 110) notes, is for decision making; the assembly is for the creation of consensus through verbal persuasion. This difference in rhetorical register may be connected to performance contexts in the archaic age (see Christensen 2007, 132–35) or to nascent political bodies in the archaic Greek world. Cf. Sealey (1969, 260) and Elmer (2006, 69–70).

50. Before his first speech in the epic the narrative introduces Nestor by valorizing his ability to speak: he is a "sweet-spoken, clear-voiced orator whose words flow more sweetly than honey from his tongue" (*Il.* 1.247–49), resonating with the be-

ginning of Hesiod's *Theogony,* where the Zeus-blessed king prevails over civil conflicts because he has been blessed by the power of the Muses (Hes. *Th.* 79–93).

51. In fact, after Achilles returns at the beginning of book 16, Nestor does not speak again until he gives advice to his son, Antilokhos, during the funeral games for Patroklos (23.301–50). His final speech in the epic is in reaction to Achilles' apportionment of a prize to him in recognition of his age and wisdom (23.624–52).

52. For Diomedes as a replacement for Achilles, see Lohmann (1970, 221) and Schofield (1999, 29) for a recent bibliography. Andersen (1978) suggests that Diomedes is a Homeric innovation—hence, the poet can manipulate his story as he wishes.

53. Martin (1989, 23–26, 124–30) offers similar arguments regarding Diomedes from a different perspective. He also emphasizes Nestor's activity as his teacher. Whitman views Diomedes' interaction with Nestor as "one of the pleasantest features [of his] character" (1958, 166–67). Querbach (1976), however, argues that Diomedes rivals Nestor in an attempt to be an adviser.

Works Cited

Andersen, Öivind. *Die Diomedesgestalt in der* Ilias. Oslo: Universitetsforlaget, 1978.

Austin, J. L. *How to Do Things with Words.* Cambridge, MA: Harvard University Press, 1975.

Bakker, E. J. *Poetry in Speech: Orality and Homeric Discourse.* Ithaca, NY: Cornell University Press, 1997.

Barker, E. T. E. "Achilles' Last Stand: Institutionalising Dissent in Homer's *Iliad.*" *Proceedings of the Cambridge Philological Society* 50 (2004): 92–120.

Beck, Deborah. *Homeric Conversation.* Washington, D.C.: Center for Hellenic Studies, 2005.

Brown, H. Paul. "Addressing Agamemnon: A Pilot Study of Politeness and Pragmatics in the *Iliad.*" *Transactions of the American Philological Association* 136 (2006): 1–46.

Chaintraine, Pierre. *Dictionnaire Étymologique de la Langue Grecque: Histoire des mots.* Paris: Éditions Klincksieck, 1997.

Christensen, Joel. "The Failure of Speech: Rhetoric and Politics in the Iliad." PhD Diss., New York University, 2007.

Clark, Matthew. "Fighting Words: How Heroes Argue." *Arethusa* 35 (1992): 99–115.

———. "Chryses' Supplication: Speech Act and Mythological Allusion." *Classical Antiquity* 17 (1997): 5–24.

Crotty, Kevin. *The Poetics of Supplication.* Ithaca, NY: Cornell University Press, 1995.

Dickson, Keith. *Nestor: Poetic Memory in Greek Epic.* New York: Garland, 1995.

Edwards, Mark W. "Homer and Oral Tradition: The Type Scene." *Oral Tradition* 7 (1992): 284–330.

Elmer, David. "The Politics of Reception and the Poetics of Consent." PhD diss., Harvard University, 2006.

Falkner, Thomas. M. *The Poetics of Old Age in Greek Epic, Lyric, and Tragedy.* Norman: University of Oklahoma Press, 1995.

Finkelberg, Margalit. "Homer's View of the Epic Narrative: Some Formulaic Evidence." *Classical Philology* 82.2 (1987): 135–38.

Foley, John Miles. *The Theory of Oral Composition: History and Methodology*. Bloomington: Indiana University Press, 1988.

———. *Immanent Art: From Structure to Meaning in Traditional Oral Epic*. Bloomington: Indiana University Press, 1991.

———. "Sixteen Moments of Silence in Homer." *Quaderni I Urbinati di Cultura Classica* 79 (1995): 7–26.

Ford, Andrew. *Homer: The Poetry of the Past*. Ithaca: Cornell University Press, 1992.

Friedrich, Paul, and Redfield, James. "Speech as a Personality Symbol: The Case of Achilles." *Language* 54 (1978): 263–88.

Graver, Margaret. "Dog-Helen and Homeric Insult." *Classical Antiquity* 14 (1995): 41–61.

Graziosi, Barbara, and Haubold, Johannes. *Homer: The Resonance of Epic*. London: Duckworth, 2005.

Griffin, Jasper. "Homeric Words and Speakers." *Journal of Hellenic Studies* 106 (1986): 36–57.

———. "Speech in the *Iliad*." *Classical Review* 41 (1991): 1–5.

Hainsworth, J. B. *The* Iliad: *A Commentary*. Vol. III; *Books 9–12*. Cambridge: Cambridge University Press, 1993.

Hammer, Dean. *The Iliad as Politics: The Performance of Political Thought*. Norman: University of Oklahoma Press, 2002.

de Jong, Irene J. F. "The Voice of Anonymity: *Tis*-Speeches in the *Iliad*." *Eranos* 85 (1987): 5–22.

Keenan, Elinor. "A Sliding Sense of Obligatoriness: The Polystructure of Malagasy Oratory." In *Political Language and Oratory in Traditional Society*, edited by M. Bloch. London: Academic Press, 1975.

Kennedy, George. *Classical Rhetoric and its Christian and Secular Tradition from Ancient to Modern Times*. Chapel Hill: University of North Carolina Press, 1980.

Kirby, John T. "Rhetoric and Poetics in Hesiod." *Ramus* 21 (1992): 34–50.

Kirk, G. S. *The* Iliad: *A Commentary*. Vol.I; *Books 1–4*. Cambridge: Cambridge University Press, 1985.

Knox, Ronald, and Russo, Joseph. "Agamemnon's Test: *Iliad* 2.73–75." *Classical Antiquity* 8 (1989): 351–58.

Lardinois, André P. M. H. "Modern Paroemiology and the Use of *Gnomai* in Homer's *Iliad*." *Classical Philology* 92 (1997): 213–34.

———. "Characterization through Gnomai in Homer's *Iliad*." *Mnemosyne* 53 (2000): 641–61.

Lloyd, Michael. "The Politeness of Achilles: Off-Record Conversation Strategies." *Journal of Hellenic Studies* 124 (2004): 75–89.

Lohmann, Dieter. *Die Komposition der Reden in der* Ilias. Berlin: de Gruyter, 1970.

Lord, Albert. *The Singer of Tales*. 1960. Reprint. Cambridge, MA: Harvard University Press, 2000.

Mackie, Hilary. *Talking Trojan: Speech and Community in the* Iliad. Lanham, MD: Rowman & Littlefield, 1996.

Martin, Richard. *The Language of Heroes: Speech and Performance in the* Iliad. Ithaca, NY: Cornell University Press, 1989.

McGlew, James F. "Agamemnon's Test of the Army in *Iliad* Book 2." *Classical Antiquity* 8 (1989): 283–95.

Meissner, Torsten. *S-Stem Nouns and Adjectives in Greek and Proto-Indo-European.* Oxford: Oxford University Press, 2007.

Minchin, Elizabeth. "Speaker and Listener, Text and Context: Some Notes on the Encounter of Nestor and Patroklos in *Iliad* 11." *The Classical World* 84 (1991): 273–85.

———. *Homeric Voices.* Oxford: Oxford University Press, 2007.

Montiglio, Silvia. "La menace du silence pour le héros de l'*Iliade.*" *Metis* 8 (1993): 161–86.

Nagy, Gregory. *The Best of the Achaeans: Concepts of the Hero in Archaic Greek Poetry.* Baltimore: Johns Hopkins University Press, 1979.

Parry, Milman. *The Making of Homeric Verse,* edited by Adam Parry. Oxford: Oxford University Press, 1971.

Person, Raymond F. "The 'Became Silent to Silence' Formula in Homer." *Greek, Roman, and Byzantine Studies* 36 (1995): 327–39.

Querbach, C. A. "Conflicts between Young and Old in Homer's *Iliad.*" In *The Conflict of Generations in Ancient Greece and Rome,* edited by S. Bertman. Amsterdam: Grüner, 1976.

Roisman, Hanna. "Nestor the Good Counsellor." *Classical Quarterly* 55 (2005): 17–38.

Roochnik, David. 'Homeric Speech Acts: Word and Deed in the Epics." *Classical Journal* 85 (1990): 289–99.

Schiappa, Edward. *The Beginnings of Rhetorical Theory in Classical Greece.* New Haven, CT: Yale University Press, 1999.

Schofield, Malcolm. *Saving the City: Philosopher Kings and Other Classical Paradigms.* London: Routledge, 1999.

Scully, Stephen. "The Language of Achilles: The *Okhth sas* Formulas." *Transactions and Proceedings of the American Philological Society* 114 (1984): 11–27.

Sealey, Richard. "Probouleusis and the Sovereign Assembly." *California Studies in Classical Antiquity* 2 (1969): 247–69.

Segal, Charles. "Nestor and the Honor of Achilles (*Iliad* 1.257–84)." *Studi micenei ed ego anatolici* 13 (1971): 90–105.

Sihler, Andrew L. *New Comparative Grammar of Greek and Latin.* Oxford: Oxford University Press, 1995.

Taplin, Oliver. *Homeric Soundings: The Shaping of the* Iliad. Oxford: Oxford University Press, 1992.

Thalmann, William G. "Thersites: Comedy, Scapegoats and Heroic Ideology in the *Iliad.*" *Transactions and Proceedings of the American Philological Association* 118 (1988): 1–28.

Thomas, Carol G., and Edward Kent Webb. "From Orality to Rhetoric: An Intellectual Transformation." In *Persuasion: Greek Rhetoric in Actions,* edited by I. Worthington. London: Routledge, 1994.

Vodoklys, E. *Blame-Expression in the Epic Tradition.* New York: Garland, 1992.

Walker, Jeffrey. "Before the Beginnings of 'Poetry' and 'Rhetoric': Hesiod on Eloquence." *Rhetorica* 14 (1996): 243–65.

Whitman, C. H. *Homer and the Heroic Tradition.* Cambridge, MA: Harvard University Press, 1958.

Wilson, Donna F. *Ransom, Revenge, and Heroic Identity in the* Iliad. Cambridge: Cambridge University Press, 2002.

Achilles' Heel: The Historicism of the Film *Troy*

Jonathan S. Burgess

Troy's downfall is its historicist conceit that it is portraying a real Trojan war, not a version of the myth of the Trojan War. The film's allusive repudiation of the motif of Achilles' heel in the death scene of the hero is indicative of *Troy*'s uneasy negotiation of history and myth. It excludes the medium of myth by which Achilles will become famous, though glory is often described as his main motivation. My argument discusses the complex mix of plotlines and character motivations in the film and sorts out the various ancient sources to which the film has recourse, notably the tradition of the epic cycle. Reception theory is employed to contrast the variant needs of ancient and modern audiences in an analysis of the film's strategic choices.

MY TITLE METAMORPHICALLY INTIMATES THAT *TROY'S* HISTORICISM IS ITS downfall. More literally, it signifies the crucial importance of the Achilles' heel motif in the film's negotiation of myth and history. *Troy's* allusivc rcjcction of thc motif is cmblematic of the film's overall narrative strategy. The film chooses not to narrate myth, but instead portray a historical war that devolved into the legend of the Trojan War. This approach raises fascinating issues about myth, history, and audience reception. Innovation of ancient tradition is entirely excusable, of course; the Homeric poems themselves attest to the malleability of myth.[1] And the film's realism can be compared to occasional Homeric suppression of supernatural elements. Nonetheless, the film's innovation and historicism remove it far from the mythopoetic world of Homer.[2] As a result *Troy's* claim to be narrating a memorable story is undercut.

AUDIENCES

Consideration of how the tale of the Trojan War would be received in different periods is essential to my analysis.[3] There is no single, monolithic audience for the fall of Troy; the general tendencies of reception change as time goes by, and to a large degree audiences dictate the way that a story is told. Audiences take their own preconceptions and expectations to a narrative; responsibilities and opportunities as well result for the storyteller. Employing reception theory, we can often reconstruct the reaction to a work at particular periods. Jauss' concept of the "horizon of expectation" refers to the system of knowledge that any particular audience generally shares.[4] Even within a single period the audience will be splintered, and different people will react to a performance with different degrees of attentiveness, comprehension, and interest. But we can certainly make major distinctions between the general ancient audience for early Greek epic and the general modern audience of *Troy*.

The original audience of the *Iliad* should be characterized in historic and anthropological terms, not as a preferred or privileged audience. Within the largely oral culture of the archaic age, an audience would have taken to the Homeric poem a working understanding of the Greek mythological system, including the tradition of the Trojan War. Greek myth, though flexible, communicated the basic outlines of narratives in a relatively stable manner. The Homeric epics were situated within this living mythological system and were composed and performed under the assumption that their audience would be mythologically informed. Though the *Iliad* narrates only a small part of the Trojan War directly, it makes frequent use of the whole story of the war and expects the audience to employ its knowledge in an active manner. There is much allusion, recollection, foreshadowing, and reflection—as well as modification and suppression—of events outside its narrative boundaries. In the performance culture of early Greek epic, the common mythological knowledge of both bard and audience is essential.[5]

Such cannot be assumed for the modern audience, which does not possess the living mythological traditions that permeated all aspects of the ancient world. Classicists, having artificially reconstructed for themselves the knowledge of the ancient audience, sometimes lose sight of *Troy's* responsibilities toward its modern audience.[6] But the moviemakers did not spend millions on the film for academics; the general public was naturally regarded as the film's intended audience. *Troy* cannot assume its audience knows more than isolated bits of the story, such as the beauty of Helen, the trick of the wooden horse, or the motif of Achilles' heel. As a result, the film must narrate not just the story of the *Iliad* but also the story of the whole war. On the other hand, its general audience's freedom from preconception allowed much opportunity for innovation. In crowded movie theaters blatant contradictions of tradition (for example, when Menelaus is killed at Troy) will not bother the audience as a whole, even if met by the gasps and groans of a classicist or two.

Between the original and modern audiences for the tales of the Trojan War there were of course many other types of audiences at different times as well. By the classical age long-standing mythological (and theological) traditions were being vigorously reinterpreted, questioned, or rejected, notably by mythographers, pre-Socratics, and early historians. Nonetheless, certain early epics that had been preserved began to serve as exemplars of dying oral traditions, and by the Hellenistic age a canonical body of literature became featured in the educational and academic systems. Audience knowledge of the Trojan War could still be assumed, but now dependent on a textual tradition consisting of a few Homeric and nonHomeric epics. During the Second Sophistic in the time of the Roman Empire there emerged radically innovative versions of Trojan myth. Sometimes labeled "anti-Homeric," these works self-consciously challenged Homer but paradoxically acknowledged the *Iliad*'s cultural preeminence while assuming audience knowledge of the literary tradition of the Trojan War.[7]

Sources

Since *Troy* cannot assume a mythologically informed audience, it needs to provide information to it. Yet it is not bound by tradition, and so it also is free to mix and match its sources for the Trojan War, as well as be innovative in its retelling of it. Several strands of material that went into its composition can be unraveled. Most obviously there is the *Iliad:* as the final images fade, the screen announces that the film had been "inspired by the *Iliad*." As the *Iliad, Troy* evokes the essential situations of tension between Agamemnon and Achilles, a relationship between Achilles and the war bride Briseis, and Hector as the main defender of Troy. Defenders of the film rightly point out that *Troy's* closing acknowledgment that it was "inspired" by the Homeric classic need not be a commitment to absolute fidelity. Much is changed—book 6's meeting between Hector and Andromache is splintered into an indoor and an outdoor scene, for instance, and some Homer-derived scenes are very pale imitations indeed (e.g., Odysseus' request that Achilles not leave, corresponding to the embassy scene in book 9). Though some minor Homeric details in the movie will register with those who know the *Iliad* well, the intended audience of the general public would not recognize these.[8]

The Screenwriter David Benioff has emphasized in interviews that the *Iliad* is not the sole source and that the film is not truly an adaptation of the *Iliad* ("the story of the Trojan War does not belong to Homer"). Besides these sources, Benioff specifies the *Odyssey,* the *Aeneid,* Ovid's *Metamorphoses,* Robert Graves's *The Greek Myths,* and Thomas Bulfinch's *The Age of Fable.*[9] These sources, especially the handbooks, indicate that the screenwriter had recourse to ancient non-Homeric traditions about the Trojan War. Essentially this means the epic cycle, whether its influence on the film was direct or indirect.[10] The epic cycle was a collection of early Greek epic poems, now lost except for a few fragments, that covered the tale of the war from its beginning until its end, continuing beyond to the return home of the Greeks.[11] The *Iliad*'s narrative is much differently centered on just one episode of a few weeks in the tenth year of the war, focusing on just a few days of fighting. Hellenistic scholars considered the cycle an innovatively derivative attempt to provide a context for the Homeric poems, a view that has persisted to modern times. But this puts the cart before the horse. Whatever the aesthetic value of the cycle poems, which can hardly be judged now that they are lost, and whatever their date of composition, which is not securely known, they clearly represent the pre-Homeric tradition of the Trojan War. This can be readily demonstrated by the manifold ways in which the *Iliad,* through allusion and reflection, displays knowledge of material also found in (I do not say belonging to or originating in) the epic cycle.[12] The pre-Homeric nature of the cycle's material is also apparent on the evidence of early Greek iconography, which demonstrates both knowledge of the broad outline of what is also found in the epic cycle and a marked preference for non-Homeric material as opposed to what is directly narrated by the *Iliad.*[13]

Ignorance of this cyclic tradition in a modern audience made it necessary for the film to convey information about the broad scope of the war in a direct way that the *Iliad* finds unnecessary. The film does not try to relate all of the many episodes in the epic cycle but rather concentrates on incidents essential to the plot of the war, such as the elopement of Helen and Paris, the wooden horse, and the sack of the city. Employment of other cyclic episodes occurs, to be sure. The desecration of Apollo's tomb and beheading of his statue by Achilles, I would suggest, have, as their source Achilles' slaughter of Troilus (in the iconography he is sometimes beheaded) at the altar of Apollo. And Briseis' reflection of multiple characters, including Cassandra and Polyxena, extends the intertextual use of cyclic material. Other elements in the film reflect the cyclic tradition in a radically changed manner. For example, the initial landing of Protesilaus ("First-Leaper") has been transferred to Achilles, the death of Ajax is completely different both temporally and circumstantially, and Agamemnon is, against all tradition, killed during the war.[14]

Though reflecting the cycle's scope, the film radically compresses the traditional ten-year length of the war to a matter of days (just six by my count, not including the twelve-day truce before Hector's funeral). The Greeks attack the day they land, Paris and Menelaus duel the next day, Patroclus is killed the fourth day, and Hector the fifth. After a truce, Troy is immediately sacked. This is shocking for a classicist, yet I would suggest that the results are rather Homeric. The film narrates the whole war but stresses the events of the *Iliad.* In ancient myth, the withdrawal of Achilles and the subsequent deaths of Patroclus and Hector constitute a minor episode of the whole war. Yet the film, as the *Iliad,* suggests (with difficulty, as we shall see later) that this episode is central to the story of the Trojan War. Whereas the *Iliad* employed the indirect means of allusion and reflection to indicate earlier and later events of the war, the film tacks these directly onto the *Iliad*'s events with a radical compression of time. Here is a comparative graph of the relative timeframes of *Troy* and the *Iliad:*[15]

Prewar: Battle scene, Mycenae scene, Phthia scene	Pre-Iliadic
Day 1: Landing of Greeks, quarrel of Agamemnon and Achilles	Pre-Iliadic, day 10
Day 2: Duels of Menelaus and Paris, Hector and Ajax	Day 22
Days 3–4: Refusal of Achilles to return, death and funeral of Patroclus	Days 25–26
Day 5: Death of Hector, release of corpse	Days 27, 41
Days 6–17: Truce (building of wooden horse)	Days 43–51
Day 18: Sack of Troy	Post-Iliadic

The wide scope of the narrative informs the modern audience of what it must know, but as well much of the traditional story is excised. The elimination of the gods and the supernatural, in keeping with the film's relentlessly rationalizing ethos, also serves to strip down the story. With no divinities, there can be no judgment of Paris, no scenes of Olympic quarreling, and no divine meddling on the battlefield. The end result is that *Troy* at once tells a more comprehensive story than that of the *Iliad* but employs a far shorter duration of time in which to do so. Some have criticized *Troy* for taking on too much material, but the radical adjustment of chronology results in a quite manageable story, at least quantitatively (some of the innovative material at the beginning and end I find lagging). Whether the mesh of cyclic scope and Homeric material succeeds qualitatively is another question.

Historicism

More significant than the innovative mix of sources for *Troy*'s ultimate meaning is the deliberately historical nature of its narrative. True, the film displays little interest in accuracy about its portrayal of ancient material culture. Fine art historians and archaeologists have been driven to distraction by the polychronistic mixture of material culture. Bronze Age, Iron Age, and classical age elements exist side by side, with a good amount of non-Greek material and lots of imagination thrown in for good measure.[16] This is somewhat comparable to Homeric epic, since the pre-Homeric oral tradition of the Trojan War haphazardly picked up and shed a wide variety of different elements from different periods as it developed through the ages. One reviewer's caustic description of the film as a "chronological train-wreck" (M. Rose 2004) could justly be applied to Homer's work. The mythological story of a war in the distant past was often employed anachronistically to address contemporary sociopolitical issues. For the Greeks heroic myth served as a type of vague history of their past culture and lineage, and only a limited number of Bronze Age details were preserved down through the centuries in the oral tradition of the Trojan War. The film actually has more historic resources at its command than the early Greek epic tradition did, since archaeological work of the last century and a half has uncovered the prehistoric Mycenaean civilization, of which historic Greeks were largely ignorant.

So though it must be conceded that the film is historically inaccurate and inconsistent, its basic approach is historicizing. *Troy* is not really interested in narrating another version of the *myth* of the Trojan War. The film actually wants to recreate imaginatively a *historic* Trojan War that it suggests eventually turned into the Greek myth. As Nick Lowe has pointed out, the screenwriter David Benioff is employing the "fairly banal conceit" by which the historical reality that lies behind a legend is revealed.[17] This trope has a long history, going back to the ancient "Euhermerist" approaches to myth.[18] For the Trojan War this approach culminated in the works by the pseudonymic Dictys and Dares, who claimed to be eyewitnesses of the Trojan War. Their flat prose accounts employ rationalized, jumbled data from Homer and the cycle (though unlike comparable "anti-Homeric" works, they do not directly challenge Homer, for they purport to be pre-Homeric documents).[19] Georg Danek compares aspects of *Troy* to Dictys and Dares, pointing out that these works were used by Robert Graves, whose handbook was one of the resources of David Benioff.[20]

Our own positivistic culture prefers to reconceive myth as history, encouraged by the sensational archaeological finds of the nineteenth century that seemed to uncover the reality under myth. In fact we live in an age that, dominated as it is by science and technology, is not very comfortable at all with myth. We prefer to replace the mythological with the historical, to find the kernel of truth that underlies the preposterous myth. Or—to interpret the situation more optimistically—myth still has its allure, but only as a guilty pleasure that must be ostentatiously corrected by discovery of "what really happened." The drive to uncover the truth behind myth is entirely earnest, but perhaps it camouflages a secret submission to the charms of myth.

As Casey Dué has persuasively argued, the producers of *Troy* encouraged the general public's historicist tendencies in their publicizing campaigns.[21] And the segment entitled "From Ruins to Reality" in the special features disc of the *Troy* DVD emphasizes the film's archaeological and historical approach. If the film does not attempt to reflect the Bronze Age in a precise manner (see Fitton 2007), it readily takes on the aura of archaeological historicity in service of the conceit that we are witnessing prelegend reality. Juxtaposition of Minoan walls and classical statues may be historically inaccurate, but the film's basic premise exactly reflects the general thesis of the most recent archaeological excavations at Hisarlik. The

Korfmann expedition posits that political and economic conflicts arose around the important city of Troy and rather favors the supposition that the destruction of level VIIa led to the Trojan War myth.[22] The film's allusions to the Iraq War, which started concurrently with the film's production, serve to confirm the plausibility of its portrayal of Bronze Age imperialism. The film assumes a positivistic desire to enjoy myth as history, even if it is not interested in detailed fidelity to archaeological truth.

What *Troy* actually does is to employ the medium of myth, boldly innovated and rationalized, to envision history. Early Greek historians such as Herodotus and Thucydides also employed myth to envision history. They were rationalistic as well, shoehorning the mythological tradition into more plausible parameters, but with faith in the essential truth of the mythological past. *Troy*'s radical rearrangement of sources and historicist tone are also comparable to the approach of Dictys and Dares, as Danek (2007) insightfully argues. But the film is more optimistic about the historic truth of the Trojan War than Dares and Dictys. Dares and Dictys engage in a type of playful fabrication, both in the dizzyingly historicist conceit of their purported origins (documents from prehistory miraculously preserved, then discovered and translated from ancient script into Greek, thence to Latin) and in the hash of Homer and the cycle. Their audience is meant to enjoy the shock of shamelessly straight-faced innovation, boldly presented as fact.[23] Pretending to present history, these works offer an alternative fiction to the myth that they regard as fiction. *Troy*'s belief in a historic Trojan War is more comparable to the refurbishing attitude of early Greek historians, and the ignorance of its audience precludes the intertextual games of Dictys and Dares.[24] The film is a project of rehabilitation, designed to transform implausible (if secretly fascinating) myth into credible history, or rather explain how this history became myth. Then we can relax and enjoy it.

Plotlines

Many have not enjoyed the film, however. To explain why, first we need to consider further the problematic nature of the film's plot.[25] It is not clear that the various elements that directly or indirectly influenced *Troy* (including the Homeric poems, the epic cycle tradition, and perhaps the "anti-Homeric" tradition) successfully cohere in the narrative. There are many strands in the plot of *Troy,* as well as multiple character motivations. I suggest that there are two main impulses in *Troy*'s narrative drive, which for the purposes of analysis I will label the "imperialism mode" and the "*kleos* mode" (*kleos* being the Greek word for "fame").[26] The imperialism mode would seem to dominate the main plot, though the film periodically returns to its *kleos* mode. Ultimately *Troy* favors the *kleos* mode, but the historicist manner in which it has pursued the imperialist mode undermines this attempt to grasp at higher significance.

The imperialism mode tells the story of a clash of political states, instigated by the ambitions of Agamemnon. The fall of Troy is this plotline's goal, in pursuit of which individuals are relegated to a secondary status. Characters lose their human identity and become reinterpreted in terms of their function for the plot.[27] Helen is not the true cause of the war, merely "useful," according to Agamemnon; the early death of the aggrieved Menelaus fails to abort the war, though Odysseus points out that it should have that effect. Briseis is a problem because she distracts Achilles from the war effort (Agamemnon later observes to Briseis that "your little romance" almost cost him the war), whereas the death of Patroclus is a boon because it refocuses Achilles' energies toward the war ("That boy just saved the war for us," Agamemnon observes with satisfaction as the pyre burns).

The *kleos* mode, on the other hand, centers on Achilles' desire for immortal fame.[28] Odysseus' claim that the coming war will never be forgotten and Thetis' prediction that the war will cause his name to be known for thousands of years convince Achilles to join Agamemnon's expedition. Thereafter Achilles often states his wish that later generations remember his name, and he repeatedly assumes that this is what others want as well (he entices his men with "immortality" as their ship approaches the beach of Troy). From his perspective, the political forces at play, both the aggressive imperialism of the Greeks and the staunch patriotism of the Trojans, are worthless—they are just a means to achieve *kleos.*

In ethical terms *Troy* seems to disapprove of both of its major modes. The film clearly signals that the war's instigator, Agamemnon, is not sympathetic, even as the imperialism mode controls the plot's direction. Achilles is somewhat more sympathetic, yet the *kleos* mode compels him to contribute his ferocious skills to the war, with dire consequences. Truly sympathetic characters like Briseis, Hector, and Andromache suffer. The film portrays the Greek desire to sack

Troy in disapproving terms, yet it also seems to have an ambivalent (and perhaps confused, as we shall see) attitude to the alternative motivation of *kleos*.

Other plotlines arise, but in the end these seem to do nothing more than complicate the film's movement forward. Briseis, who threatens to become the moral center of the film despite her limited screen presence, becomes an obstruction to the *kleos* mode as well as the imperalism mode. Achilles participates in the sack of the city only in order to protect her—war and fame now forgotten. This might be described as the romance plotline, but it is rudely interrupted by the death of Patroclus, which leads to Briseis' being pushed forcefully down onto the beach by her neck. Many, thinking of post-Homeric developments, would suggest that Patroclus is the true love interest.[29] But the film here rather seems to posit clan loyalty as character motivation, one that trumps love.

Reviewers have sometimes mocked the idea that a cousin would inspire such devotion,[30] yet the film does repeatedly emphasize family loyalty. Besides Achilles and Patroclus, there are the brother relationships of Agamemnon/Menelaus and Hector/Paris, another pair of loyal cousins in Hector and Briseis, and in general the family loyalty of the Trojan royal family.[31] There is ideological positioning at play here; *Troy* presents the clan mentality of Achilles and the Trojans as ethically preferable to, and even socially subversive of, the internally repressive and externally aggressive large political state.

Agamemnon's machinations obviously represent post-9/11 American foreign policy, but alternative motifs in American mythology are suggested as well. Achilles is the loner with his own powerful yet confused moral code who ambiguously has the power either to save or to destroy his social community. The Trojan extended family, though royal, reflects the "just-folks" demeanor of the supposedly class-free American audience. If only the Trojans were left alone, the film implies, they would live the good life, one of god-fearing family values and an isolationist foreign policy (Hector's "simple" code of living, he tells his troops, is to "honor the gods, love your woman, and protect your country").[32] Some deflation and nuance are allowed to creep into the film's portrayal of clan ideology, however. Achilles' loyalty to Patroclus is of no use to the communities to which he nominally belongs, the Myrmidons and the Greeks, and it is destructive to the community with which he seems most comfortable, the Trojan one (bonding with Priam as well as with Briseis).

And the trust that the Trojans have in the gods turns out to be willfully naïve.

It is not surprising that a story of epic scale would have multiple motivations and causalities, or that these would clash. But the film seems to have trouble deciding how to balance its various plot strands. The imperialism mode asserts itself as the main plotline, and that leads to the sack of Troy. But the film goes out of its way to portray this conclusion not just negatively, but as senseless. The (mythologically innovative) death of Agamemnon in the course of the sack makes the imperialist plotline meaningless in one blow (just as mythological motivation for the war, Greek outrage at Helen's abduction, suppressed and discredited from the start of the film, suddenly becomes pointless at Menelaus'—also untraditional—early death). The escape of some sympathetic Trojan characters, which weakens the tragic tone yet in no way constitutes a happy ending, fails to convert the aborted imperialist plotline into something more moving.

As for the romance plotline, Briseis provides Achilles with some moments of peace, as he puts it, but her relationship with Achilles essentially fizzles when Patroclus is killed. Achilles' clan mentality then motivates a vengeance plotline that leads to the death of Hector. Then this plotline peters out. Priam requests and Achilles grants the corpse of Hector, which accomplishes nothing in terms of the big picture. Hector suggests to Andromache, while showing her the city's escape route, that his death will lead to the fall of Troy. But he is wrong, even if *Troy* cannot quite bring itself to admit this. It is the walls of Troy that are holding back the Greeks, necessitating the trick of the wooden horse. Achilles is in the horse, but he is only there for the ride, motivated now by a desire to protect Briseis, in an unconvincing resurgence of the romance plotline.[33] The Greeks, trusting the wiliness of Odysseus, not force, now have no need for Achilles. In the cyclic tradition the insignificance of Achilles to the fall of Troy is recognized; he is killed before the sack.[34] In the end neither Achilles nor Hector really has a decisive impact on the dominant plotline, the fall of Troy.

Many have attributed such difficulties to *Troy*'s attempt to narrate the stories of both the *Iliad* and the epic cycle.[35] It is not true that the story of the Trojan War cannot be narrated well, as those beholden to Aristotelian concepts of unity would suggest.[36] Aristotle well praises the *Iliad* for expansively exploring an episode of the Trojan War while indirectly making use of the larger Trojan cycle, but the possible success of more straightforward chronicles of the war need not be denied.[37] That is not to say that *Troy* should be focused only on the tradition of the epic cycle. As we saw earlier, the film's radically foreshortened temporal scheme created space for Homeric as well as cyclic material.

The trick is to harmonize the *Iliad*'s plot with the larger plot of the Trojan War. The *Iliad*'s theme of wrath and vengeance does not lead logically to the story to which the film is committed, the fall of Troy. It is the premise of the *Iliad*'s plot that Zeus, at Thetis's request, aids the Trojans during Achilles' withdrawal. This occurs slowly and haphazardly, and eventually Achilles returns to kill Hector after he has killed Patroclus. The *Iliad* through its magic makes it seem as if Hector's death does signal the end of Troy, but this is foreshadowing, not causal logic. The Homeric poem unfolds as a powerfully expansive episode that cloaks the status of its plot as a bleeding chunk of a larger narrative with illusionary poetics and allusive intertextuality. *Troy* does not have the Homeric resources to disguise narrative disjunctions.[38]

In an attempt to provide unity to all these competing motivations and plot interruptions, *Troy* eventually returns to the *kleos* mode. After the failure of the imperialism mode, the *kleos* mode takes over at the film's end. Odysseus in a voiceover speaks of his desire to be remembered along with Hector and Achilles. This wish obviously comes true; *Troy* in and by itself is evidence that this is so. But the *kleos* mode is not really any less of a failure than the imperialism mode, for film has trouble explaining how the heroic fame of Troy came about. The difficulty stems from the conceit that we are witnessing historical events that were eventually transformed to myth.

Agamemnon taunts Achilles after the initial victory with his argument that "history" will remember the commander and not the soldiers.[39] But why should either think that history will remember them? The Trojan War as a historic event, if there actually was such a thing, would not have been remembered outside myth. After three millennia archaeologists uncovered evidence that allows some to suppose that the Trojan War did actually occur. But the archaeological evidence has not proved that there was a historical war. And the archaeological evidence lacks narrative.[40] The Trojan War belongs to myth.

Achilles' Heel

By pretending to uncover prelegendary history, by relating the tale with Bronze Age imagery and mundane political causality, *Troy* undercuts its *kleos* plotline. Toward the end, though, there is a moment in which this problem seems to be realized. Achilles is shot through the back of his ankle by Paris, then killed by subsequent arrows. Before he dies, Achilles pulls out all but the arrow in his ankle. Other soldiers arrive and gaze with wonder at the corpse with a single arrow in its ankle. The modern audience can be counted upon to recognize this motif: Achilles' heel. And thereby the film has its cake and eats it too. Achilles is portrayed as just a mortal who died by multiple arrows. Subsequently, we are led to believe, a myth arose that he was invulnerable except for a spot by his ankle. By an unforeseen and trivial twist of fate he enters mythological tradition and acquires fame.

This scene had been set up in the early goings of the film when a boy asks Achilles whether it was true that he cannot be killed. Achilles sardonically denies it.[41] The moment serves as a programmatic announcement that the film will not attempt to depict the supernatural, which is fair enough. But the exchange also throws the baby out with the Styx water. One might suppose on the basis of the boy's hearsay that Achilles is becoming legendary—in Greek epic rumor is sometimes designated as *kleos,* apparently in the conception that talk might, in time, morph into glory.[42] But Achilles does not believe that rumors will lead to the immortality of his name; otherwise he would not pursue the military career that he thinks will lead to true glory. Trapped in protolegendary history, Achilles remains ignorant as to how he will become famous. The medium of myth will grant him heroic stature. But *Troy* portrays myth as failure of history, a process whereby a trivial fluke leads to a misunderstanding of what really happened. Achilles has no interest in myth, and therefore he has no credible means to achieve *kleos,* his main motivation.[43]

In its historicist disregard for mythopoetic tradition the film is quite un-Homeric. Homeric poetry, with self-consciousness and self-confidence, continually trumpets the role of epic traditions in creating mythological fame. The Homeric poems would have us know that as they recall the fame of heroes of a past age they themselves contribute to this fame and pass it on. They depict bards in the midst of the heroic milieu, reminding heroes of previous heroic generations and transforming heroic deeds into legend as they happen (Odysseus hears a bard sing of him in the *Odyssey*). But as Mendelsohn rightly complains, the film never depicts a bard.[44] Poetry and myth have been banished from this grimly rational world—a world very unlike our own.

Ironically the motif of Achilles' heel, to which *Troy* alludes to explains how we proceed from history to myth, is not Homeric.[45] In the *Iliad* Achilles is not invulnerable; at one point he is even wounded (*Il.* 21.166–67). Evidence for the familiar story in which Thetis dipped Achilles by his ankle (heel in the medieval transmission of the story) in the Styx to make him (almost completely) invulnerable first occurs in the time of the Roman Empire. In some early Greek stories Thetis tested the mortality of Achilles or tried to make him immortal by dipping him in boiling water or in fire (and feeding him nectar, as Demeter does with Demophoon in the *Homeric Hymn to Demeter*), but these tales, though undoubtedly leading to the Styx story, are fundamentally different from it. It is also true that at an early date the death of Achilles involved a lower leg wound. Apollodorus, who may be following the *Aethiopis* of the epic cycle, states that he was struck in the ankle, and several images on Greek vases seem to depict such a wound. Arguably the motif of Achilles' heel—in other words, incomplete invulnerability—was already in existence by the time the Homeric poems were being composed.[46] There are other explanations for a lower wound that do not involve the late-attested Styx story, however. A poisoned arrow might explain death by an ankle wound, for example, or the hero's life forces being in the ankle.[47]

My own theory has been that the ankle wound is to be linked to the swiftness of Achilles that is repeatedly invoked by the *Iliad.* Once immobilized, the hero could be more easily killed by other arrows. This explanation may seem rather pedestrian if it is not realized that Achilles' inhuman swiftness (in the cyclic tradition he runs down Troilus riding on horseback) is a supernatural advantage (suppressed a little in the *Iliad,* as the fantastic often is). Death would follow the unexpected failure of a magical ability, which is the essence of the later Achilles' heel motif. The correspondences between early and later stories about Achillles' infancy and death would not be coincidental. The innovation of (near-) invulnerability, according to my proposal, would have been motivated by an innovation in the story of Achilles' death, in existence by the Hellenistic age, in which he is ambushed in the temple of Apollo, where he has gone intending to marry Polyxena.[48] The preexisting ankle motif would have been preserved from earlier tradition, but now an explanation not involving immobilization would be necessary in order to explain the stationary hero's death.

Troy's depiction of Achilles' death has many points of contact with my argument. The scene is clearly based on the version of Achilles' death that is motivated by the hero's love for Polyxena.[49] In that story, Achilles is shot by Paris in a temple of Apollo where he has met Polyxena; in *Troy,* Achilles is shot by Paris in a temple of Apollo where he has found Briseis (who is reminiscent of Polyxena, among many female characters in the Trojan War myth).[50] It is my thesis that the motif of Achilles' heel was invented to explain why a now-stationary Achilles is shot in the ankle; the film scene rejects the Styx-dipping tale but acknowledges it with its demonstrative rationalization of how it came about. *Troy* also rather implausibly indicates that the lower wound prevents Achilles from killing Paris (this is emphasized more in the late script by Benioff, where Briseis' pleas are also required), whereas I have argued that immobilization was the point of earlier versions of Achilles' death. Whether or not the makers of *Troy* were aware of speculation about the nature of Achilles' death in early Greek myth, they realize that it is the celebrated Styx-dipping version that their audience knows. Yet in recognition of our culture's dismissive attitude toward myth, the motif is portrayed as a falsehood that devolved from a trivial happenstance. The death scene of Achilles reveals that the hero's fame depends not on the historical Trojan War that *Troy* depicts but rather on mythological traditions that the film studiously excludes.

After the mythopoetic tradition has been pushed away in this penultimate scene, *Troy*'s final few words belatedly grasp at what is otherwise lacking in the film. Odysseus closes the film by wishing to be remembered as a contemporary of "Hector, breaker of horses" and Achilles. Homeric epithets (e.g., "king of kings") appear occasionally throughout the film, apparently in order to suggest a grandiose if stilted protocol at work among prehistoric royalty. But "Hector, breaker of horses" is significant; the noun-epithet phrase concludes the *Iliad.* Revealingly, Odysseus makes no mention of Agamemnon, the prosaic character responsible for the realistic war that we have just witnessed.

In the special features disc of the DVD Peter O'Toole quotes Bernard Shaw to the effect that no boundary has been satisfactorily established between myth and history. Troy does place a boundary between the two, quite unsatisfactorily, by favoring history over myth. In and of itself, the decidedly forgettable geopolitical struggle that is depicted can only produce mute rubble for archaeologists to uncover thousands of years later. Without the medium of myth, *Troy*'s protolegend cannot quite transform itself into something that will be remembered.

Notes

A version of this paper was presented at the 2005 annual meeting of the Classical Association of Canada in Banff, Alberta. I thank the audience for helpful responses. Nick Lowe and Robin Mitchell-Boyask generously provided me with their presentations on *Troy* at the 2005 annual meeting of the American Philological Association in Boston. Thanks also to Jane Aspinall for discussion and for commenting upon a draft.

1. See Winkler (2007c passim), Morrissey (2004; I thank David Mirhady for this reference). My analysis is primarily of the theatrical release, though when relevant I will take note of variants in the "director's cut" release and in a late but not final script by David Benioff, available online at http://www.dailyscript.com/scripts/troy_by_david_benioff.pdf and discussed at Lowe (2004a). Since the theatrical release is a result of shared responsibilities, I do not single out the screenwriter or director when discussing *Troy*'s characteristics.

2. *Pace* Danek (2007, 70–76), who suggests a continuous line of rationalizing myth from Homer to early Greek historians, the later approach of Euhemerus, and Dictys and Dares. For the essential differences between Dictys/Dares and earlier mythological rationalism, see Merkle (1983: 183–84). For the limited suppression of the supernatural in Homeric verse, see Burgess (2001: 169–70).

3. For comments on the ancient and modern audience of the Trojan War, cf. Winkler (2007b: 44, 47–48), Danek (2007: 76–77, 84), Shahabudin (2007: 108–12).

4. Jauss (1982). Relevant is the concept of the "implied reader," on which see Iser (1978); for surveys of the various kinds of reception theory, see Holub (1984) and Schmitz (2002, 86–97).

5. This understanding is central to my study on Achilles (Burgess 2008). For more skeptical portrayals of the stability of myth and the knowledge of the ancient audience, see Andersen (1998) and Scodel (2002).

6. I have found undergraduate students to be the harshest critics of *Troy;* recent initiates can be the fiercest guardians of antiquity. In a *New York Times* article of October 9, 2005 ("In a Classical World, Nerds Walk with Gods"), a first-year student gives *Troy* a −7 on a scale of 10 to −10 (Orlando Bloom lifts the film up a bit from rock bottom). "It made too many changes to the story," adds another student; "the *Iliad* existed thousands of years and didn't need anyone to tamper with it." Winkler (2007c) presents a spirited defense of *Troy*'s need to innovate.

7. See Merkle (1983, 193–94, 1996, 578–80), Danek (2007, 74–75), Burgess (2001, 45; where I unaccountably use the term *anti-Homerist,* perhaps succumbing to the characteristically Homerist tendency to elide the difference between poet and scholar and to think it is all about us).

8. On the film's allusions to details of the *Iliad,* see Danek (2007, 76–78). On the fragmented audience for cinema inspired by classical themes, see Goldhill (2007, esp. 267).

9. The interviews are discussed at Lowe (2004a), Winkler (2007a, 9; 2007b, 61), Danek (2007, 69, 84), and Shahabudin (2007, 107); some can be found at <http://www.bbc.co.uk/films/webaccess/david_benioff_1.shtml>, <http://www.screenwritersutopia.com/modules.php?name=Content&pa=showpage&pid=2686>.

10. Discussion of the epic cycle's role in *Troy* has been mostly inadequate. Latacz (1997) helpfully if vaguely provides a general reconstruction of the content of the

epic cycle. Cyrino (1997) cites the outdated edition of Allen. Mendelsohn (2004) employs Aristotle's comparison of cyclic and Homeric plot as an organizational principle, naming the cycle poems the *Cypria* and the *Little Iliad,* but not the equally relevant *Iliou Persis,* which Aristotle did not happen to mention.

11. See Burgess (2001); more briefly, Davies (1989) and Burgess (2005). For editions of the fragments and *testimonia,* see Bernabé (1987), West (2003; a Loeb edition with translation).

12. Kullmann (1960) is the most thorough scholarly demonstration of this; for further discussion see Burgess (2001, 2008). As much is concisely indicated at Latacz (2007, 28–30), a summary of Trojan War myth with italics indicated Homeric knowledge of it; see also Scully (2007, 125–28).

13. Cf. Snodgrass (1998); Lowenstam (2007).

14. On Briseis' reflection of multiple characters, cf. Danek (2007, 80–81), Allen (2007, 149, 156–57), and Dué (2007, 251). The elopement of Helen and Paris and the deaths of Protesilaus and Troilus occur in the *Cypria* of the epic cycle. Achilles dies in the cyclic *Aethiopis,* but before the sack of Troy. The cyclic *Little Iliad* told of the suicide of Ajax and the wooden horse; *Iliou Persis* also told of the wooden horse and the sack of Troy, including the murder of Priam at an altar, the dragging of the priestess Cassandra from a statue of Athena (her prophetic abilities were also featured in the *Cypria*), and the slaughter of Polyxena over the grave of Achilles. Menelaus arrives home safely with Helen, and Agamemnon is killed at home by his wife in the cyclic *Nosti.* So much is indicated by a surviving summary of events from antiquity; ancient testimony and a few quotations give further details (for which, consult the editions of the epic cycle noted). The *Odyssey,* as the *Iliad,* alludes to many of these events; the second book of the *Aeneid* presented a memorable account of the sack.

15. I have modified a graph in Lowe (2004) for the days of the *Iliad* I follow Latacz (2007, 31–32). See also Danek (2007, 81–82). The Marvel Comics' "The Iliad" (2008), which is obviously influenced by *Troy,* marvelously sets the scene from the wedding of Helen through the first nine years of the war in three pages, juxtaposing on each page multiple select scenes of different time and place with irregular and subtle borders (thanks to Kevin Lawson for bringing this to my attention).

16. For discussion by the archaeologist consulted by the producers, though she is careful to disavow any official role, see Fitton (2007).

17. Lowe (2004); cf. Shahabudin (2007, 117–18).

18. In the Hellenistic age Euhemerus composed a fantastic tale in which is was claimed that the Olympians had originated as historical, mortal men whose status was gradually elevated in the course of time.

19. See Frazer (1966); Merkle (1983, 1996). The accounts are in Latin, claiming to be translated from Greek; a papyrus fragment of an earlier Greek version of Dictys demonstrates that they in fact originated as Greek compositions, probably in the late first century C.E.

20. Danek (1997, esp. 75–76, 79–84). Lowe (2005) refers to Robert Graves as "Dictys-obsessed." Graves (1955, 2:302) displays a historicizing and economical approach to the Trojan War. The theory of Allen (1924, 130–76) that Dictys and Dares stem from a long-standing prose tradition has been rejected.

21. Dué (2007, esp. 248–49, 252–55).

22. The late Manfred Korfmann, the most recent excavator of Hisarlik (the mound in modern-day Turkey identified as ancient Troy), comments tolerantly on *Troy*'s divergences from the archaeological record (Korfmann 2007). The Korfmann expedition, begun in 1988, has published timely reports on its results; see <http://www.uni-tuebingen.de/troia/eng/index.html> and the periodical *Studia Troica.* For a recent historicist approach to the Trojan War, see Latacz (2004). For more skeptical approaches, cf. Burgess (2006) and Dué (2007). But I do not lack appreciation for the enormous amount of valuable information uncovered by archaeological excavation at Hisarlik.

23. See Merkle (1996, 570–71, 577–80), who admits that some readers, and even perhaps the late Latin translators, may not have been in on the joke. A text does not control its audience, of course; ironically, Dictys and Dares began to dominate the mediaeval romance tradition of the Trojan War when the decline of Greek led to the neglect of Homer—a type of resurgence of the cyclic tradition, distorted and transformed to the romance genre, over the once and future domination of the Homeric epics.

24. Cf. Danek (2007, 83–84).

25. On classical and Homeric plot, cf. Lowe (2000), Rabel (1997), and Wilson (2007).

26. For epic *kleos,* see Nagy (1979, index, s.v. *kleos*).

27. Cf. the discussion of Simone Weil's essay on the dehumanizing role of force in the *Iliad* at Dué (2007).

28. See Shahabudin (2007, 117).

29. Note that the seashell necklace given to Achilles by Thetis is worn by Patroclus but then eventually given to Briseis (an interesting reflection, with a twist, of the first set of armor of Achilles, passed on in the *Iliad* from Peleus to Achilles to Patroclus to Hector). In the late script by Benioff Achilles' choice of revenge over Briseis is more emphasized.

30. Mendelsohn (2004, 47). A running gag in the amusing "Troy in 15 Minutes" by "Cleolinda Jones" (*nome de web,* <http://cleolinda.livejournal.com/99710.html>) is the defensiveness with which Achilles and the film insist that Patroclus is just the hero's cousin. The late script by Benioff has Odysseus say to Patroclus that "every boy in Greece must be jealous" of his training under Achilles; in the film this becomes "kings would kill for the honor."

31. See Shahabudin (2007, 113).

32. Achilles as loner: Ahl (2007, 180). Rabel (2007) provides a helpful analysis of the character of Agamemnon and Achilles in *Troy* by reference to "hard" and "soft" power in realist politics. For Homer and American ideology, cf. Belsky (2007) and Schein (2007). The cold war era film *Helen of Troy,* a major influence on *Troy,* portrays the Greeks as threatening communists and Trojans as Americans, according to the astute analysis of Mitchell-Boyask (2005). Ahl (2007) makes an analogy between *Troy* and the later stages of World War II, noting the German origin of *Troy*'s director, Wolfgang Petersen. For the political implications of another recent Hollywood blockbuster about antiquity, *Gladiator,* see Cyrino (2004) and P. Rose (2004).

33. By taking up the romance plotline once more, *Troy* makes Achilles more central to the story, as Dictys does with its Achilles and Polyxena romance plotline: Merkle (1983, 186–91; 1996, 568–70) and Danek (2007, 80–81). The *Iliad* also pro-

vides a model for Achilles as central to the plot (Shahabudin 2007, 116), though its vengeance plotline pushes Briseis completely out of the picture. The late script by Benioff more explicitly emphasizes that Achilles' motive in joining the wooden horse expedition is to save Briseis. In the late script by Benioff there are no voice-over musings by Odysseus about fame as he lights Achilles' pyre, and the film ends with Briseis looking back to the smoke rising over Achilles' pyre. The theatrical release ends with Odysseus' voiceover, with no final shot of Briseis looking back. The director's cut has the shot of Briseis looking back but closes with Odysseus' voice-over. These variants of *Troy* reflect different conceptions about how the plotlines should be balanced.

34. From the perspective of the epic cycle, where the war is motivated by the plan of Zeus to destroy the Heroic race (see Burgess 2001, 149–50), Achilles is useful for causing many deaths of Trojans, as well as many deaths of Greeks by his withdrawal.

35. In an interview, Benioff states that his original conception was very Iliadic, focusing only on Achilles and Hector (<http://www.screenwritersutopia.com/modules.php?name=Content&pa=showpage&pid=2686>).

36. Mendelsohn (2004). Aristotle contrasted the cycle large-scale scope unfavorably with the *Iliad*'s relative focus (*Poetics* chapter 23). The anticycle formalism of Aristotle was deepened into an anticyclic ideology by Hellenistic scholars, who, subscribing to the notion that Homer was a purely inventive fountainhead of all literature, tried to remove him from even a protocycle traditional context. Until recently many classicists have also sought to prove fidelity to Homeric epic by belittling non-Homeric epic. At the beginning of Mendelsohn's review one finds the old trope that no one ("apart from the most scrupulous philologue," 46; ouch!) minds that the epic cycle poems were lost.

37. The *Iliad* was not designed to make the cycle's tradition obsolete, for the poem's full meaning depends on its audience's ability to appreciate its intertextual dependency, through a multiplicity of allusions and reflections, on the tradition of the Trojan War. The epic cycle *did* become obsolete—but this resulted from the anticycle agenda, not from the poetic program of the *Iliad*. The *Iliad* can be appreciated, it is true, with no consciousness of its cyclic intertextuality, but Homer-centric praise of the poem for that is a celebration of ignorance, not a manifesto of superior aesthetics.

38. Part of the problem is the visual emphasis of mass fighting, as opposed to the *Iliad*'s focus on heroic duels. The film never convincingly demonstrates why individuals like Achilles and Hector really matter. Sometimes it is suggested that their military strategy and morale building are essential—this must be the explanation of the curious scene in which Achilles mutters strategic advice as he watches the Greek army attack Troy.

39. In the initial voiceover Odysseus suggests that posterity will remember "how bravely we fought" (in a nod to the romance plotline, he adds, "how fiercely we loved"). In the late script by Benioff a stage direction in reference to Greeks watching the duel between Achilles and Hector notes that "each of them knows this fight will be remembered forever."

40. Hittite documents, as historicists have emphasized, may provide some clues, but a complete picture does not begin to emerge from them. See Latacz (2004) for a recent overview.

41. For discussion, see Danek (2007, 68–69) and Shahabudin (2007, 116–18).

42. See Finkelberg (1998, 74–88).

43. Though the film alludes to the mythological foreknowledge of Achilles' mother, its historicism exposes Thetis as being just as clueless about *kleos* as her son. She predicts that if he stays home, his name will be remembered for a few generations, but that if he goes to Troy, the world will know it for thousands of years. But as seen through *Troy*'s historicist lense, the Trojan War is more likely to be remembered for just a few generations.

44. Mendelsohn (2004, 47). The late script and the director's cut release depict singers, but not of heroic narrative. More relevant in the script and in the director's cut is Nestor's suggestion to Achilles (before his first duel with the "Thessalonian" champion) that soldiers will sing many "songs" in his honor. It is not clear that a mythopoetic tradition is hinted at when Thetis says to Achilles that stories will be written about him *(told* about him in the late script by Benioff), or when Achilles claims to Hector that there will be future talk about the war, or when Odysseus wonders in the final voiceover whether "they will tell my story." Cf., in the late script by Benioff, the argument between Achilles and Patroclus over what stories will be told about them in Hades.

45. For a review of the ancient evidence for the motif, with discussion and bibliography, see Burgess (1995); an updated version of this appears as part of Burgess (2008). For a concise discussion, see Gantz (1993, 625–28).

46. So Danek (2007, 70), where it is suggested that the ineffective wounding of Diomedes' foot in *Iliad* 12 is a polemic rejection of the motif. This is a striking idea, but I understand the passage to contribute to Diomedes' role as an Achilles doublet through reflection of a lower wound of Achilles that did not involve incomplete invulnerability (cf. Kullmann 1984, 313–15). Danek's argument is in line with the correspondence he sees between the relative realism of Homeric verse and the historicism of Dictys and Dares, which I have disputed earlier.

47. Poison: Bullfinch, *The Age of Fable,* chapter 28 (qtd. at Danek 2007, 69–70), Rose and Robertson (1970, 5), Burgess (1995, 224 n. 29, 232–34.) Life force: Gantz (1993, 627). Parallels to these explanations can be found in some non-Greek myths.

48. Explicit evidence for Achilles' romantic interest first occurs in the Roman Empire, but many suppose it originated in the Hellenistic age (just as I am supposing that the Styx story somewhat predates its first evidence). Grosshardt (2005, 238–39) dates it to the first half of the fourth century BCE. Already in the archaic age Polyxena was somehow involved in the story of the death of Troilus, and she was sacrificed over Achilles' grave; it is arguable, as at Danek (2007, 80), that then Achilles had an erotic interest in her. But there is no early evidence for the ambush in the temple.

49. Probably indirectly from Dictys and Dares (Danek 2007, 69). These works ignore the Achilles' heel motif. The film's rationalistically allusive omission of the motif might be considered a rare instance of correspondence to the intertextual method of Dictys and Dares.

50. Morrissey (2004) describes the film's Briseis as Achilles' fatal weakness (Achilles' heel?).

Works Cited

Ahl, F. "Troy and the Memorials of War." In *Troy: From Homer's* Iliad *to Hollywood Epic,* edited by M. M. Winkler. Malden, MA: Blackwell Press, 2007.

Allen, A. "Briseis in Homer, Ovid, and Troy." In *Troy. From Homer's* Iliad *to Hollywood Epic,* edited by M. M. Winkler. Malden, MA: Blackwell Press, 2007.

Andersen, O. "Allusion and the Audience of Homer." In *Homerica,* Proceedings of the 8th International Symposium on the *Odyssey,* edited by M. Païsi-Apostolopoulou. Ithaca, Greece, 1998.

Belsky, S. A. "The Poet Who Sings through Us: Homer's Influence in Contemporary Western Culture." *College Literature* 34, no. 2 (Spring 2007): 216–28.

Bernabé, A., ed. *Poetae epici Graeci. Testimonia et fragmenta.* Vol. 1. Teubner: Leipzig. 1987.

Burgess, J. S. "Achilles' Heel: The Death of Achilles in Ancient Myth." *ClassAnt* 14, no. 2 (1995): 217–43.

———. *The Tradition of the Trojan War in Homer and the Epic Cycle.* Baltimore: The Johns Hopkins University Press, 2001.

———. "The Epic Cycle and Fragments." In *The Blackwell Companion to Ancient Epic,* edited by J. Foley. Oxford University Press: Oxford, 2005.

———. "Tumuli of Achilles." In *The Homerizon: Conceptual Interrogations in Homeric Studies,* Center for Hellenic Studies. 1996. http://chs.harvard.edu/publications.sec/classics.ssp.

———. *The Death and Afterlife of Achilles.* Baltimore: The Johns Hopkins University Press, 2008.

Cyrino, M. "Gladiator and Contemporary American Society." In *Gladiator: Film and History,* by M. M. Winkler. Malden, MA: Blackwell Press, 2004.

———. "Helen of Troy." In *Troy. From Homer's* Iliad *to Hollywood Epic,* edited by M. M. Winkler. Malden, MA: Blackwell Press, 2007.

Danek, G. "The Story of Troy through the Centuries." In *Troy: From Homer's* Iliad *to Hollywood Epic,* edited by M. M. Winkler. Malden, MA: Blackwell Press, 2007.

Davies, M. *The Greek Epic Cycle.* 2nd ed. Bristol, England: Bristol Classical Paperbacks, 1989.

Dué, C. "Learning Lessons from the Trojan War: Briseis and the Theme of Force." *College Literature* 34, no. 2 (Spring 2007): 229–62.

Finkelberg, M. *The Birth of Literary Fiction in Ancient Greece.* Oxford: Oxford University Press, 1998.

Fitton, J. L. "Troy and the Role of the Historical Advisor." In *Troy: From Homer's* Iliad *to Hollywood Epic,* edited by M. M. Winkler. Malden, MA: Blackwell Press, 2007.

Frazer, R. M. *The Trojan War: The Chronicles of Dictys of Crete and Dares the Phrygian.* Bloomington: Indiana University Press, 1966.

Gantz, T. *Early Greek Myth.* Baltimore: The Johns Hopkins University Press, 1993.

Goldhill, S. "*Naked* and *O Brother, Where Art Thou?* The Politics and Poetics of Epic Cinema." In *Homer in the Twentieth Century,* edited by B. Graziosi and E. Greenwood. Oxford: Oxford University Press, 2007.

Graves, R. *The Greek Myths.* 2 vols. Edinburgh: Penguin Books, 1955.

Grosshardt, P. "Zum inhalt der HEKTOROS LYTRA des Dionysios I. (TGrF 1,76 F 2A)." *RhM* 148 (2005): 225–41.

Holub, Robert. *Reception Theory.* Methuen: London, 1984.

Iser, W. *The Act of Reading.* Baltimore: The Johns Hopkins University Press, 1978.

Jauss, Hans Robert. *Toward an Aesthetic of Reception.* Minneapolis: University of Minnesota Press, 1982.

Korfmann, M. "Was There a Trojan War? Troy between Fiction and Archaeological Evidence." In *Troy: From Homer's* Iliad *to Hollywood Epic,* edited by M. M. Winkler. Malden, MA: Blackwell Press, 2007.

Kullmann, W. *Die Quellen der Ilias.* Wiesbaden: Hermes Einzelschriften 14, 1960.

———. "Oral Poetry Theory and Neoanalysis in Homeric Research." *GRBS* 25 (1984): 307–24.

Latacz, J. *Troy and Homer.* Oxford: Oxford University Press, 2004.

———. "From Homer's Troy to Petersen's Troy." In *Troy: From Homer's* Iliad *to Hollywood Epic,* edited by M. M. Winkler. Malden, MA: Blackwell Press, 2007.

Lowe, Nick. *The Classical Plot and the Invention of Western Narrative.* Cambridge: Cambridge University Press: 2000.

———. "Writing Troy." American Philological Association Annual Conference, Boston: 2005. 2004a.

———. "Beware Geeks Bearing Scripts: Hollywood's Homer and the Battle to Preserve a Tragic Credibility." *Times Literary Supplement,* June 4, 18–19, 2004b.

Lowenstam, S. *As Witnessed by Images.* Baltimore: The Johns Hopkins University Press, 2007.

Mendelsohn, D. "A Little *Iliad.*" *The New York Review of Books,* June 24, 46–49, 2004.

Merkle, S. "Telling the True Story of the Trojan War." In *The Search for the Ancient Novel,* edited by J. Tatum. Baltimore: The Johns Hopkins University Press, 1983.

———. "The Truth and Nothing but the Truth: Dictys and Dares." In *The Novel in the Ancient World,* edited by G. Schmeling. Leiden: Brill Academic, 1996.

Mitchell-Boyask, Robin. "Troy Story." Presented at the American Philological Association Annual Conference, Boston, 2005.

Morrissey, C. S. "'Pomo Homer': A Review of the *Troy* Movie." At *Chronicles of Love and Resentment* 304 (6/26/04), 2004. http://ww.anthropoetics.ucla.edu/views/vw304.htm

Myrsiades, K., ed. "Reading Homer in the 21st Century." Special Issue. *College Literature* 34, no. 2 (Spring 2007).

Nagy, G. *The Best of the Achaeans.* Baltimore: The Johns Hopkins University Press, 1979.

Rabel, R. J. *Plot and Point of View in the* Iliad. Ann Arbor: Universitiy of Michigan Press, 1997.

———. "The Realist Politics of *Troy.*" In *Troy: From Homer's* Iliad *to Hollywood Epic,* edited by M. M. Winkler. Malden, MA: Blackwell Press, 2007.

Rose, H. J., and C. M. Robertson. 1970. "Achilles." In *Oxford Classical Dictionary,* 2nd ed. 1970.

Rose, Mark. "Troy's Fallen." *Archaeology,* May 14, 2004. www.archaeology.org/online/reviews/troy/.

Rose, P. "The Politics of Gladiator." In *Gladiator: Film and History,* by M. M. Winkler. Malden, MA: Blackwell Press, 2004.

Schein, S. "An American Homer for the Twentieth Century." In *Homer in the Twentieth Century,* edited by B. Graziosi and E. Greenwood. Oxford: Oxford University Press, 2007.

Schmitz, T. A. *Modern Literary Theory and Ancient Texts.* Malden, MA: Blackwell Press, 2002.

Scodel, R. *Listening to Homer.* Ann Arbor: University of Michigan Press, 2002.

Snodgrass, A. *Homer and the Artists.* Cambridge: Cambridge University, 1998.

West, M. L. *Greek Epic Fragments.* Loeb Classical Library. Cambridge, MA: Harvard University Press, 2003.

Wilson, J. "Homer and the Will of Zeus." *College Literature* 34, no. 2 (Spring 2007): 150–73.

Winkler, M. M. *Gladiator. Film and History.* Malden, MA: Blackwell Press, 2004.

———. "Editor's Introduction." In *Troy: From Homer's* Iliad *to Hollywood Epic,* edited by M. M. Winkler. Malden, MA: Blackwell Press, 2007a.

———. "The *Iliad* and the Cinema." In *Troy: From Homer's* Iliad *to Hollywood Epic,* edited by M. M. Winkler. Malden, MA: Blackwell Press, 2007b.

———, ed. *Troy: From Homer's* Iliad *to Hollywood Epic.* Malden, MA: Blackwell Press, 2007c.

Redefining Homeric Heroism in Wolfgang Petersen's *Troy*

Charles C. Chiasson

Wolfgang Petersen's film *Troy,* although inspired by Homer's *Iliad,* redefines Homeric heroism in two fundamental ways. First, it adds romantic love to bravery in battle as a constituent element of heroism; second, it diminishes the power of the Homeric gods, who delineate by contrast the nature of the human condition. The public sphere of battle and the private sphere of love prove irreconcilable in the *Iliad* but are inextricably intertwined in *Troy*. The film's climactic scene features a confrontation between Paris, who demonstrates his love for Helen in mortal combat, and Achilles, who saves his beloved Briseis by sacrificing his own life. The finale also contrasts divine impotence and human heroism in an inversion of the Homeric hierarchy whereby mortal heroes aspire to immortal divine power. The gods prove powerless to save Troy from the Greek assault, just as Apollo failed to punish the peerless Achilles for desecrating his statue.

VIEWERS OF WOLFGANG PETERSEN'S *TROY* WHO ARE FAMILIAR WITH THE *Iliad,* its acknowledged "inspiration," realize from the outset that fundamental Homeric values have not survived their translation to the big screen intact. The first utterance in the film, an introductory voiceover by Odysseus, gives fair warning that the director has modified the basic standards of Homeric heroism. Odysseus asserts, "Men are haunted by the vastness of eternity. And so we ask ourselves: will our actions echo across the centuries? Will strangers hear our names long after we're gone and wonder who we were? How bravely we fought? *How fiercely we loved?*" (my emphasis). Although the mention of bravery in battle recalls Sarpedon's famous justification of the heroic code in book 12 of the *Iliad,* the assumption that a hero's love life would help to determine his posthumous reputation signals one way in which the film substantially modifies the notion of Homeric heroism, with remarkable consequences for characterization and plot alike. A second fundamental departure from the *Iliad* that affects the concept of heroism in *Troy* is the absence of the gods—or, to be more precise, the absence of effortlessly powerful gods, whose status underscores by contrast not only the weakness of the human condition but also, paradoxically, its strength. While the prominence of romantic love in Petersen's film modifies the essence of heroism from within, as a new constituent element, the diminution of the Homeric gods modifies a framing device that defines mortality from without, by embodying what the human condition is not.

Homeric Heroism

Our logical starting point is the statement of the Lycian commander Sarpedon mentioned earlier, which explains what Iliadic heroes do and why.[1] Homer makes Sarpedon's extraordinary status and importance for the Trojan cause explicit from the outset, claiming that the Trojans would not have breached the wall of the Greek camp "if cunning Zeus had not set his own son, Sarpedon, upon the Argives, like a lion upon cattle with twisted horns" (*Il.* 12.292–93).[2] Sarpedon thus enters the fray as a paradigmatic hero: close to deity on the one hand as a direct descendant of Zeus, but animalian on the other as possessing the fury of a deadly predator.[3] Before allowing Sarpedon to speak, the poet develops the latter point by means of an extended simile, in which the lion's "excessively manly spirit" (*thymos agênôr,* 12.300) compels him to risk death—just as a hero does—as he enters a farmstead in search of food. After the simile, the "godlike" (12.307) Sarpedon summons the aid of his fellow Lycian, Glaucos, with a speech that explains the need for heroic prowess in battle from two different perspectives, the communal and the personal. From a communal perspective, heroes fight in order to earn the material honors (choice food and drink at banquets, choice land) bestowed upon them by their fellow citizens, who look upon them "like gods" (12.312). Sarpedon's second justification acknowledges that, despite Homer's repeated description of various warriors as "godlike," there remains an unbridgeable gap separating even the greatest of the heroes from the immortals:

> My friend, if only we could flee from this war
> And were destined to be ageless and deathless for all time,

> I would neither fight in the front ranks myself
> Nor would I send you into battle that bestows glory upon men.
> But as things are, since demons of death beset us
> In numbers beyond counting, which no mortal can flee from or avoid,
> Let us enter battle, whether to offer glory to an opponent, or he to us.
> (*Il.* 12.322–28)

Two recurrent formulaic phrases are of special interest for our purposes. First, the description of battle as "bestowing glory upon men" (*kûdianeiran,* 12.325) occurs on seven other occasions in the *Iliad,*[4] suggesting that this is a characteristic, even essential feature of battle for the poet. Moreover, since "ageless and deathless for all time" (12.323) is Homer's formulaic description of the blissful state of the gods, Sarpedon is saying that the glory won in war is in effect a kind of "surrogate immortality," a way of extending human life after the inevitable visitation of death.[5] The human heroes of the *Iliad* thus aspire to the divine prerogative of deathlessness and pursue it by means of warfare, which mitigates mortality in the long run while precipitating it on the battlefield.

Heroism and Romantic Love

Although love has no place in Sarpedon's description of undying glory won through deadly combat, this is not to say that love has no place in the *Iliad.* On the contrary—two of the couples whose romantic relationships are central to Petersen's film (Paris and Helen, Hector and Andromache) are clearly based on their Homeric counterparts, while even the third (Achilles and Briseis), though deviating markedly from the *Iliad,* may yet claim some small basis in the text. I begin by focusing on the Trojan couples, who in the epic are not only prominently featured but also pointedly juxtaposed. We first make the acquaintance of Paris and Helen in book 3 of the *Iliad,* where Homer implicitly invokes the beginning of the war by staging a duel between Paris and Menelaus for high stakes—not only Helen and her wealth but an end to the fighting as well. Paris cuts an altogether unimpressive figure: after challenging the best of the Greeks to mortal combat, he retreats before Menelaus' advance, only to be shamed into fighting by the insults of his brother Hector. The fact that Paris, an archer, must borrow his brother Lycaon's breastplate to fight at close quarters[6] portends victory for Menelaus, but this outcome is forestalled by the physical intervention of the goddess Aphrodite, who whisks Paris away from the battlefield to his bedroom. In the meantime we have met in Helen a far more sympathetic figure, filled with regret for having abandoned her family and homeland, and for the suffering she has caused Troy as Paris's consort. When Aphrodite urges Helen to join Paris in the bedroom, she refuses at first, in anger and shame, fearing the recriminations of the Trojan women, but her fear of the wrathful goddess proves greater still. In the bedroom, Helen's scorn for Paris' shortcomings as a fighter gives way to anxiety for his welfare, and finally to passion, as the presence of Aphrodite manifests itself in the lovemaking of human characters who are dear to her. While Paris and Helen indulge themselves behind closed doors, however, the war that sprang from their reckless passion is destined to break out anew outside the city walls.

Hector's subsequent visit to the city in book 6 gives Homer the opportunity to draw a pointed contrast between the selfish, self-destructive *erôs* (lust) shared by Paris and Helen and the lasting marital *philia* (affection) shared by Hector and Andromache.[7] As we shall see, the latter relationship involves not only a private, mutual commitment to one another, but also a public commitment to the broader civic community of Troy. Homer notes the disparity in civic awareness between the two couples by means of concrete details. So it is that Hector encounters Paris and Helen relaxing in the privacy of their bedroom, but he fails to find Andromache at home; instead she occupies the public space of the city wall, where she anxiously observes the progress of the fighting. Moreover, Andromache has with her their son Astyanax, another sign of the couple's contribution and commitment to the community, in significant contrast with the childless "marriage" of Paris and Helen. Indeed, as Homer points out explicitly (6.402–03), the very name *Astyanax,* literally "lord of the city," incorporates the leadership role that the Trojans anticipate for Hector's infant son. On the present occasion, however, Andromache begs her husband to place his familial responsibilities before his communal responsibilities. In reply Hector emphasizes his duty to his fellow Trojans, as well as the glory (*kleos*) men gain by distinguishing themselves in battle:

> To be sure all that you say is a concern to me, wife, but I would
> Feel terribly ashamed before the men of Troy and the women in their long robes

> If like a coward I were to lurk far from battle.
> Nor does my spirit bid me do so, since I have learned to be valiant
> Always and to fight in the front ranks of the Trojans,
> While striving to win great glory (*kleos*) for my father and myself.
> (*Il.* 6.441–46)

To fight for *kleos* in war is thus a lesson passed down from father to son, and Hector presently prays to the gods that the infant Astyanax may learn this lesson in his turn:

> Zeus and the rest of you gods, grant that this son of mine too
> Be outstanding among the Trojans, as I have been,
> And as valiant in his might, as he rules Troy in power.
> And one day someone will say, "This man is far better than his father,"
> As he returns from war, bearing the bloody spoils
> Of the enemy he has killed, and his mother will rejoice in her heart.
> (*Il.* 6.476–81)

The poignancy of this prayer is intensified by its irony, since (as Homer's audience well knew) the Greeks killed Astyanax during the sack of Troy to prevent him from growing up to avenge the death of his father and the fall of his city.

Such then is the contrast that Homer draws between the relationships of Paris and Helen, on the one hand, of Hector and Andromache, on the other. The film *Troy,* however, mitigates this contrast, so that Paris and Helen become more sympathetic characters, and both male heroes become more appealing to a modern, mass moviegoing audience: Hector is sexier though no less responsible and valiant, and Paris is more responsible and valiant though no less sexy. While Petersen's portrayal of Hector and Andromache remains essentially faithful to its Iliadic model, their relationship becomes more physically demonstrative, more overtly erotic, on screen. Steven Scully (2007, 128) has pointed out that Petersen "domesticates" the scene involving Hector, Andromache, and Astyanax on the city wall by moving it indoors to the bedroom, where husband and wife share a passionate kiss while their irresistibly large-eyed son plays in his crib with a toy lion made of wood. I would add that in the dialogue preceding their kiss Petersen has also thoroughly "domesticated"—which is to say, thoroughly compromised—Hector's commitment to heroic warfare, and his vision of its place in his son's future. For when Andromache begs Hector to abstain from fighting, he responds:

> You know I don't want to fight. I want to see my son grow tall.
> I want to see the girls chasing after him.

Thus Hector on the big screen has become a reluctant warrior, and a homebody to a degree that his Homeric predecessor could scarcely have imagined. He appears to fight only because the people of Troy expect and need his protection, and without any awareness that warding off the Greeks would enhance his own reputation as a warrior. Meanwhile, the transgenerational continuity of Homer's sanguinary heroism has fallen victim to a sentimentality more in keeping with modern sensibilities: Petersen's Hector envisions his grown son being pursued by girls rather than pursuing and slaughtering enemies on the battlefield. And grow up Astyanax will, since the film's screenplay, unlike the *Iliad,* allows him and his mother to depart from the city unscathed, by an escape route Hector has previously disclosed to Andromache. As a result, the cinematic Hector's decision to fight for his community does not have the tragically high Homeric price of his wife's freedom and his son's life.

Despite such changes as I have mentioned, Petersen's Hector, in his concern to reconcile the competing demands of domestic and civic, private and public responsibilities, bears an unmistakable resemblance to his Homeric counterpart. The more dramatic departure from Homeric precedent concerns his brother Paris, who in the *Iliad* is a lover not a fighter, maddeningly irresponsible and oblivious to the deadly havoc he has caused his family and his city by stealing Helen away from Menelaus. As such he is a relatively minor character for Homer, more important for the origins of the war than its progression, and prominent in just the two early scenes discussed (his duel with Menelaus in book 3 and his visit from Hector in book 6). Thereafter, there are only occasional references to his battle exploits in books 7 through 15, and only five mentions of him in the last nine books of the *Iliad.*[8] In Petersen's *Troy,* by contrast, Paris is transformed into a central character who professes a love of surprising depth for Helen—a love that (more surprisingly still) he proves in battle at the risk of his own life, as a warrior hero with no precedent in the *Iliad.*

From his first bedroom scene with Helen in Menelaus' Spartan palace, Paris professes a love for her that is not merely the momentary gratification of *erôs,* but a lifetime of devotion that will, he vows, withstand the opposition of gods and men alike. The film recasts Helen's infidelity in rationalized—indeed, strikingly modern—

dress, as a desperate escape from a loveless marriage to a brutal older man, arranged by her parents (rather than by Aphrodite herself).[9] Thus Paris is Helen's savior no less than her seducer and is established early on as a more sympathetic character than his Homeric predecessor. Moreover, upon arriving in Troy he shows a willingness to accept responsibility for his actions by volunteering—without pressure from Hector, as in the *Iliad*—to face Menelaus in a duel. In that duel Paris humiliates himself before Helen, his family, and all of Troy, before Hector finally intervenes, in another rationalizing deviation from Homeric tradition, to protect his brother by killing Menelaus. Paris' final act in this otherwise shameful affair, however, portends a significant development in his character. For as the outraged Greek troops advance upon the city walls Paris scrambles into no-man's-land to fetch the talismanic sword of Troy, which guarantees a future for the city's people as long as it is possessed by a Trojan. Later, as Helen tends to a wound Paris sustained during the duel with Menelaus, Paris expresses genuine remorse for his behavior, such as never passed his lips in the *Iliad:*

> Paris: You think I'm a coward. I am a coward. I knew he would kill me. You were watching . . . my father, my brother, all of Troy. Shame didn't matter. I gave up my pride, my honor . . . just to live.
> Helen: For love. You challenged a great warrior—that took courage.
> Paris: I betrayed you.
> Helen: Menelaos was a brave man; he lived for fighting. And every day I was with him I wanted to walk into the sea and drown. I don't want a hero, my love—I want a man I can grow old with.

Helen threatens to subvert the values of Homeric heroism entirely in voicing her preference for Paris' love rather than Menelaus' fighting skills. Yet Paris remains perturbed by his own cowardice, and in a subsequent scene, on the night before Achilles returns to battle to avenge the death of Patroclus, we see Helen rise from bed to watch Paris practicing his archery in the courtyard below. Paris finally puts that skill to good use on the night of Troy's fall, when his courageous decision to stay and defend the city is motivated by his love for Helen. As she begs him to flee with her to safety, Paris asks Helen, "How could you love me if I ran now?" When he assures her that they will be together again, in this world or the next, Paris anticipates his own death in the siege, and with it the fulfillment of his pledge to give Helen a lifetime of devotion. His redemption through the love of and for a good woman reaches a conclusion both heroic and ironic when Paris, mistakenly thinking that he is saving his cousin Briseis from enemy capture, slays her secret lover Achilles with a volley of arrows. This is a scene I discuss later for the light it casts on the film's central romantic relationship, that between Achilles and Briseis.

As we have seen, Paris becomes a fighter as well as a lover in Petersen's film; conversely, Achilles becomes a lover as well as a fighter.[10] In fact Achilles' cinematic love for Briseis could be said to have shallow but suggestive roots in the *Iliad.* After Agamemnon appropriates Briseis, Achilles' warprize, in a disastrous breach of heroic etiquette, Achilles complains to the king's embassy that he has been robbed of his bedmate, his *alochos,* whom he loved from his heart even though she was captured by the spear (9.336–43).[11] Briseis herself, in her lament for the dead Patroclus (19.287–300), recalls his promise to make her Achilles' lawfully wedded wife upon their return to Phthia from Troy. This view of Briseis as Achilles' beloved rather than (or as well as) his warprize, though a minority view in the ancient tradition, is also reflected in poems by Bacchylides, Propertius, and Ovid, as well as in the *Ilias Latina,* a Latin abridgment of the *Iliad* dating to the first century AD that was influential throughout the Middle Ages.[12] Petersen's greatest departure from the Homeric tradition, then, lies not in suggesting that Achilles has deep feelings for Briseis, but in making those feelings central to Achilles' character, and to the story of the fall of Troy.

Another great departure that facilitates this shift of emphasis is the transformation of Briseis from Achilles' low-profile, virtually voiceless captive in the *Iliad* to a central cinematic character in her own right. Recast as a member of the Trojan royal family and a virginal priestess of Apollo, Briseis is captured by the Myrmidons and presented to Achilles, in conversation with whom she proves defiant, courageous, articulate, and thoughtful. In a scene of pivotal importance for both characters, after Hector has killed Menelaus and the Trojans have driven the Greeks back to their ships, Achilles and Briseis discuss their lives and their understanding of the relationship between human beings and the gods. Alone together in Achilles' tent, they each criticize the life that the other has chosen to lead—she as a virgin devoted to Apollo, he as a warrior. When their conversation culminates in lovemaking, it is clear that Briseis has forsaken her commitment to the god. Achilles too has a fundamental change of heart, announcing his intention the next morning to lead the

Myrmidons back to Greece, thus forsaking the war that would secure his reputation. Briseis has made Achilles see that he was not simply born to be a warrior, as he claimed; he had chosen to be a warrior and could choose otherwise if he wished. (Earlier in the film Achilles' mother, Thetis, had in fact outlined his options, familiar from the *Iliad,* either to live a long inglorious life in Phthia or to fight at Troy and win lasting renown by dying young.) Nonetheless, even though Briseis has persuaded Achilles to reevaluate his priorities in life, the prospect of domestic bliss with his Trojan princess vanishes when Hector kills Patroclus. As Odysseus says fatefully in the wake of Patroclus' death, "I don't think anyone's sailing home now."

Petersen's integration of love and warrior heroism in the portrayal of Achilles finds its ultimate expression in the film's rousing final scene, a rendition of the fall of Troy that departs from Greek tradition (the sack itself is post-Iliadic) in several particulars, including the very presence of Achilles and the death of Agamemnon. In the film Briseis returns to Troy with Achilles' permission when Priam ransoms the corpse of his son Hector, and as the city burns, Achilles is determined to save Briseis yet again from his fellow Greeks, even at the cost of his own life. Briseis is threatened first by Agamemnon, whom she herself kills, stabbing him in the neck; and then by a pair of nameless soldiers, whom Achilles dispatches in short order. It is at this juncture that the love-driven heroism of Paris ironically intersects with that of Achilles. Mistakenly thinking that Achilles too poses a deadly threat to Briseis, Paris brings him down with a volley of arrows—one in the heel and a series of four in the chest, despite Briseis' frantic plea for her cousin to stop. Thus Achilles is portrayed as a warrior to the last, but in the end he fights for the sake of love rather than fame, which is merely an incidental benefit of his final combat: when the Greeks find Achilles lying dead in the palace courtyard, only the single arrow in his heel remains, and we witness the birth of Achilles' best-known (albeit non-Homeric) legend.[13] The hero's own final thoughts, however, remain focused on the safety of Briseis, who made a lasting impact by giving him, he says gratefully, "peace in a lifetime of war." From Petersen's revisionist perspective, therefore, it is not merely female characters who welcome respite from war, or indeed the domesticated Hector, but even the greatest of the heroes, Achilles, who achieves his crowning triumph while dying on the battlefield in an act of selfless love.

In retrospect, for Homer warrior heroism and romantic love seem to represent inherently conflicting spheres of interest. In the *Iliad,*

Paris's ability as a lover corresponds to his weakness as a warrior: in his case, at least, the two skill sets seem mutually exclusive. His brother Hector is both a loving family man and a committed military defender of the community, but when push comes to shove, he must abandon his wife and son in order to protect his fellow Trojans. His parting words to Andromache, in which he distinguishes between the male realm of war and the female realm of the home (6.490–93), suggest that we understand the conflict between heroism and love as a conflict between public and private interests. Indeed, even the greatest of the heroes, Achilles, expresses his affection for Briseis by refusing to fight.

In Petersen's *Troy,* by contrast, romantic love supplements martial valor as a constituent element of heroic *kleos,* triggering profound changes in characterization, especially for Paris and Achilles. There is reason to believe that Homer himself might have regarded this broadening of the hero's nature or experience as a kind of "humanizing" effect, although this need not imply improvement, since in the archaic mythic tradition the primeval heroes, as "demigods" (*hêmitheoi*), are unquestionably more powerful than the later generation of purely, merely human beings. The Homeric evidence I adduce is the description in *Iliad* 18 of Achilles' shield, fashioned by Hephaestus to contain scenes of peace as well as war, including a wedding celebration and the joyous climactic image of the dance, with young boys and maidens, "beauties courted with costly gifts of oxen."[14] The inclusion of the river Okeanos (believed by the Greeks to surround the world) as the outer rim of the shield encourages us to understand the shield, with Bernard Knox (1990, 62), as "an image of human life as a whole," as opposed to the narrow life of heroic combat led by those fighting before Troy. In other words, the tableau created by Hephaestus represents what Achilles and his fellow heroes left behind in joining Agamemnon's expedition. By this standard Petersen's heroes, defined to no small degree by their experience of love, may be judged more fully human, better balanced emotionally, certainly more appealing to modern sensibilities. Nonetheless, it is Homer's warrior heroes who, having made hard, exclusive, irrevocable choices, linger in the memory with a weight that is both tragic and timeless.

Heroism and the Gods

Another feature of Petersen's film that influences his conception of heroism is his representation of the gods. I begin with some prefatory remarks on the Homeric gods, the most powerful forces in the Homeric universe, one of whose important functions in the *Iliad* is to help define the human condition.[15] The gods perform this function by means of what they do, as anthropomorphic characters directly involved in the action of the poem, and by means of what they say, as a divine audience observing the struggles of the heroes engaged in combat before Troy. A brief survey of the divine presence in the first book of the *Iliad* will demonstrate the nature of the Homeric gods and some of the ways in which they shed light upon both the power and the weakness of the human condition.

The first of the gods to make his presence felt in the *Iliad* is Apollo, who inflicts a deadly plague upon the Greek camp to punish Agamemnon for insulting his priest. The plague precipitates a quarrel between Agamemnon and Achilles in which Athena plays a crucial role: when Achilles is on the verge of killing the king for his threat to take Briseis for himself, the goddess appears to Achilles and persuades him to settle for abusing Agamemnon verbally instead. Nestor's attempt to broker a reconciliation fails, and Agamemnon reaffirms his decision to appropriate Briseis. In response, Achilles withdraws from the fighting and asks his mother, the sea goddess Thetis, to intervene with Olympian Zeus himself, so that the Trojans might prevail on the battlefield in Achilles' absence. The interaction between Achilles and Thetis, here and elsewhere in the *Iliad,* underscores both his extraordinary proximity to deity as the son of a goddess and his tragic remoteness from it as a mortal, indeed a "hypermortal" bound to die young. On Olympus, Thetis' supplication of Zeus precipitates a second quarrel, between Zeus and his wife, Hera, who is hostile to the Trojan cause. This quarrel, however, reaches a peaceful conclusion thanks to the god Hephaestus, who laments his parents' squabbling over mere mortals, advises Hera to acknowledge the superior power of Zeus, and restores good cheer among the Olympians by serving them nectar. In summary, I would emphasize three aspects of the Homeric gods that are especially important for our comparative purposes: (1) the swift, severe punishment of human offenses against deity exemplified by Apollo's plague; (2) the definition of Achilles' mortal status by comparison and contrast with his mother's immortal status; (3) the more generalized definition of mortality suggested by the significant juxtaposition of the human quarrel in the Greek camp (unresolved and bound to result in the loss of many lives) and the divine quarrel on Olympus (short-lived and without lasting consequence).

The apparent omission of the Homeric gods in Petersen's *Troy* has elicited the disapproval of many classicists. For example, Stephen Scully (2007, 120) has singled out the absence of divine machinery as one of the reasons why *Troy* fails to achieve true epic greatness. By contrast, Joachim Latacz (2007, 42) insists that—on the contrary—Petersen has not omitted the gods from his film, since the gods may be found inside the human characters. I wish to stake out a third position in this debate, since the status of the gods in *Troy* is more complex and interesting than the bare binary opposition of "presence" and "absence" would suggest. On the one hand, the Greek gods do exist in the film, to the extent that humans (primarily the Trojans) believe that they exist and act in accordance with this belief—a belief that is physically embodied in the images of the gods that adorn Apollo's temple and Priam's palace. On the other hand, Petersen's gods exist as utterly debased versions of their Homeric counterparts—as paradoxically impotent deities who prove powerless both to punish the humans who are disrespectful to them and to protect the humans who revere them. In other words, these are gods who lack what the ancient Greeks considered the essence of deity, namely, power: effective and indeed transcendent power. While such divine fecklessness would have mystified and indeed scandalized those ancient Greeks who held traditional religious views, it has little impact upon a modern audience, for whom the Olympian pantheon is no longer part of a living belief system. In this new cultural context, the relationship between heroes and gods assumes a different significance, whereby the very fact of belief or disbelief in the gods becomes one index of heroic stature. At the communal level the skeptical Greeks prove more powerful than the pious Trojans, while at the individual level the greatest hero, Achilles, is the hero most openly dismissive of the gods. Petersen's *Troy* could be said to represent the logical conclusion of the modern tendency noted (and lamented) by Mary Lefkowitz to aggrandize the heroes of Greek mythology at the expense of the Greek gods.

The concept of immortality first surfaces early in the film, with regard to the ontological status of Achilles and his mother, Thetis. The young boy dispatched by Agamemnon to summon Achilles for his duel with the Thessalian giant Boagrius addresses him with awe, telling Achilles that people claim he is the son of a goddess and cannot be killed. Achilles himself dismisses the latter notion with the ironic observation that he would not be bothering to carry a shield if he were immortal. When the boy concedes that he for one would not want to fight Boagrius, Achilles replies matter-of-factly, "That's why no one will remember your name." We learn from this response that, for Petersen as well as for Homer,[16] Achilles is not a god but strives to win a reputation that will outlive him—the film's understated equivalent of the "undying renown" (*kleos aphthiton*) that Homeric heroes seek. In the Iliadic passage quoted at the beginning of this paper, the Lycian commander Sarpedon explicitly recognizes this goal as the ultimate achievement for mortals, but one that nonetheless falls short of the literal immortality enjoyed by the gods. The Homeric formulation and concept thus indicate both human achievement and limitation simultaneously, acknowledging the superior power of transcendent deities who no longer exist in the world of Petersen's film.

Achilles does not directly address the question whether he is the son of a goddess, as he is most pointedly (and poignantly) in the *Iliad.* Nor, unfortunately, is the matter much clarified when Thetis herself appears on the seashore to discuss the prospect of Achilles' joining the Greek expedition against Troy. The role of Thetis is played by the British actress Julie Christie, who has aged gracefully since her Hollywood heyday but has aged visibly nonetheless. She looks old enough to be Achilles' (Brad Pitt's) mother, which will seem only appropriate to a modern audience unacquainted with Greek mythology but will call to any contrarian classicist's mind the formulaic Homeric description of the gods as "ageless and deathless for all time." On the other hand, this aged Thetis does have prophetic powers worthy of a Homeric deity. She claims to have known long before Achilles was born that his fellow Greeks would summon him to battle and proceeds to predict what the future holds for him under either scenario, whether he goes to Troy or not. The matter of Thetis' alleged immortality appears to remain curiously unresolved, then, and critics are divided: Steven Scully (2007, 120) considers the scene an "odd cameo" representing Thetis as an aging goddess, while Georg Danek (2007, 68) judges her to be a merely human woman with prophetic powers. Doubtless for the majority of the film's intended audience the distinction is of little importance. In any event, if Thetis is to be thought of as a goddess, the deity that she possesses is an attenuated sort, consistent with the diminished powers of the Olympian gods portrayed elsewhere in the film. Petersen's Thetis thus becomes a far less affecting figure than her Homeric counterpart, whose deity both explains the origin of Achilles' unparalleled power and serves as a constant, pathetic reminder of its limitations.

Among the diminished deities I have just mentioned, the Olympian god with the most prominent role in *Troy* is Apollo, identified early on as the sun god and the patron god of Troy. As such he alone of the Olympians is given a temple of his own, perched on a bluff overlooking the Trojan shore. In front of the temple stand two statues: a larger-than-life-size *kouros* and a gold statue of the god himself, crouching to shoot an arrow, as if to ward off enemies arriving by sea. In fact, however, Apollo proves unable to perform even this basic tutelary function, as the Greeks, led by Achilles, storm the temple. Achilles urges his men to take whatever treasure they can find from the enemy's patron god. When his pious companion Eudorus cautions that it might be unwise to offend all-seeing Apollo, Achilles responds with a breathtaking expression of his disdain for the god, lopping the head off his statue with a single, swift stroke of his sword. Audience members familiar with Homer or with Euripidean tragedy[17] might well react as Eudorus does—with bug-eyed, open-mouthed incredulity—and the moreso since this outrageous act remains unpunished by the god. This is decidedly not the fatally vengeful Apollo we met in the first book of the *Iliad*. Moreover, throughout the *Iliad* one of Apollo's characteristic functions is to chasten heroes who threaten to erase the distinction between god and man, including Achilles himself at the beginning of book 22.[18] When taunted by Apollo with the disparity between divine and human capabilities, Achilles answers that he would punish the god for protecting the Trojans if only he had the power (22.8–20). This discrepancy between mortal weakness and immortal power, which is fundamental to the *Iliad* and to traditional Greek religious belief, is turned on its head by Petersen's Achilles. Thus the hero's decapitation of Apollo's statue assumes a programmatic importance, heralding a thoroughly secular revision of Troy's fall, in which the actions of men prove far more important than the will of the gods.

By no means is the disdain Achilles expresses for Apollo merely a momentary madness induced by the stress of battle. In subsequent scenes with Briseis Achilles calmly reflects upon, generalizes, and justifies his disrespect for deity. Their first scene together follows the sacking of Apollo's temple and the capture of his priestess, whom Achilles' men deliver to his tent for his "amusement." When a defiant Briseis warns that Apollo will yet have his revenge, Achilles wonders what the god is waiting for, declares that Apollo is afraid of him, and claims greater knowledge of the gods than priests possess, because he has seen gods with his own eyes.[19] In the crucial later scene that culminates in Briseis' decision to forsake her devotion to Apollo and surrender her virginity to Achilles, the hero explains his emphatically un-Homeric perception of the relationship between gods and mortals:

> Achilles: I'll tell you a secret—something they don't teach you in your temple. The gods envy us. They envy us because we're mortal, because any moment might be our last. Everything's more beautiful because we're doomed. You will never be lovelier than you are now. We will never be here again.
>
> Briseis: I thought you were a dumb brute. I could have forgiven a dumb brute.

Achilles effectively inverts the metaphysical justification for heroic warfare argued by Sarpedon, quoted at the beginning of this paper. Homeric warriors aspire to the immortality and eternal potency of the gods, but since they themselves are bound to die, they must settle for immortal existence in the memories of men, the result of extraordinary military prowess. The gods of *Troy,* by contrast, are such that they envy humans their transience and mortality.[20]

This startling "secret" prompts comparison with a scene from the Battle of the Gods in book 21 of the *Iliad* that supports precisely the opposite conclusion. The Homeric theomachy follows Achilles' harrowing battle against the river Xanthus and precedes his climactic duel with Hector. Zeus for one is delighted by the sight of his fellow Olympians' pairing off against one another in combat; nonetheless, the episode offers more than mere comic relief.[21] The fact that gods who back the Greeks (Athena, Poseidon, Hera) defeat those who support the Trojan cause (Aphrodite, Apollo, Artemis) anticipates the outcome of the war itself, while the nonmortal nature of divine conflict points up what is at stake for human combatants. Of special interest for our purposes is the abortive contest between Poseidon and Apollo (*Il.* 21.435–69). Poseidon challenges Apollo to fight, criticizing his support for the Trojans, but Apollo declines to do so:

> "Earthshaker, you would say that I am out of my mind
> If I were to join battle with you for the sake of mortals,
> Wretches, who like leaves at one moment enjoy
> The prime of their lives, eating the fruit of the earth,

> But the next moment dwindle and die. No, let us cease fighting
> Immediately, and let the mortals themselves fight to the end."
> (*Il.* 21.462–67)

The fact that human life is ephemeral, like that of leaves on a tree, makes mortals *deiloi,* wretched—creatures to be scorned, perhaps pitied, but by no means envied or admired, and certainly not worth fighting over. Apollo's words demonstrate that from a divine perspective human beings—even the most heroic warriors—are insignificant. And yet Apollo's action or rather inaction, his declining to fight even though he is immortal, implicitly underscores the courage of those human beings who do choose to fight at the risk of their lives.

Thus the Homeric Apollo's decision not to fight for the sake of mortals manifests both superhuman power—he need not fight to achieve immortality—and inferiority to heroes who must strive to overcome the limitations of the human condition. Petersen's Apollo, however, manifests only impotence in failing to punish Achilles for his impiety and to protect his own devotees, the Trojans, from the Greek military assault. The emphasis that Petersen places on the piety of the Trojan community also represents a significant deviation from the *Iliad,* where the Trojans are guilty of condoning Pars' abduction of Helen, which violates the code of guest friendship (*xenia*) dear to Zeus himself. Moreover, the archer Pandarus renews Trojan guilt in this regard when he shoots an unsuspecting Menelaus, thus violating the oaths sworn before Zeus by both sides as a solemn preliminary to the king's duel with Paris. In the film, by contrast, the Trojans' devotion to and dependence upon Apollo find striking visual expression in the statue of the god poised before his seaside temple, seeming to form the first line of defense against enemies approaching by sea. Petersen amplifies this visual effect when the Trojans debate their war strategy, in the wake of the Greek attack, in a room ringed by commanding statues of the gods. An important issue in the debate itself concerns the relationship between divine and human responsibility for protecting the city. After Glaucus has given king Priam a positive assessment of the Trojans' (human) military resources, the high priest confirms the likelihood of success by recounting what he interprets to be a favorable omen from Apollo. Hector proclaims his habitual devotion to the gods but remains skeptical in this particular instance, especially since he witnessed Achilles' desecration of Apollo's statue, which was not punished by the god. "The gods," he cautions, "won't fight this war for us." Hector does not doubt the existence of the gods, but rather their effective power in battle against something that he has seen with his own eyes, Achilles' extraordinary ability to hurl a spear. It is not merely in the impious opinion of Achilles, therefore, that human power trumps divine power.

The fall of the city demonstrates vividly the unfortunate result of the Trojans' belief in ineffectual gods. First, the treacherous wooden horse fabricated by the Greeks enters the city as the result of a misguided attempt to honor deity. A contingent of Trojans led by the high priest mistakenly believe that the horse is a Greek offering to Poseidon and urge that it be placed in his temple in Troy. (This marks a significant variation from the best-known version of this incident, in the second book of Vergil's *Aeneid,* where the Trojan priest Laocoön shrewdly urges that the horse be destroyed.) Then, under cover of darkness, the Greeks emerge from the horse and, in an enthusiastic display of godlessness, topple the majestic statues of the deities that frame the Trojans' council chamber. Now it is well attested in ancient tradition that the Greeks were disrespectful to the gods (though less obviously so) in their sack of Troy, as exemplified by Neoptolemus' killing of Priam at the altar where he sought asylum, and by the rape of Cassandra in Athena's sanctuary by Locrian Ajax. The crucial difference lies in the ancient sequel to such outrageous behavior—namely, the punishment that the Greeks endured for their impiety in the course of their various voyages home.[22] Petersen too might have made a similar point easily enough in the film's climactic scene had he wished to, since the deaths of both Agamemnon at the hands of Briseis and Achilles at the hands of Paris take place in the vicinity of a statue of Apollo (indeed, Briseis kills Agamemnon directly after offering a silent prayer to the god). Had Paris, for example, invoked Apollo's name as he shot arrow after arrow into Achilles, the god's divine potency might have been salvaged at last by means of a collaborative killing with an authentic Homeric pedigree.[23] However, the director's interest lies not in ancient perceptions of the Olympian pantheon, but in modern expectations of his human heroes as shaped to a significant degree by the conventions of Hollywood epic filmmaking. What matters, finally, is Paris' power, not Apollo's impotence.

In conclusion, we see that the Greek gods exist in Petersen's *Troy* as the souls of deceased mortals in the Homeric underworld, as powerless entities upon whom the Trojans rely with disastrous consequences. And if nonetheless some of Petersen's Trojans live to fight another day as proto-Romans, we discern here too the modern secularization of a story that for its ancient audience had a fundamental religious dimension. For Greco-Roman tradition held that the safety of Troy depended upon possession of the Palladium, a small wooden image of Athena believed to have fallen from the sky. In the most common Greek version of the story Odysseus and Diomedes carried it away, thus precipitating the capture of Troy; in the canonical Roman tradition Aeneas rescued it and took it to Lavinium, whence it ultimately reached Rome.[24] Both versions of the story reflect the ancient belief in the power of the divine, since Troy did not and could not fall as long as Athena's image remained on the citadel. In Petersen's film, this manifestation of divine presence, potency, and protection has been replaced by the so-called sword of Troy, a more utilitarian symbol of purely human military prowess, passed down from Priam to Paris and ultimately to Aeneas, who makes an unexpected cameo appearance during the sack of the city. Thus *Troy* secularizes in one fell sword's swoop not merely the demise of its eponymous city but also the foundation story of Rome.

Coda

In this paper I have argued that Wolfgang Petersen's film *Troy,* although inspired by the Homeric *Iliad,* develops a distinctive view of heroism by adding romantic love as a characteristic feature and by recasting the relationship between gods and men for an audience with no investment in the power of the Olympian pantheon. I close by briefly noting how each work's view of heroism informs its climactic scene.

The emotional climax of the *Iliad* is the scene in book 24 in which Achilles agrees to accept ransom from King Priam for the return of Hector's corpse. On this occasion the concept of warrior heroism explicated by Sarpedon serves as a paradigm that Achilles struggles to transcend by recognizing the common ground that he shares with his enemy, Priam, and pitying him. He does so, significantly, by contrasting the lives of suffering they both lead as mortals with the carefree existence of the gods. To this end he tells the story of the two jars of Zeus—one jar of blessings, one of troubles—from which the god dispenses the fate of human beings (24.527–33). A fortune consisting of mixed good and evil is the best that a human being can hope for. While it is possible for a luckless mortal to receive nothing but misfortune, from a single jar of Zeus, the opposite fate lies outside the realm of human possibility, since only the gods live free of suffering. And yet while Priam and Achilles both shoulder the burden of mortality in this scene by grieving for their loved ones, Homer also underscores at the same time their proximity to deity. Priam is described as *theoeidês,* "godlike," eight times in this book, but nowhere else in the *Iliad* and addresses Achilles in his turn with similar phraseology (*theois epieikel[e],* "resembling the gods," 486).[25] After Achilles has prepared Hector's body for burial and shared a meal with Priam that symbolizes the end of their shared grief, they gaze at one another in mutual admiration.

> But when they had put aside their desire for drink and food,
> Priam the son of Dardanus gazed in wonder at Achilles,
> At his size and beauty; for he was like the gods to look upon.
> And Achilles gazed in wonder at Priam the son of Dardanus,
> Looking at his noble visage and listening to his speech.
> (*Il.* 24.628–32)

As the poet indicates explicitly, such wonder is the characteristic human response to divine presence. While this postprandial scene is unparalleled in Homer, it is characteristic of the *Iliad* in suggesting both the strength and the weakness of the human hero by comparison with the blessed existence of the gods.

Although Priam's visit to Achilles for the sake of ransoming Hector finds a place in Petersen's *Troy,* there is no mention of the gods as a standard for measuring heroic achievement. Nor does the ransoming scene, for all its emotion, mark the climax of the film: while the *Iliad* is focused on the wrath of Achilles and merely alludes to the future fall of Troy, the sack of the city is the natural conclusion of Petersen's more diffuse narrative. As we have seen, the film's finale pointedly juxtaposes divine impotence and human heroism as defined at the outset by Odysseus to include both courage in battle and romantic love. Without the collaboration of Apollo attested in ancient Greek tradition, Paris braves death to prove his love for Helen, while his victim, Achilles, sacrifices his own life in order to save the life of his beloved Briseis. Even in Petersen's gentler vision of heroism, mitigated by such solace as love may afford, mortality exhausts human effort in the end—and exalts it all the while.

Notes

Oral versions of parts of this paper were delivered at conferences of the American Philological Association (January 7, 2007) and the Classical Association of the Middle West and South (April 12, 2007); my thanks to constructively critical audiences at those venues. Thanks as well to Kostas Myrsiades for his interest; to Jim Perry for unflappable technical support (as ever); and to my wife, Susan, for (*multa inter alia*) helping me to clarify the main outline of my argument.

1. Helpful recent discussions of this important passage include Hainsworth (1993, 352–54), Rutherford (1996, 40–41), and Clarke (2004, 77–78).

2. All translations of Homer are my own unless otherwise noted; their primary aim is closeness to the original text.

3. See Clarke (2004, 80–81) for the raging warrior as poised between the extremes of divine blessedness and the self-destructive fury of beasts, and characterized by an excessive level of male energy (*agênoriê*).

4. See Kirk (1985, 105), commenting on *Il.* 1.490, where the adjective is for the only time in Homer applied to *agorê*, "assembly."

5. For the formulaic description of deity see Clay (1982); for fame as "surrogate immortality" see Clarke (2004, 78).

6. This distinctive feature of Paris' arming scene is discussed by Edwards (1987, 194).

7. For the distinction between *erôs* and *philia*, see Skinner (2005, 4, 159–60); for *erôs* as a potentially obsessive, destructive force, Skinner (2005, 28, 56–59, 161–62, 171, 183–85).

8. For additional details see Scully (2007, 122, n. 1 and 2).

9. See Cyrino (2007) for a general discussion of Helen as represented in the film, Homer's *Iliad*, and other ancient sources.

10. See King (1987, 171–217) for Achilles as a lover (of Patroclus, Briseis, Deidameia, Penthesilea, and Polyxena, among others) in sources ranging from ancient Greece through medieval Europe. For Achilles as lover of Briseis in particular see also Allen (2007).

11. The literal meaning of *alochos* is "bedmate," but the term usually has the more specific sense "wife" in Homeric and other Greek poetry. Achilles' use of the term in this context is calculated to equate his depth of feeling for Briseis with Menelaus' for Helen, the proximate cause of the Trojan War. See Hainsworth (1993, 106–07) for further discussion.

12. See King (1987, 172–74) for further details and discussion.

13. The scene is so understood by Danek (2007, 69) and Shahabudin (2007, 116–18).

14. Fagles' (1990) admirable translation of *parthenoi alphesiboiai* (*Il* 18.593).

15. Enlightening recent discussions of the Homeric gods include Griffin (1980, 144–204), Edwards (1987, 124–42), Rutherford (1996, 44–49), and Kearns (2004).

16. See especially Griffin (1977; 1980, 165–67) for Homer's restriction of uncanny, supernatural elements (such as the indestructibility of Achilles or his armor) by comparison with the other poems of the so-called epic cycle, which complete the narrative of the Trojan War from beginning (the marriage of Achilles' parents, Peleus and Thetis) to end (the return of the heroes).

17. The most striking Greek literary precedent for the conversation between

Achilles and Eudorus is a scene (lines 88–120) from the prologue of Euripides' tragedy *Hippolytus*. Hippolytus returns from the hunt with high praise and a garland for his beloved goddess Artemis but fails to acknowledge the statue of Aphrodite that stands at the entrance to the royal palace. In response to his servant's oblique suggestion that it would be unwise to ignore Aphrodite, Hippolytus contemptuously bids the goddess good riddance and departs the stage. However, we know from Aphrodite's opening speech that Hippolytus will pay for his contempt with his life, while Petersen's Achilles is unpunished for his more outrageous act.

18. Apollo must remind Diomedes and Patroclus as well of their human limits—Diomedes when he assaults the god himself in battle (*Il.* 5.431–42), Patroclus when he persists in attacking the walls of Troy, even though it is not his fate to capture the city (*Il.* 16.784–92). Both of these incidents share a formulaic structure, in which the hero rushes at his target three times before a fourth attempt that elicits Apollo's intervention. On this final attempt the hero is described as *daimoni îsos,* "equal to a god," just before the god pointedly proves otherwise. See Janko (1992, 400) for further discussion.

19. Achilles' curious claim to have seen gods with his own eyes may support the case for regarding his mother, Thetis, as immortal, although the context in which he has seen a plurality of gods remains unexplained.

20. Achilles' theory of divine envy must not be confused with the post-Homeric belief of some Greeks in divine *phthonos,* often misleadingly translated as "envy of the gods." According to this view, attested most memorably in the *Histories* of Herodotus, the gods do not envy human frailty but on the contrary resent human prosperity and power of such magnitude that it threatens to transcend mortal limits and transgress upon the realm of divine privilege.

21. For insightful remarks on the theomachy see Richardson (1993, 85–86 and 91 for the clash between Apollo and Poseidon as the "central scene" of the episode that "makes a deeply serious point").

22. For details of the Greeks' suffering see the ancient testimonia and fragments of the cyclic epic *Nostoi* ("Returns") in West (2003, 153–63), to be supplemented by Apollodorus's *Library*. VI.1–30.

23. In the last words that he speaks before dying (22.359–60), Hector predicts Achilles' death at the hands of Paris and Apollo, an event narrated in the cyclic poem *Aithiopis* (West 2003, 113).

24. For a concise conspectus of the various ancient traditions concerning the Palladium see Austin (1964, 83–85); for further discussion of the political significance of the Palladium see Erskine (2001, Index s.v. "Palladion").

25. For Priam and Achilles as "godlike" see Macleod (1982, 127). In discussing their gaze of mutual admiration (24.629–32) he emphasizes their equal stature, since Priam is "as much the hero as Achilles is."

Works Cited

Allen, Alena. "Briseis in Homer, Ovid and Troy." In *Troy: From Homer's* Iliad *to Hollywood Epic,* edited by Martin Winkler. Malden, MA: Blackwell, 2007.

Austin, R. G., ed. *Aeneidos Liber Secundus.* Oxford: Clarendon Press, 1964.

Clarke, Michael. "Manhood and Heroism." In *The Cambridge Companion to Homer,* edited by Robert Fowler. Cambridge, MA: Cambridge University Press, 2004.

Clay, Jenny Strauss. "Immortal and Ageless Forever." *Classical Journal* 77 (1982): 112–17.

Cyrino, Monica S. "Helen of *Troy*." In *Troy: From Homer's* Iliad *to Hollywood Epic,* edited by Martin Winkler. Malden, MA: Blackwell, 2007.

Danek, Georg. "The Story of Troy through the Centuries." In *Troy: From Homer's* Iliad *to Hollywood Epic,* edited by Martin Winkler. Malden, MA: Blackwell, 2007.

Edwards, Mark W. *Homer: Poet of the* Iliad. Baltimore and London: The Johns Hopkins University Press, 1987.

Erskine, Andrew. *Troy between Greece and Rome.* Oxford: Oxford University Press, 2001.

Fagles, Robert, trans. Homer, *The Iliad.* New York: Penguin, 1990.

Griffin, Jasper. "The Epic Cycle and the Uniqueness of Homer." *Journal of Hellenic Studies* 97 (1977): 39–53.

———. *Homer on Life and Death.* Oxford: Clarendon Press, 1990.

Hainsworth, Bryan, ed. *The Iliad: A Commentary.* Vol. III. Cambridge: Cambridge University Press, 1993.

Janko, Richard, ed. *The Iliad: A Commentary.* Vol. IV. Cambridge: Cambridge University Press, 1992.

Kearns, Emily. "The Gods in the Homeric Epics." In *The Cambridge Companion to Homer,* edited by Robert Fowler. Cambridge: Cambridge University Press, 2004.

King, Katherine Callen. *Achilles: Paradigms of the War Hero from Homer to the Middle Ages.* Berkeley: University of California Press, 1987.

Kirk, G. S., ed. *The Iliad: A Commentary.* Vol. I. Cambridge: Cambridge University Press, 1985.

Knox, Bernard. "Introduction." In *Homer, The Iliad.* Translated by Robert Fagles. New York: Penguin, 1990.

Latacz, Joachim. "From Homer's Troy to Petersen's *Troy*." In *Troy: From Homer's* Iliad *to Hollywood Epic,* edited by Martin Winkler. Malden, MA: Blackwell, 2007.

Lefkowitz, Mary. *Greek Gods, Human Lives: What We Can Learn from Myths.* New Haven: Yale University Press, 2003.

Macleod, Colin, ed. *Homer: Iliad Book XXIV.* Cambridge: Cambridge University Press, 1982.

Richardson, Nicholas, ed. *The Iliad: A Commentary.* Vol. VI. Cambridge: Cambridge University Press, 1993.

Rutherford, R. B. *Homer.* Oxford: Oxford University Press, 1996.

Scully, Steven. "The Fate of Troy." In *Troy: From Homer's* Iliad *to Hollywood Epic,* edited by Martin Winkler. Malden, MA: Blackwell, 2007.

Shahabudin, Kim. "From Greek Myth to Hollywood Story: Explanatory Narrative in *Troy*." In *Troy: From Homer's* Iliad *to Hollywood Epic,* edited by Martin Winkler. Malden, MA: Blackwell, 2007.

Skinner, Marilyn. *Sexuality in Greek and Roman Culture.* Malden, MA: Blackwell, 2005.

West, Martin L., ed. and trans. *Greek Epic Fragments: From the Seventh to the Fifth Centuries B.C.* Cambridge, MA and London: Harvard University Press, 2003.

The *Odyssey* and Frank Capra's *It's a Wonderful Life*

Bruce Louden

Part of *It's a Wonderful Life*'s ability to move audiences results from its use of motifs common to classical myth, and especially prominent in the *Odyssey*. As does Homer's epic it begins with a divine council that includes, in Clarence, a mentoring immortal who intervenes in and guides the affairs of George Bailey much as Athena does for Odysseus. The film's keynote sequence, what Bedford Falls would be like if Bailey never existed, is an adaptation of two traditional structures also used in the *Odyssey*, the hero's descent to the underworld and *the vision*. The film transforms these and other mythical structures with a Christianizing modality to construct a distinctly American subgenre of myth.

REGARDED BY MANY AS *THE* CLASSIC AMERICAN MOVIE, *IT'S A WONDERFUL Life* is a film of considerable depth and power. Its small-town setting and everyman protagonist, as brought to life by Jimmy Stewart, have connected with audiences for sixty years, though the film was only a modest financial and critical success in its initial release. While celebrated as classic Americana, the film's most moving sequences are composed of elements common to ancient myth, and particularly prominent in the *Odyssey*. I would not argue for any genetic relationship between the two works. It is unlikely, in my view, that the several writers who contributed to the film's script had the *Odyssey* in mind in any conscious way.[1] Nonetheless, the role of Clarence, George Bailey's guardian angel, is quite close to that of Athena, Odysseus's mentor, in the *Odyssey*. Even more intriguing is the film's keynote sequence. George Bailey's vision of what his town would be like if he had never been born is clearly an adaptation of the hero's traditional descent to the underworld, as Odysseus undergoes in *Odyssey* book 11. The *Odyssey* thus provides an unexpected context for the film's pivotal episodes. Analysis of those elements and type scenes the film has in common with the *Odyssey* helps explicate its classic quality, the emotional power of its climactic episodes, and the way it bestows a particularly American modality upon the traditional elements. Conversely, such an analysis increases our understanding of how the same elements function within the *Odyssey* itself.

Sacred Narratives, or Myth

After the opening credits, the first words spoken in the film, while the camera shows snow falling on the streets in Bedford Falls, are eight rapid one-line prayers on behalf of George Bailey, the protagonist. The camera then ascends to the heavens, settling on a group of stars and galaxies. Angels, figured as the twinkling celestial forms, speak the next words. The opening immediately establishes the religious or sacred dimension of the film, which will only increase in the later interventions by the angel Clarence. The date on which the plot opens, and on which the film's key scenes take place, is Christmas Eve, which gains in importance as the film unfolds.

The *Odyssey*'s first line addresses the Muse, a goddess who is to be understood as the real source of the epic, "Muse tell me of the man of many ways." The *Odyssey* emphasizes to its audience that it is *the word of God,* or, in a more common sense, a myth. I have elsewhere defined myth as follows: "A sacred, traditional, narrative, that depicts the interrelations of mortals and gods, is especially concerned with defining what is moral behavior for a given culture, and passes on key information about that culture's institutions" (Louden 2006, 9). *It's a Wonderful Life* meets all of these criteria except that it is not traditional, in the sense of having evolved anonymously from an oral tradition, its plot set in the distant past. The film has its genesis in a short story, "The Greatest Gift," by Philip Van Doren Stern, which four different writers, including Capra himself, later developed, with alterations or additions.

Though it is not traditional, I classify Capra's film as myth because of the several divine characters, one of whom, the angel Clarence, has a major recurring role, and because of the importance of Christian myth throughout the film. I suggest *It's a Wonderful Life* should be seen as a specifically American subtype of myth, set in an almost contemporary era, depicting the circumstances of a middle-class businessman in a heroic light, thematically recasting a central Christian dynamic, the hero as savior overcoming death. Both the *Odyssey* and *It's a Wonderful Life* may also be regarded as romances,[2] which I would characterize as follows:

> The protagonist, a moral man, through his own mistake becomes separated from his family for many years, usually a generation. He is trapped in a foreign land, a marvelous, exotic place, for all or much of this period. His imprisonment suggests thematic parallels with being in the underworld. Because of his piety the gods help reunite him with his family, who presume he is dead. His return from such a long absence and reunion with family resembles a triumph over death. Romances climax in a recognition scene, in which the protagonist, in highly emotional circumstances, is reunited with a beloved family member.

Though *It's a Wonderful Life* lacks the standard element of the passage of twenty years (e.g., the myth of Joseph: Genesis 42:24, 43:30, etc.; sixteen years in *The Winter's Tale*), instead suggesting it within the *Descent to the Underworld* (discussed later).

Both protagonists are characterized as wanderers, typical of a romance protagonist. In Odysseus's case this is a trademark quality. So it is for George Bailey. He is thematically depicted as desiring to travel to exotic foreign lands ("Tahiti—Fiji islands, the Coral Sea! . . . Only us explorers can get it . . . I'm going out exploring someday, you watch"; "I'm shaking the dust of this crummy little town off my feet and I'm going to see the world. Italy, Greece, the Parthenon, the Coliseum"; "a whole week in Bermuda"; etc.),[3] repeatedly shown looking over travel brochures and posters from all over the globe. But as part of the film's thematic inversion of conventional heroic acts, the motif is reversed: he never leaves Bedford Falls.

George's conversation with his father, shortly before his stroke, articulates the movie's dominant heroic paradigm. Eager finally to have the opportunity to travel, and then go to college, George emphasizes his larger concerns to his father, "I want to do something big and something important" (Basinger 1987, 143). His father replies, framing his own view from his position as director of the Bailey Building & Loan, which has rarely made any money to speak of but has helped dozens of local residents buy their own homes, "You know, George, I feel that in a small way we are doing something important" (143). This is the film's new paradigm of heroism: the details of middle-class existence in a small American town have a larger significance that can take on epic dimensions, with heavenly powers observing and intervening in the hero's struggles.

Each time George expresses such wanderlust, events conspire to keep him in Bedford Falls. In reality, he could leave but repeatedly chooses to remain out of a sense of responsibility and a desire to help others. Though Odysseus goes to the equivalents of all the places George dreams of, it should be emphasized that he does so involuntarily, that he spends his entire epic, and the preceding ten years, attempting to return to his own relatively obscure, out-of-the-way home. A prisoner on Ogygia,[4] he would rather return home than stay in Kalypso's paradise, immortal as she is. On Skheria he ignores Alkinoos's offer of Nausikaa's hand, turning down comfortable residence in yet another paradise, to return to his wife and remote kingdom. The hero whose adventures in books 9–12 give us the word *odyssey* is at heart the homebody that George Bailey is.

Both narratives have intricate chronologies with complicated flashbacks or retrospective scenes. Both begin their stories with the action well advanced, *in medias res,* if you will, but later switching to events many years earlier in the protagonists' lives. The present time of the *Odyssey* takes up forty-one days (de Jong 588), but all of books 9–12 are a flashback, or retrospective account, of the preceding ten years. Other flashbacks go back to shortly after Odysseus was born (*Od.* 19.399–412), and again at a time in his youth when he first showed himself a hero (*Od.* 19.392–467). With a similar complexity, *It's a Wonderful Life* opens on December 24, 1945, but after the opening scene (discussed later), flashes back to 1919, when George was twelve. The film then brings the external audience, and the divine internal audience, up to date on the protagonist's life and his current crisis, not returning to December 24, 1945, until an hour and sixteen minutes have elapsed.

The Opening Divine Council

After only the briefest openings, both narratives begin with the same type scene, the divine council, in which two or more gods meet to discuss the fate of the protagonist. The divine council is a standard feature of epic in particular, from *Gilgamesh* on, but also occurs in other subgenres of myth. The Book of Job, for instance, opens with two exchanges between Yahweh and Satan (Job 1:6–12, 2:1–7). Most divine councils belong to one of two basic subtypes.[5] The chief god, Zeus in Homeric epic, is in dialogue with either the mentor god, Athena in the *Odyssey,* or a god with a divine wrath against the protagonist, Poseidon in the *Odyssey* (13. 125–58), as is the case with the divine councils in Job, between Yahweh and Satan. The *Odyssey*'s opening divine council (1.26–96) is the former type. Though all the Olympians except Poseidon are said to be present, only Zeus and Athena speak. Zeus has called the assembly to articulate his complaint about mortals, that they blame the gods when in difficulty, when in fact their own recklessness has caused their problems. Athena agrees, noting, however, that Odysseus does not fit this category of mortal behavior. She then steers the council to a discussion of his current dilemma (discussed later).

The divine council that opens *It's a Wonderful Life* (Basinger 1987, 111–15) is the same type, discussion with the immortal who serves as the protagonist's mentor, though with modifications to continue the film's interest in constructing an American subgenre of myth. An angel named Franklin presides over the council. Franklin, Benjamin, that is, in serving as the guiding spirit of this heavenly group typifies how the film constructs a specifically American subgenre of myth. Fully aware of the crisis that is unfolding for George, he summons Clarence, who will serve as George's guardian angel. As the *Odyssey*'s opening divine council turns its gaze upon Odysseus, in *It's a Wonderful Life* Joseph and Clarence, through a divine kind of sight, now watch earlier episodes in George's life.

The Crisis That Generates the Story

A myth often begins with a problem that the rest of the plot answers or solves, the mysterious plague at the beginning of *Oedipus the King*, the people of Uruk's complaints about Gilgamesh's behavior (*Gilgamesh* 1.67–76). The *Odyssey* opens with two problems, both involving the protagonist's return home. Object of Poseidon's divine wrath, Odysseus is unable to cross the sea and return home, though it is ten years since the Trojan War ended. He is prisoner, kept against his will by the goddess Kalypso on her island Ogygia, off the known map, presumed dead by many characters. Back home in Ithaka the suitors have taken over his palace and are forcing the household to serve them, as Athena will shortly witness.

It's a Wonderful Life begins with George Bailey, object of the eight opening prayers, in a desperate circumstance. He fears his reputation is destroyed over a mistake someone else made, his uncle Billy, who misplaced $8,000 ("Do you realize what this means? It means bankruptcy and scandal, and prison!").[6] It is this moment, when George Bailey is about to take his life by jumping from the bridge into a rushing river, with which the film's opening prayers coincide, though none of those praying know he is about to commit suicide,[7] only that he is in desperate circumstances. Both opening divine councils address the protagonists' respective crises.

The Mentoring Immortal: Athena and Clarence

Each opening divine council features a heavenly being who champions the protagonist throughout the rest of his narrative. A god serving as the hero's mentor is a standard feature of ancient heroic myth, with Shamash for Gilgamesh, Hera for Jason, and Athena for not only Odysseus, but Achilles and Heracles (see *Il.* 8.362–69).[8] Key among the typical acts by the mentor god are speaking up on the hero's behalf at divine councils, as Athena does at *Il.* 1.48–62, 81–87, and helping arrange a solution to his crisis. Hereafter she will intervene repeatedly on Odysseus' behalf, first by doing so for Telemachos.

In *It's a Wonderful Life*'s opening divine council the angel Clarence, sent for by Franklin, quickly becomes the third divine participant. Extending the film's thematic development of a specifically American subgenre of myth, Clarence has with him a copy of *The Adventures of Tom Sawyer.* Both divine mentors mirror the defining qualities of their respective protagonists. They are in heaven as he is on earth. In a well-known scene in the *Odyssey* Athena defines the nature of her relationship with Odysseus,

> We both know
> cunning ways, since you are best of all the mortals
> in plotting and speaking, while I among all the gods
> am renowned for my devices and my cunning ways.
> (*Od.* 13.296–99)[9]

Clarence's own situation, bypassed by more successful peers (Basinger 1987, 111–12), closely parallels George Bailey's position in life. Having chosen to stay in Bedford Falls and keep his father's building and loan out of Potter's hands, George watches his contemporaries, his brother Harry and Sam Wainwright, leave town, go off to college, and enter into successful, even lucrative business opportunities.

Clarence remains wingless, needing to earn his wings by saving George. Even George, though at first refusing to believe Clarence is his guardian angel, nonetheless sees the parallels:

> "That's what I was sent down for. I'm your guardian angel" . . .
> "Well, you look about like the kind of an angel I'd get. Sort of a fallen angel, aren't you?" (Basinger 1987, 279)

The parallels extend to the end of the film: Clarence's promotion is simultaneous with George's happy ending (322–23).

Both narratives have further divine councils. The *Odyssey* has two more between Zeus and Athena (*Od.* 5.3–43, 24.472–87), one between Zeus and Helios (*Od.* 12.376–88), and one between Zeus and Poseidon (*Od.* 13.125–64). *It's a Wonderful Life* has further brief divine councils that mark the key turning points in George's life. The second depicts a grown-up George Bailey in 1928 (Basinger 1987, 131–32), the day he chooses not to go see the world but to remain and run the building and loan. A third marks Harry's return from college, four years later, with a glamorous wife and exciting business prospects (168), traditional American signs of success that so far elude George. A final divine council summarizes Bedford Falls's passage through World War II, taking the film, and audience, back up to the day on which it began, 10 AM, Christmas Eve, 1945 (232–37).

The Villains: Potter and the Suitors

Both narratives feature highly negative characters, the moral opposites of the protagonist, who in effect are besieging his home and city, threatening his very existence. Such moral stratification of characters into patently good or bad is a standard tendency of romance.[10] Though there are 108 suitors and only one Potter, the two are close equivalents in their respective narratives, both highly oppressive, negative examples of the myths' central ethical propositions. The *Odyssey* depicts the suitors as systematically violating hospitality, an institution whose sanctity is guarded by Zeus himself (*Od.* 9.270, 14.57–58). In the frame of reference closest to that used in *It's a Wonderful Life* the suitors are constantly attempting to take possession of others' goods. Every day for years they have eaten their meals in Odysseus' palace, not only violating hospitality, but without ever offering any recompense (*Od.* 1.160, 1.377 = 2.141, 14.377,

14.417, 18.280; cf. 1.250–51, 2.55–79, 21.331–33, 22.36). George's father offers a succinct characterization of Potter that offers a thematic parallel, "Hates everybody that has anything he can't have" (Basinger 1987, 140). In the climactic instance of this tendency Potter winds up in possession of $8,000 that George's uncle Billy foolishly misplaces (245–46). Peering through the window blinds (251) when George and Billy look for it frantically, by keeping the money that is not his, Potter precipitates the crisis that provokes George's suicide attempt. He is an instantiation of selfishness as George is an ideal of selflessness.

Both the suitors and Potter intimidate others through speaking abusively, and both verbally abuse the protagonists. The suitors dominate the *Odyssey*'s assembly in book 2 by threatening those who criticize or speak against their position (*Od.* 2.178–93, 243–51). In a close parallel, Potter dominates meetings of the board of directors of the building and loan (Basinger 1987, 162–65; cf. 125–27). Claiming the town has no need for the institution, he advances a motion to close it down. His real motive, that the town's poorer citizens would have no other option than to rent from him, becomes obvious in the subsequent dialogue, however. The suitors, or various members of their party including the servants Melanthios and Melantho, repeatedly insult Odysseus (*Od.* 17.217–18, 17.446–52, 18.15–31, 18.321–36, 19.65–69). Potter is thematically depicted as speaking abusively (Basinger 1987, 125–27, 163–65, 204, 223–24, 266–69, 313), and is not above uttering ethnic slurs, as he characterizes what he views as George's wasted choices in life, "trapped into frittering his life away playing nurse-maid to a lot of garlic-eaters" (227). In his most dishonest scene, when George goes to him begging for help, with Potter all the while in possession of the $8,000 that prompts the crisis, he knowingly lies about what George could have done with the money, playing the market or spending it on a mistress (265–66). Instead, pretending to play the role of honest citizen, he declares he will call the police: "I'm going to swear out a warrant for your arrest. Misappropriation of funds—manipulation—malfeasance" (267).

At a deep, if implicit, level the suitors and Potter are both associated with death or the underworld. An almost vampirish quality is suggested in the suitors when they are figured as ticks on the dying Argos (*Od.* 17.300), as de Jong notes (2001, 421): "The dog's body is covered with vermin, just as the palace is infected by the parasitic suitors." In his prophecy of their coming destruction the prophet

Theoklymenos sees them in their feasting as if they are already ghosts flitting about Hades (*Od.* 20.351–70), the palace walls running with their blood. In book 24 the narrative follows the slain suitors down to Hades, depicting their reception there, and dialogue with Agamemnon. Potter's very name suggests connections with the underworld (discussed later in The Descent to the Underworld). His remark to George about his life insurance policy, "You're worth more dead than alive" (Basinger 1987, 267), indirectly prompts his suicide attempt. Potter associates himself with death when he refers to his attempts to gain control of the Bailey Building & Loan: "You know, also, that for a number of years I've been trying to get control of it . . . or kill it" (226).

Potter's thematic association with death and the underworld also has diabolic overtones. In an earlier episode his employee Reineman points out that he is losing customers, and considerable revenue, to George's own housing development, Bailey Park, where low-income citizens can become homeowners rather than renters under Potter. As a result Potter invites George to his office (Basinger 1987, 226–30) to offer him a job at a princely salary.[11] Not only is he attempting to buy him off, remove competition, but Potter's offer to have George work for him for such a high salary, with irresistible perks, clearly implies that he is offering to buy George's soul. The theme is sounded even more firmly during an earlier crisis when the bank, for unexplained reasons, calls in its loan to the Bailey Building & Loan. To pay it back they deplete most of their reserves, causing a run by their customers. Potter exploits the situation by offering George's customers fifty cents to the dollar for their accounts. When some start to think it is an attractive offer, George tries to dissuade them: "Don't you see what's happening? Potter isn't selling. Potter's buying!" (208). Epic has a close parallel in Ishtar's offer to make Gilgamesh her lover, which, as Abusch argues (149, 152, 159, 174), would transform him into some kind of functionary in the underworld. The *Odyssey* echoes this in Kalypso's offer to make Odysseus immortal on Ogygia (*Od.* 5.208–09), the same subgenre of myth as the episode in *Gilgamesh.*[12]

The Hero Triumphs over Death

Central to the depiction of the hero in ancient myth is his ability to transcend death in some way, and to take others back from it. In

Greek myth Heracles embodies this defining theme more than any other hero, not only in the last few of his labors, but in his rescue of Alcestis.[13] In the *Odyssey* Odysseus' ability to triumph over death is thematic throughout the epic. It is implicit in episodes such as that of the Lotus Eaters, from whose island he successfully takes all his men back alive, though against their will. The escape from Polyphemos' cave, which suggests a miniature of the underworld, is perhaps the most emphatic instance. Except the six the Cyclops eats, Odysseus saves all of his crew who entered the cave with him. On Aiaia, where half the crew are turned into swine, he saves them by having Circe restore their proper form. They would have otherwise been slaughtered, possibly eaten, if remaining in their porcine state, shut in pens to be fattened. After consulting Teiresias Odysseus rescues all his crew from Hades (other than Elpenor, who had earlier gone by himself), a literal return from death (discussed later).

A thematic ability to triumph over death is also at the core of George Bailey's character, though depicted in a less swashbuckling manner and in a Christianizing modality. In the film's earliest episode, which serves to introduce him to Clarence, George saves the life of his brother, Harry, who has fallen through the ice on a frozen lake (Basinger 1987, 114–15). The episode is pivotal, frequently referred to in later scenes, key to establishing George as the figure who even at twelve years of age saves the others in his town. The *Odyssey* offers a parallel in Eurykleia's reminiscence about Odysseus on the boar hunt at Parnassos (*Od.* 19. 392–467). In Greek myth boar hunts are typically dangerous, often lethal. At an unspecified age, but clearly young, Odysseus takes part in a hunt, is dangerously wounded in his thigh, but slays the boar, a triumph over death. Both episodes serve as rites of passage for the protagonists, establishing them as the heroes they will become.

A short time afterward, while recovering from the ear infection he develops from diving in the icy waters to save Harry (cf. Odysseus's thigh wound), George prevents Gower, the pharmacist he works for, from accidentally poisoning a customer. Distraught over the sudden death of his son, Gower has been drinking heavily and accidentally places poison in capsules he then orders George to deliver to a household where a boy has diphtheria. Aware of the deadly error, but realizing Gower will not listen to him because of his condition, George seeks advice from his father but finds him locking horns in a quarrel with Potter, unable to speak with him. When George returns to Gower to attempt to reason with him, the pharmacist, enraged because George has still not delivered the "medicine," boxes him on his sore ear. Only when he cries out in pain does George break through to Gower, who now, realizing what he almost did, tries to hug George in gratitude (Basinger 1987, 122–29).

In these ways and more George instantiates a Christianizing form of heroism and acts out the notion of savior, as associated with Christ. When Clarence jumps into the river to forestall George's suicide attempt, he does so to trigger this central hallmark of George's character, "I jumped in to save George. . . . I knew if I were drowning, you'd try to save me . . . and that's how I saved you" (Basinger 1987, 276). By jumping into the river in a snowstorm Clarence essentially replicates the circumstances when George saved Harry, dead of winter, snow, icy body of water. His jumping into the lake to save his brother from death established him as the selfless man who saves others. His divine mentor here prompts George, who has always put others first, to save himself unknowingly.

The Crisis Falls on a Holy Day

In the *Odyssey* the confrontation between Odysseus and the suitors reaches a climax on a day sacred to Apollo (*Od.* 20.156, 21.258; cf. 20.276–78). In this confrontation Odysseus has the implicit support of Zeus, as god of hospitality; the explicit aid of Athena (*Od.* 13.393–96); and now, as the preeminent archer of his time, Odysseus will use the bow against the suitors on a day sacred to the god of archery, suggesting implicit aid from Apollo as well. The night before Apollo's sacred day, Odysseus prays to Zeus for help in the coming encounter,

> Zeus Father, if it was your will to bring me over land and sea
> to my homeland, after I had suffered exceedingly,
> let someone, of those awake within, speak an omen to me,
> and let a sign show outside from Zeus.
>
> (*Od.* 20.98–101)

In *It's a Wonderful Life* George's crisis with Potter takes place on Christmas Eve. The date, which gathers momentum throughout the movie, implicitly underscores the divine aid that George receives: that the eight prayers that open the film are answered, and George's own, "God . . . God . . . Dear Father in Heaven, I'm not a praying man, but if you're up there and you can hear me, show me the way. I'm at the end of my rope. Show me the way, God" (Basinger 1987, 269).

The Vision

In the film's crucial scene Clarence persuades George his life has been important, by *showing* him what the whole town would be like if he had never existed. He does so by conducting George through a traditional subgenre of myth, *the vision,* in which the protagonist is removed from the mortal plane, accompanied by an otherworldly guide, who reveals to him a larger truth, the "big picture," previously hidden from his view. This basic structure, familiar from texts such as Cicero's "Scipio's Dream," book 6 of the *Aeneid,* and Dickens's "A Christmas Carol," is also the central organizing device in the Book of Revelation, which is largely an extended instance of *the vision.* By *removed from the mortal plane* I mean that in the vision the heavenly guide takes the protagonist up to a heavenly setting (an *anabasis*), as in Scipio's Dream and the Book of Revelation, or down to an underworld setting (a *catabasis*), as in *Odyssey* 11, *Aeneid* 6, and *It's a Wonderful Life.*

After consulting Teiresias, his reason for going to Hades, as instructed by Circe, Odysseus speaks with the shade of his mother, Antikleia (*Od.* 11.152–224). At the end of their dialogue she directs him to remember everything *he sees* in order to tell Penelope when he returns. Then a procession of shades of women approach him, the Catalogue of Heroines, each telling her story. In keeping with the visual nature of the vision Odysseus introduces each woman with the expression "and then I saw *X*" (*Od.* 11.235, 260, 266, 271, 281, 298, 305, 321, 326).[14] This is the *Odyssey*'s less developed instance of the vision, with Antikleia, who suggests a certain omniscience in knowing the state of affairs in Ithaka since Odysseus left, serving as his otherworldly guide. Though Odysseus does not here undergo as dramatic a transformation as George Bailey does, his narration of his meeting with his mother, and the subsequent Catalogue of Heroines, to Arete, queen of the Phaiakians, is crucial for securing his homecoming. The epic twice earlier specifies that if he is to reach home, Arete's decision to help him do so is crucial (*Od.* 6.313–15 = 7.75–77). Immediately after describing the Catalogue of Heroines, Odysseus briefly halts his narration of his wanderings, the only such pause in all of books 9–12. Queen Arete then asks the Phaiakians to give him gifts and intimates that she will now help bring about his homecoming (*Od.* 11.335–41), which he had asked of her back in book 7. A consensus seems to be emerging[15] that she does so because of his narration of his dialogue with his mother and subsequent meetings with the heroines, the vision.

In *It's a Wonderful Life* Clarence is unable to help George to see the value of his life, the purpose of his divine intervention, until the protagonist's chance remark, "I suppose it would have been better if I'd never been born at all" (Basinger 1987, 280). Seeing the possibilities that would result, Clarence quickly responds, "You've got your wish. You've never been born." Clarence's granting of his wish is reminiscent of folk tales, in particular some of those collected by the Brothers Grimm (e.g., "The Fisherman's Wife"), in which a mortal is granted a wish that goes awry. With his remaining wish he is just able to restore conditions to where they were before his first foolish wish. As in *Odyssey* 11, the visual nature of what George will experience here is emphasized,

> "You'll see a lot of strange things from now on." (287)
> "Well then, why am I seeing all these strange things?" (291)
> "You've been given a great gift, George. A chance to see what the world would be like without you." (293)
> "You're screwy, and you're driving me crazy, too! I'm seeing things." (293)

While several incidents George experiences will be discussed in the following section, we can note some larger parallels here. For both Odysseus and George their witnessing the vision is key to their being able to return home. As a result of what he sees in his vision George will ask Clarence to help him return to his family. The *Odyssey* and *It's a Wonderful Life* are further tied in both setting their versions of the vision within a *catabasis,* whereas Scipio's Dream and the Book of Revelation set theirs within *anabases.* The two works differ, however, in the way they structure the vision with respect to the descent to the underworld. In the *Odyssey* the descent, to the underworld is the larger structure and the vision is an element within the descent whereas in *It's a Wonderful Life* the vision is the larger structure and contains the descent to the underworld.

The Descent to the Underworld

In ancient myth the hero's descent to and successful ascent back from the underworld instantiate his triumph over death and constitute a resurrection of sorts. In Greek myth in addition to Heracles, Theseus and Orpheus make the descent. Though Odysseus's descent is the fullest depiction of this subgenre in Greek myth, it is unusual in several respects. Technically Odysseus does not *descend* to the underworld, but sails there because the *Odyssey* subsumes his *catabasis* under its larger rubric of *the fantastic voyage,* which provides the overarching framework for all of books 9–12.[16] As directed by Circe, Odysseus goes to Hades to learn from the prophet Teiresias how to return home.[17] But only a small portion of his encounter involves Teiresias. His dialogue with his mother is longer (seventy-four lines to sixty-one, respectively), the first sign of the episode's unexpected focus on the feminine. In other descents the hero typically meets with male comrades (e.g., Bacchylides 5), suggesting that the *Odyssey* innovates in having Odysseus meet with not only his mother, but the subsequent heroines of the Catalogue.

Though in earlier scenes Clarence offers a close parallel to Athena, as the hero's divine mentor, within the descent Clarence parallels Teiresias, the figure with divine knowledge, familiar with the underworld, who tells the protagonist how to return home. In the film's most far-reaching statement of its Christianizing theme, in a world without George Bailey, his town is not only completely dominated by all that Potter represents, it becomes an equivalent of the underworld.[18] His thematic role as the man able to save others nonexistent, the entire town has now gone over "to the dark side of the force," as George Lucas would say. Ancient myth typically depicts the underworld as a city, including the Old Testament underworld, Sheol.[19] Bedford Falls is now Potterville, with Potter himself clearly serving as a Hades figure. There is no Bailey Park. A cemetery lies where George expects to find it.

The town's new name, *Pottersville* (Basinger 1987, 283), suggests an allusion to Potters' Field (*ton Agron tou Kerameos*), a burial place for foreigners (*tois xenois*), mentioned in Matthew 27:7 (cf. Acts 1:18–19). The chief priests, having received the thirty pieces of silver from Judas for betraying Christ, decide the money cannot be put in with temple funds: "It is blood money." Instead they use the funds to purchase "Potter's Field."[20] An earlier episode refers to the section of Bedford Falls dominated by Potter's rental units as "Potter's Field." When Martini is able to buy a home in Bailey Park, thanks to George's help, he declares, "No more we live like pigs in thisa [*sic*] Potter's Field" (Basinger 1987, 220, and again at 297). The apparent allusion strengthens the episode's connection to an underworld setting, in being a burial place, and offers yet another tie to Christian myth.[21] By implication the entire town is now accursed, purchased with blood money, a burial ground for strangers.

More like Dante and his guide in the *Inferno* than Odysseus, who is comparably immobile in his underworld, George is quite mobile, going from one area to another. Consequently, Clarence is here more like a combination of the Sibyl and Anchises, or even Virgil, as Dante uses him in the *Inferno*. Associations with death are everywhere, not only in the cemetery that stands where he thinks Bailey's Park should be, but in the unexpected sight of the gravestone of his brother, Harry. Not only did he die as a boy, without a George to save him, but all the men whom he had saved as a World War II hero died as well, without him there to save them (Basinger 1987, 303).

There is much heavier drinking in Pottersville than there had been in Bedford Falls. The bar now serves hard liquor exclusively, "for men who want to get drunk fast" (Basinger 1987, 286), as the hardened, less-than-hospitable Nick informs George and Clarence. *It's a Wonderful Life* uses drinking and the town's bar in much the same way that the *Odyssey* uses the incident of Elpenor, drunk, falling to his death, to frame Odysseus' descent to Hades. At the end of book 10, Elpenor, drunk, sleeping it off on Circe's roof, is startled out of his sleep by the sounds of Odysseus and the others preparing to go to Hades. Waking up suddenly and forgetting where he is, he falls off the roof, breaking his neck. In Hades he begs Odysseus to bury him when he returns to Circe's isle, and the protagonist does. Elpenor thus frames Odysseus' entrance to and return from the underworld.[22] In the last episode before his suicide attempt, and Clarence's intervention, George, out of despair over the financial scandal, is drinking heavily at Martini's bar (269–72). A patron bloodies his lip, recognizing him as the man who spoke rudely to his wife. Later, he sees that as his last "normal" moment before the vision began, "The last man I talked to before all this stuff started happening to me was Martini" (302).[23] When the vision starts, his lip is no longer bleeding; the incident never happened. When the vision concludes, his lip is bleeding again.

Odysseus and George both encounter their mothers in their descents, instead of the hero's more typical meeting with his father (as Aeneas in *Aeneid* 6, and Scipio the Younger with the Elder in *Scipio's Dream*). The episodes are otherwise quite different in tone. As noted, Antikleia serves as Odysseus' otherworldly guide in his vision, and brings him up to date on developments in Ithaka. George's mother does not know him, shutting the door in his face. George is a stranger, as Clarence had said ("You're nobody. You have no identity" [Basinger 1987, 292]), even to his family and friends. As such he parallels Odysseus after he has returned to Ithaka, disguised as a wanderer, addressed throughout as "stranger." He has a series of what could be called nonrecognition scenes, as his close friends and associates: Gower the pharmacist, who without George to save him from poisoning the neighbor boy is now a broken-down bum (289); Ernie the taxi driver (296–97); then his mother (300–02); and finally Mary (303–07), all declare they do not know him.

While a sense of what his life has meant to others has been building throughout the scene—Harry's premature death, Gower's lapse into alcoholism, Uncle Billy in an insane asylum, Mary a spinster—it is the loss of his wife and children (who no longer exist) that makes him want to live again: "Clarence! Clarence! Help me, Clarence! Get me back. Get me back. I don't care what happens to me. Only get me back to my wife and kids. Help me, Clarence, please! I want to live again!" (Basinger 1987, 308). Clarence's guidance in the vision has made George realize he values his family more than he fears possible ruin from the financial scandal.

Reunited with His Wife in a Recognition Scene

While romances in general climax in highly emotional recognition scenes between the protagonists and family members, both these works feature the same subtype, recognition scenes with the protagonists' wives.[24] There is a key difference in the interval of time that has passed. Usually the recognition scenes are as emotional as they are because the protagonist, as has Odysseus, has been gone for twenty years (cf. Joseph, the sixteen-year gap before Leontes meets Perdita, etc.). Though *It's a Wonderful Life* has no lengthy absence, the emotions are strong because of everyone's concern for him, and the film employs many of the traditional features. For instance, after

Odysseus first realizes he is back on Ithaka (after Athena scatters the mist with which she has cloaked the island), he kisses the ground (*Od.* 13.354). When George realizes he is back home, no longer in Pottersville, he addresses the city excitedly, "Hello, Bedford Falls!" (Basinger 1987, 310).

Both works use earlier scenes to prepare for the climactic recognition scenes with the wives. As *It's a Wonderful Life* the *Odyssey* has an earlier "nonrecognition scene" between Odysseus and Penelope, Penelope's interview of the mysterious stranger in book 19. In this episode Odysseus tests Penelope, as earlier directed by Athena (*Od.* 13.335–36, 402–03). She is unable to penetrate his god-given disguise, much as Joseph's brothers are unable to recognize their presumably long dead brother, though in his very presence, twenty years later (*Genesis* 42:6–25, 43:15–44:34). When Odysseus successfully passes her test, "proving" he recently met with Odysseus by accurately describing an article of clothing Penelope had earlier given him, she breaks down and cries, the strong emotional reaction like that a true recognition scene provokes.

Two earlier scenes in *It's a Wonderful Life* between George and Mary anticipate their climactic recognition scene. The day George learns that Harry has married is also the day he realizes he will wed Mary. His decision, which occurs after a complicated sequence of events (Basinger 1987, 183–97), is a recognition scene of sorts, since George recognizes that he loves Mary (while she has been aware of her feelings for him throughout the film). A closely related scene follows, the run on the bank, when George and Mary spend their honeymoon money to keep the Bailey Building & Loan solvent. At day's end, instead of taking him to begin his honeymoon, Ernie takes George to where Mary has directed, the abandoned house at 23 Sycamore. The old house is tightly connected to their marriage, almost like the olive tree in Odysseus's marriage (*Od.* 23.190–204). In an earlier scene, long before they married, Mary had silently wished that they would someday live in the house. While he spent the day keeping the Building & Loan open, she somehow managed to move furnishings into the house. When Ernie takes him there, travel posters for all the exotic places George has wanted to go are hanging on the walls. Mary welcomes him home (218–19). This first welcome home closely anticipates his return home in the film's final episode. Both times they embrace deeply ("Mary! Let me touch you! Oh, you're real!" [318]), much as Penelope melts into Odysseus's arms when she recognizes him (23.205–08).

The Richest Man in Town

The protagonist in romance typically returns home with fabulous riches. Joseph, when his brothers and father are reunited with him, is now fabulously wealthy, pharaoh's right-hand man. Odysseus had earlier been wealthy as king of Ithaka and surrounding lands. But the suitors, in their multiyear depredations, have significantly reduced his holdings. Though all the gold Odysseus had earned as the sacker of Troy is now at the bottom of the sea, after winning over Arete, who directs the Phaiakians to give him lavish gifts (*Od.* 11.338–41), he nonetheless returns home with fabulous riches (*Od.* 8.387–406; 13.10–15, 217–18), greater in value, according to Zeus (*Od.* 5.39–40), than his plunder from the war. Though the *Odyssey* is often seen as validating an aristocratic ideology, balanced reflection on its depiction of the suitors should dispel such a view.[25] If anything, the *Odyssey,* in its resolutely negative portrayal of the 108 suitors, and the *Iliad,* in its emphatically flawed Agamemnon,[26] should be seen as thematically associating the ruling class with abuse of power.

The *Odyssey* figures the suitors, who essentially comprise all the nobles from Ithaka and nearby lands, as using intimidation and violence to attempt to seize goods belonging to another man. In doing so they violate the key institutions of their culture, particularly the sanctity of hospitality, which the *Odyssey* employs throughout as a litmus test of a given character's morality. When Penelope tricks them into paying her back unaware, for much of what they have plundered from the palace (*Od.* 18.206–303), she is able to do so because of their lust for her (*Od.* 18.212–13), parallel to Zeus's exemplum of Aigisthos (*Od.* 1.39). In all these ways the *Odyssey,* in its relentlessly negative depiction of the wealthy suitors, and its locating examples of moral behavior in the poor (Eumaios, Philoitios, Eurykleia), prefigures central qualities of New Testament myth, in which Christ associates with fishermen, and the like, while a corrupt power structure threatens him.[27] Quite the contrary to validating an aristocratic ideology, the *Odyssey* for much of its narrative identifies with common laborers, spending a notable part of its second half with the swineherd Eumaios, the only character whom the narrator addresses in apostrophe.[28]

It's a Wonderful Life engages in a dialogue about what constitutes the proper acquisition of material goods, what is the meaning of wealth. In one respect the film suggests an opposition between two affluent characters, Sam Wainwright, who is seen as a proper capitalist, and Potter, a close equivalent of the *Odyssey*'s suitors in his greed. But George Bailey, in a final instance of the film's Christianizing tendency, redefines success and wealth as one's relations with others.

Notes

1. For Philip Van Dorn Stern's original short story from which the plot derives, discussion of earlier versions of the screenplay, and the four credited screenwriters, one of whom is Capra himself, see Basinger (1987, 94–108, 339–54).

2. For discussion of the *Odyssey* as a romance see Louden (unpublished, chapter 3).

3. Quotations taken respectively from Basinger (1987, 119, 157, 199).

4. On the island setting, cf. the phonograph playing "Song of the Islands" in *It's a Wonderful Life* (Basinger 1987, 216).

5. Discussion in Louden (2005, 90–94).

6. Basinger (1987, 253).

7. Odysseus is also considering suicide as his narrative begins, *Od.* 1.59; cf. 10.51, 10.496–99.

8. On the functions of the mentor god, and on Athena as most frequently serving this position in Greek heroic myth, see Louden (2005, 90–96).

9. Translations of the *Odyssey* are my own.

10. See Louden (1999, 203) for discussion of how *The Tempest* and Plautus's *Rudens* instantiate this standard romance tendency.

11. Potter offers $20,000; George apparently makes $2,340 (= $45 × 52).

12. Discussion in Louden (unpublished, chapter 5). Cf. Agamemnon's attempts to buy off Achilles by marrying him to one of daughters (*Il.* 9.120–57) and giving him seven cities as dowry.

13. On which see Louden (2008).

14. Cf. *Gilgamesh* 12.90–153; *Aeneid* 6.695: *imago,* 6.703: *videt Aeneas;* 6.710: *visu,* 6.716: *ostendere,* 6.760: *vides,* 6.779: *viden,* 6.788: *aspice,* 6.818: *videre,* 6.825: *aspice,* 6.826: *cernis,* 6.855: *aspice,* 6.860: *videbat*). Discussion in Louden (unpublished, chapter 9).

15. See for example Doherty (1991) and Louden (1999, 11–13).

16. Again, for discussion, see Louden (unpublished, chapter 9). Cf. the Book of Jonah for a rough parallel in Old Testament myth.

17. Cf. Saul's consultation with the shade of the deceased prophet Samuel in 1 Samuel 28.

18. Cf. the *Beavis and Butt-head Christmas Special* (1995), which parodies the vision in *It's a Wonderful Life* by having a guardian angel show that if Butt-head did not exist, his town would be a virtual utopia.

19. See Dahood (1968, 194): "Among the numerous texts which depict the realm of the dead as a city with gates (*Isaiah* 38:10; *Job* 24:12, 38:17; *Eccl* 51:9, *Mat* 16:18). . . . In Canaanite mythology, Death's subterranean domain is termed *qrt,* 'city.'"

20. See Albright and Mann (1971, 341) for discussion of some significant problems in the Greek text.

21. The original short story mentions only a "Potter's studio" (Basinger 1987, 99) from which George and Harry returned the day Harry would drown.

22. For further discussion of how the *Odyssey* uses Elpenor to frame the descent to the underworld see Reece (1995) and Louden (1999, 43–45).

23. Cf. "Look here, Ernie, straighten me out here. I've got some bad liquor or something" (Basinger 1987, 296).

24. As opposed to recognition scenes between siblings, as in Euripides' *Iphigeneia in Taurus,* and the myth of Joseph, or between mother and son, as in Euripides' *Ion,* or father and daughter, as Shakespeare prefers.

25. "It is usually assumed that the Homeric poems support an aristocratic ideology. I disagree; it is monarchy that appears most prominently in both epics. In the *Iliad* Agamemnon misuses his power, and in the *Odyssey* Odysseus regains his kingdom from a bunch of aristocratic usurpers" (Janko 1998, 13).

26. Discussion in Louden (2006, 158–67).

27. Discussion in Louden (unpublished, chapter 13).

28. Kahane (1994, 85–107) notes that the positioning of the apostrophe, internal in all thirteen instances to Eumaios, is the mode "by which special attention to the addressee is revealed."

Works Cited

Abusch, Tzvi. "Ishtar's Proposal and Gilgamesh's Refusal: An Interpretation of *The Gilgamesh Epic,* Tablet 6, Lines 1–79." *History of Religions* 26 (1986): 143–87.

Albright, W. F., and C. S. Mann. *The Anchor Bible: Matthew: Introduction, Translation, and Notes.* Garden City, NY: Doubleday, 1971.

Basinger, Jeanine. *The* It's a Wonderful Life *Book.* New York: Alfred A. Knopf, 1987.

Crane, Gregory. *Calypso: Backgrounds and Conventions of the* Odyssey. Frankfurt am Main: Athenäum, 1988.

Dahoud, Mitchell, S. J. *The Anchor Bible: Psalms II 51–100: Introduction, Translation, and Notes.* Garden City, NY: Doubleday, 1968.

de Jong, Irene J. F. *A Narratological Commentary on the* Odyssey. Cambridge: Cambridge University Press, 2001.

Doherty, L. E. "The Internal and Implied Audience of *Odyssey* 11." *Arethusa* 24, no. 2 (1991): 145–76.

George, A. R. *The Babylonian Gilgamesh Epic: Introduction, Critical Edition and Cuneiform Texts.* Vols. I & II. Oxford: Oxford University Press, 2003.

Janko, Richard. "The Homeric Poems as Oral Dictated Texts." *Classical Quarterly* 48 (1998): 1–13.

Kahane, A. *The Interpretation of Order: A Study in the Poetics of Homeric Repetition.* Oxford, 1994.

Louden, Bruce. *The Odyssey: Structure, Narration, and Meaning.* Baltimore: The Johns Hopkins University Press, 1999a.

———. "The *Tempest,* Plautus, and the *Rudens.*" *Comparative Drama,* vol. 33 (1999b): 199–233.

———. The Iliad*: Structure, Myth and Meaning.* Baltimore: The Johns Hopkins University Press, 2006.

———. "Reading through *The Alcestis* to *The Winter's Tale.*" *Classical and Modern Literature* 27, no. 2 (2008).

———. The Odyssey *and the Near East.* (forthcoming).

Reece, Steve. "The Three Circuits of the Suitors: A Ring Composition in *Odyssey* 17–22." *Oral Tradition* 10 (1995): 207–29

Suggs, M. Jack, Katharine Doob Sakenfield, and James R. Mueller. *The Oxford Study Bible.* New York: Oxford University Press, 1992.

Reading *The Gunfighter* as Homeric Epic

Kostas Myrsiades

This paper examines the progress of the warrior's glory and his homecoming through a comparison of Henry King's *The Gunfighter* (1950) and Homer's eighth-century B.C.E. *Iliad* and *Odyssey*. It explores the themes of the hero's cunning, the destination, homecoming, and reunion in the *Odyssey* and his being condemned to glory, his self-recognition, and the roles of irony and fate in the *Iliad*. This is a tale about the gunfighter as warrior, the hero who desires honor, receives it through gifts, and ends in achieving glory through those gifts. It is a tale of discovery through self-recognition that ends in the repudiation of that glory so dearly won. It is a tale of the hero's realization as he turns homeward from the wars and inward, away from the externals that glory represents, to discover that his humanity lies in the importance to him of family.

IN 1967 JORGE LUIS BORGES WROTE IN *THE PARIS REVIEW,* "I THINK NOWAdays, while literary men seem to have neglected their epic duties, the epic has been saved for us, strangely enough, by the Westerns . . . has been saved for the world by of all places, Hollywood" (1967). Andre Bazin, one of the most important and influential film critics, places the western in the epic category "because of the superhuman level of its heroes and the legendary magnitude of their feats of valor," which has even turned the Civil War "into the Trojan war of the most modern of epics" (1971, 148). The communications scholar Doug Williams concurs that the Western has become the American epic, for just as John Wayne stands as an icon of the American identity, so once stood Odysseus for the Greeks (1998, 93). The historian Richard Slotkin finds compatibility between Homer and the western because the western, as the Homeric epic, deals with a nation's culture and its past and thus acts as a paean to the greatness of that nation (1992). The film historian Philip French argues that there is no theme or situation that cannot be examined in terms of the western, as "the Trojan War turned into a Texas range conflict" (1974, 23). Dealing with Clint Eastwood's *Unforgiven,* Mary Whitlock Blundell and Kirk Ormand assert that Eastwood's film "lies squarely within a tradition that questions, but ultimately reaffirms, an ethic of violence . . . the tradition of the Western European epic, beginning with the *Iliad*" (1997, 543). Dealing with the heroic nature of the title hero, Robert Warshaw in his 1954 classic essay "The Westerner" calls the westerner "a more classical figure" (154), while Jim Kitses speaks of the western hero "as a latter-day knight, a contemporary Achilles (1970, 1), and Andre Bazin sees Billy the Kid "as invulnerable as Achilles" (1971, 147). Martin M. Winkler, who has done more than anyone else in pointing out Homeric parallels in the American western, deals with Homer's influence in several films (1985, 1996, 2001) and especially at some length with John Ford's *The Searchers,* where he notices that "Ford's understanding of heroism places especially the figure of Ethan Edwards and the film's ending in the cultural tradition of Homeric epic" (2004).

This paper hopes to add to this body of literature by examining the progress of the warrior's glory and his homecoming through a comparison of Henry King's *The Gunfighter* (1950)[1] and Homer's eighth-century B.C.E. *Iliad* and *Odyssey.* It explores the themes of the hero's cunning, the destination, homecoming, and reunion in the *Odyssey* and his being condemned to glory, his self-recognition, and the roles of irony and fate in the *Iliad.* This is a tale about the gunfighter as warrior, the hero who desires honor, receives it through gifts, and ends in achieving glory through those gifts. It is a tale of discovery through self-recognition that ends in the repudiation of that glory so dearly won. It is a tale of the hero's realization as he turns homeward from the wars and inward, away from the externals that glory represents, to discover that his humanity lies in the importance to him of family. The discovery is qualified, however, by a stipulation. He cannot possess what he now knows to be his true desire; he cannot be other than what he has become: a warrior whose glory has a cost that is part of the larger gift. The cost, as he has always known, cannot be escaped. It is his fate to be so indelibly stamped with the glory he sought that others find in him the road to their own glory. The gunfighter's homecoming is not a reunion with family but losing a title and gaining a tomb.

Three terms best define the values men live and die for in the Homeric epics, although to a higher degree in the *Iliad* than in the

Odyssey: timê, kleos, and *geras.*[2] Homeric warriors fight for *timê* (honor), which is expressed through the *geras* (gifts) they receive for their prowess and excellence on the battlefield. The quality and the number of gifts received in turn assure them of *kleos* (glory)—to be remembered after death as great warriors and thus to achieve the only type of immortality available to mortals. In the Homeric epics these values are achieved through the warrior's performance (*aristeia*) in battle where he strives to be, and demonstrates that he is, *aristos Achaiôn* (the best of the Achaians).[3] A warrior's material wealth, the booty won at war, becomes the manifestation of his *timê,* which will outlive him as *kleos aphthiton* (unperishing glory).

The Gunfighter as Warrior

The Gunfighter preserves the tightness of plot that endeared Homer's epics to Aristotle, as the Aristotelian unities of time, place, and action remain intact. As in a Greek tragedy, the plot is resolved in less than twenty-four hours (in film plot time from about 8:00 A.M. to 10:30 A.M.). The driving action is the gunfighter's efforts to reunite with his wife and son. Focusing on the title character Jimmy Ringo's final two and a half hours of life, *The Gunfighter* story line unfolds largely on a single set—the Palace Bar Saloon in the gunfighter's destination town, Cayenne. The gunfighter is an Achilles-like warrior searching for the true meaning of "the fastest gun alive" by first embracing the values of his gunfighter society—*timê, kleos,* and *geras*—and finally rejecting them as he comes to terms with the constraints of mortality, the value of *oikos* (home), and the determinism of fate. But he is also an Odysseus, surviving his years as a gunfighter in a nineteenth-century world by using the same cunning and wits by means of which he will work to reclaim his wife and son. The incompatibility of Ringo's roles—the gunfighter, the character in search of himself, and the cunning warrior—and the transformations through which Ringo must pass constitute a nuanced view of the Homeric hero coming to terms with the great myth of the American West.

On the face of things, and in the tradition of a Homeric hero, Ringo is a larger-than-life figure whose hubris—his desire to be the best, "the fastest gun alive"—instigates his downfall. It occurs at a moment of the hero's greatest disconnection from his previous life, when he comes to realize that what he desires is different from who he is, that he cannot profit from his change of heart because his character has, after all, been determined by his life as a gunfighter. When he finally realizes the kind of life the gunfighter's title entails, and in spite of his great desire to change, fate—psychologically, the necessary working out of his own character—has written his end. And in the tradition of Greek tragic irony, at the point where he finally recognizes the kind of life he wants to lead and is capable of understanding the moral distinctions that would make such a life possible, at the moment he is able, and even willing, to accept his mortality, he is struck down.

Ringo's crowning realization occurs when, determined to change his life, he leaves the Palace Bar, mounts his horse, and vows to return in a year's time to retrieve his family and begin a new life. Precisely at that moment he is shot in the back. The fate the audience has been tracking—in the guise of three brothers pursuing him throughout the film—appears to have been averted, for they have been apprehended. But as in Homer, who constantly misdirects and retards the main story line and leads us toward unexpected tangents only to return to pick up a plotline he had discarded, the unexpected occurs. At that moment, a minor figure in the film, Hunt Bromley, shoots him in the back. Fate catches up with Ringo, not face to face in the classic gunfighter mode, but unexpectedly in a backshooting, an inverse symmetry that delivers a left-handed reflection of Ringo's deserved end.

The Gunfighter as a Reading of the Odyssey

The Hero's Cunning

Each delay Ringo encounters on his odyssey to Cayenne and the resistance he meets while in Cayenne become adventures that his cunning must help him overcome. Ringo averts danger whenever he can but does not shrink from it. At the Santa Fe Bar outside Cayenne he deflects the goading insults of a young usurper, a character named Eddie, until his harasser draws and Ringo shoots him dead. On his way out of town, his cunning surprises Eddie's three brothers, who pursue him to avenge Eddie's death. He disarms them and scatters their horses so they have to chase him on foot. Whereas his reputation as a gunfighter always precedes him, he tries throughout the journey, as Odysseus does, to conceal his identity and remain anonymous. For the greater part of the film, he stays out of sight in Cayenne until he can decide how to proceed. He must still undergo a number of tests, which again require Odyssean cunning. He must disarm a father, Jerry Marlowe, intent on gunning him down to reprise, mistakenly, the murder of his son some years earlier. Ringo tucks him into a jail cell for safekeeping. In the process, a deputy, assigned by the town marshal to keep Ringo away from those who would challenge him, is himself pushed out of harm's way. Ringo's searching glance had caught the reflection of Marlowe's rifle from across the street. Hiding his identity, Ringo patiently hears the complaints and appeases the anxieties of Mrs. Pennyweather and the townswomen who are seeking the marshal to demand he keep the town free of gunfighters. In the bar waiting for a pre-arranged visit from his wife, who resides surreptitiously in the town, he is confronted by another upstart, Hunt Bromley. Sitting passively at a table, his hands hidden under it, Ringo warns Bromley that a gun is pointed at his belly. As Bromley, uncertain, turns and leaves the bar defeated and humiliated, Ringo withdraws his hands to reveal a small pocket knife he has been using to clean his nails. Years as a gunfighter anticipating others' moves, suspicious of the intentions of those he meets, have made this "man of twists and turns" (*Od.* 1.1) cautious and sharpened his wits. He weighs each situation and "learns men's minds" (*Od.* 1.4) before deciding on a plan of action, using intelligence before force as a first line of defense.

The Destination

As a western *Odyssey, The Gunfighter*'s destination is always toward *oikos* (home). From the film's opening, a horse and rider race across the dunes, which change into plains and then mountains as day becomes night and day again. The rider races toward the home he abandoned years before and is now attempting to regain. As Homer expresses the sentiment,

> And may the good gods give you all your heart desires:
> husband, and house, and lasting harmony too.
> No finer, greater gift in the world than that
>
> (*Od.* 6.198–200)[4]

Oikos is the goal of the ex-gunfighter and now town marshal Mark Stepp. He renounced his lawless life to attain a home and a town that he could be part of, that he can call his own. *Oikos* is what Molly, the saloon girl, hoped to have with her husband, Bucky Harris, before he was shot in the back in Abilene. *Oikos* is what Mrs. Pennyweather and her entourage are trying to preserve in Cayenne by insisting on protection from gunfighters like Ringo. *Oikos* is what most impresses Ringo when he listens to a simple farmer, Tommy, describe his idyllic life. It is constituted by the very life of Cayenne with its school and church, its truant children, the neighbors who recognize them and reprimand their behavior, the marshal looking after his "family," and the closeness and familiarity of its inhabitants as they go about their daily chores. All this activity creates a unity, a family, a community, in contrast to Ringo's sterile and lonely existence. The longer he remains in Cayenne waiting to meet with his wife, Peg, and his son, Jimmy, Jr., the more Ringo wants to become part of the town's life. At the same time, he recognizes the difficulty of the transition from his life as a gunfighter. The most he can hope for is a home with his family in some isolated spot far away from anyone who might recognize him as Jimmy Ringo. Trading the hard-won glory associated with his life as a gunfighter for the anonymity of family life, Ringo's choice can be considered in light of Odysseus when he renounces Calypso's gift of immortality for a chance to see his home once again. "Preside in our house with me / and be immortal" (*Od.* 5.230–31), Calypso begs Odysseus, but he replies,

> Nevertheless I long—I pine, all my days—
> to travel home and see the dawn of my return.
> And if a god will wreck me yet again on the wine-dark sea,
> I can bear that too, with a spirit tempered to endure.
> (*Od.* 5.242–45)

As did Ringo in his early years, Odysseus reflects his belief in both *timê* and *kleos* by rejecting Calypso, for remaining with her would secrete him from the real world and the glory it confers. But as Ringo in his later years, Odysseus has also had time to reevaluate the relation of the life of the warrior to domestic life, having left the warrior life ten years ago (the Calypso episode is his penultimate adventure). Both Odysseus in the *Odyssey* and Hector in the *Iliad* understand the counterbalance of the two ways of life, as does Hector in the *Iliad,* as Foley points out (2007). Hector's response to Andromache's plea that he remain at home rather than return to the battlefield forces him to consider her desire for *oikos* against his own for *kleos:*

> Yes, soon they will kill you off,
> all the Achaean forces massed for assault, and then,
> bereft of you, better for me to sink beneath the earth.
> What other warmth, what comfort's left for me,
> once you have met your doom? Nothing but torment!
>
> (*Il.* 6. 486–90)

Hector's choice for *kleos* means the death of his son, Astyanax, who will be flung from the walls of Troy to his death by Odysseus, and the destruction of his *oikos*. Ringo's original break with his home (*oikos*) results as well from his pursuit of *timê, geras,* and *kleos*. When he decides to seek his fame, he gives up his *oikos* and can only regain it after he has abandoned his need for *kleos*. Young and full of hubris, unable to command both of the opposed values, he opts for glory. Now that he is older and disappointed with his gunfighter life, seeing the possibilities of another kind of life in those of his close friends Buck Harris and Matt Stepp, Ringo recognizes that his turn to domesticity can only be achieved by repudiating who he has become as a warrior.

The Homecoming

The Gunfighter belongs to the genre of *nostos,* the homecoming of a warrior returning from an absence of many years to reclaim family and rejoin community. Ringo's wife, Peg, a Western Penelope, stands for the world he longs to enter but to which he no longer belongs. Once he joins the warrior society, open only to men, the world of the gunfighter, he must relinquish the domestic world of women, a choice with which Hector himself struggles when implored by his wife to remain with her and their son in Troy:

> All this weighs on my mind too, dear woman.
> But I would die of shame to face the men of Troy
> and the Trojan women trailing their long robes
> if I would shrink from battle now, a coward.
>
> (*Il.* 6.522–25)

Ringo's reunion with his wife presents a comparable dilemma. As his son storms unannounced into the room where Ringo is waiting, the father is taken aback by the boy's brashness, which both impresses and concerns him. His warrior self admires the boy's fearlessness; seeing himself in his son, he smiles. Hector's parting words to his infant son echo Ringo's smile of recognition:

> Zeus, all you immortals! Grant this boy, my son,
> may he be like me, first in glory among the Trojans,
> strong and brave like me, and rule all Troy in power
> and one day let them say, "He is a better man than his father!"
> (*Il.* 6.568–71)

But Ringo recognizes how futile his past life has become. He has heard the confession of his fellow gunfighter Strepp. A stray bullet in one of his robberies had killed a young girl, leading him to turn his back on his old life. Another child, his own son, leads Ringo to consider the value he gives life when the boy asks him about Wyatt Earp, whom the boy idolizes:

> Jimmy Jr.: "Did you ever meet Wyatt Earp?"
> Ringo: "Yeah. I've seen him once or twice."
> Jimmy Jr.: "Who is the toughest one you ever saw?"
> Ringo: "You mean the real toughest?"
> Jimmy Jr.: "Yes sir, besides you."
> Ringo: "Well, I guess I haven't seen anybody any tougher than a fellow you have right here in your own town. A fellow by the name of Mark Strepp."
> Jimmy Jr.: "You mean marshal Mark Strepp?
> Ringo: "He's the toughest man I ever met."
> Jimmy Jr.: "But he don't even carry a gun."
> Ringo: "Well he don't have to, son. He can handle them bare-handed."[5]

The picture Ringo paints for his son is not that of a gunfighter, but of the man who needs no gun, a man strong enough to step out of the spotlight of the Western gunfighter. The dilemma for Ringo, as he tries to rehabilitate himself in Jimmy Jr.'s eyes, is that Ringo must give up the only legacy he has to give his son—his reputation as a gunfighter—in order to rejoin him as part of a family. His son cannot be allowed to continue Ringo's way of life by taking over for him where he left off, a prospect that the boy seems to have instinctively been drawn to in his hero worship of Wyatt Earp. This break in the continuity of the father-son relationship does not auger well for Ringo, for it prefigures a disconnection between the two that is prescient. Ringo might not, unlike Odysseus, be going home again, as what he has to leave behind—a legacy—is what he needs to make a meaningful connection with his son.

Still, Ringo's stay in Cayenne has slowly begun to reintegrate him into society, awakening him to the world he forsook for *timê* and *kleos* and making him conscious of the disjunction between the two worlds. He has become one with those warriors in the *Odyssey* who reach home only after great suffering, a suffering that earns them the right to return, to reintegrate gradually into society. Odysseus is allowed to return to Ithaca only after a decade of wandering, rising slowly out of a world of monsters to the more human world of the Phaeacians and finally to the social world of Ithaca. By the same argument, Ringo integrates incrementally into the world of the home he has left, having experienced his own monsters—the usurpers Eddie and Bromley, the death of his friend Harris, and Strepp's confession and reform.

The Reunion

As a warrior returning home after a long absence, Ringo has the goal of carrying out his reunion as unobtrusively as possible. While his presence becomes known as soon as he arrives in town, only Strepp and Molly know the connection between Ringo and Peg. Now the town schoolteacher, Peg has assumed a new identity, leaving her past and the stigma of the gunfighter behind to raise her son within a community. Before he tries to meet her, Ringo, as Odysseus, cunningly questions others, the marshal and Molly, about her life and her feelings toward him. The marshal is recruited to intercede with Peg. Molly is interrogated about possible suitors:

> "Is it somebody else?" asks Ringo.
> "You ought to know better than that," Molly responds.
> "No, I don't; it's been a long time."
> "There will never be anybody else for Peg."
> "Anybody else tried?"
> "Of course. Pretty girl like that. Young squirt named Hunt Bromley got after her; thought she couldn't take care of herself. Boy you should have heard her tell him off."
> "What did he do to her?"
> "Nothing really. Just one of those loud mouth barroom loafers who try to move in on a woman without a husband."

Presented by Molly with the dilemma of meeting Ringo, the Penelope-like Peg is unsure of her own feelings and reluctant to face this stranger who claims to be her husband. Not knowing how the intervening years and the life he has led as a gunfighter have changed him, she admits, "He scares me Molly, he really does." To Molly's query about any suitors, Peg is clear: there have never been any. "Then it's still Jim," Molly says. "I guess it always will be," responds Peg, faithful to her charge as a warrior's wife and mother of his son. Throughout Ringo's absence, she has shunned the company of men, remained faithful to the gunfighter, and protected their son. Suddenly she is confronted with Penelope's dilemma—she must face the man for whom she has waited for years, reluctant to accept him before making certain he is truly the man she once knew. Molly might have persuaded her to meet with Ringo, but she will not yield to him before she questions his intentions.

Ringo, for his part, has passed the time with the young farmer Tommy as he awaits word from Molly. A man of action, he seizes upon the idea of a farm of his own, something palpable he can envision resolving the puzzle of his life. His proposal becomes a beacon, a place where the three of them can live out their lives in solitude—but not until he can prove himself by one more test, a test that will ensure his clarity of vision and his sincerity of purpose. A return to the social from the world of the monsters is not an automatic move. Ringo must pass a test before Peg will finally accept him, a test like that of Penelope's axes:

> I mean to announce a contest with those axes,
> the ones he would often line up here inside the hall,
> twelve in a straight unbroken row like blocks to shore a keel,
> then stand well back and whip an arrow through the lot.
> Now I will bring them on as a trial for suitors.
> The hand that can string the bow with greatest ease,
> that shoots an arrow clean through all twelve axes—
> he's the man I follow, yes, forsaking the house
> where I was once a bride. . . .
>
> (*Od.* 19.644–52)

Peg's test gives Ringo a year to forsake his gunfighter life. If he can stay free of trouble, he can return to claim her and the boy. Only then will she follow. Ringo's return to society must be sanctified by the experience of returning to the wilderness, surviving there as a new man, leaving his monsters behind, and then rejoining society. It is a challenge that Ringo gratefully accepts.

The Gunfighter as a Reading of the *Iliad*

Condemned to Glory

The film begins with a note to the audience:

> In the Southwest of the 1880s the difference between death and glory was often but a fraction of a second; this was the speed that made champions of Wyatt Earp, Billy the Kid, and Wild Bill Hickok. But the fastest man with a gun who ever lived, by many contemporary accounts, was a long, lean Texan named Ringo. This is the story of a warrior in the mythic West, Jimmy Ringo. An exemplar of a time when one's reputation was made by the way one handled a gun, he was simply "the fastest man with a gun who ever lived.

As the film opens, Jimmy Ringo, after an absence of twelve years, is returning home to reclaim his wife and the eight-and-a-half-year-old son he has not seen for eight years. The gunfighter interrupts his journey to stop in Santa Fe for a drink at a bar where, his fame already legendary, everyone recognizes him by name—the old man outside the bar, the bartender, the men playing poker. A young upstart at the card table named Eddie goads him. "How fast can he be?" he asks; "he's just a man like everyone else. Have a drink Mr. Frazzelbottom, isn't that your name Mr. Frazzelbottom? You don't want to drink with me Mr. Frazzelbottom?" Ringo does his best to ignore the insults: "Why is it that everywhere I go I have to meet up with a squirt like you?" Eddie draws but immediately crumbles to the ground dead. Everyone in the saloon agrees Eddie drew first, but a bystander warns Ringo that the young man has three brothers who will not ask questions how he died. Ringo leaves the bar and continues his journey toward Cayenne and the Palace Bar.

Ringo thus establishes himself in this first appearance in the film as a famous gunfighter, justly feared and grudgingly respected. This early scene with Eddie has a binary aspect to it, for just as he reminds us that he has a reputation that is the envy of every young man in the West who wants to make a name for himself, it becomes clear that Ringo himself is weary of his title and dissatisfied with the honor and fame it has accorded him. Tired of the predictable challenges that provoke shoot-outs that kill ambitious boys like Eddie, Ringo has been mellowed by time, and he has begun to question the values for which he has forsaken his wife and son. He senses there should be more to life than a reputation as the fastest gun alive, and for some time now, he has been trying to run from his past. In this light, Ringo puts on the aspect of a western Achilles, a man whose choices have been few—either to win glory by being the fastest gun alive or to live an uneventful life. It was fear of the latter that drove Ringo to seek the gunfighter's reputation that he is beginning to reconsider, as the Cayenne marshal will later remind him.

This change of heart is cemented through three crucial scenes occurring midway through the film: first, when he meets the Palace Bar saloon singer Molly, wife of his friend, the gunfighter Bucky Harris; second, when he comes in contact with Tommy, the young farmer; finally, when he speaks to Marshal Strepp. Ringo has not been a thoughtful man. He has never considered a life other than the one he led, and his trip to Cayenne has little purpose other than to meet face to face with his wife and son, without any idea of what might happen as a result. In the short time that passes during his conversations with Molly, Tommy, and Mark Strepp, however, he recognizes the falseness of the values he has pursued up to this point, he discovers what he wants, and he arrives at a plan for making the changes that will alter his life.

Self-Recognition (anagnorisis)

The first of these three crucial scenes occurs when the marshal delivers the disappointing news that Ringo's wife does not want to meet with him. As he prepares to leave the saloon, he meets Molly, who is surprised to see him. The saloon-singer wife of Ringo's friend and fellow gunslinger Bucky Harris seems surprised that Ringo has not heard that Harris, foreshadowing Ringo's own fate, was killed six months ago in Abiline, shot in the back of the head in an alley. When Ringo inquires why Molly has to work in a saloon, she says, "I have to eat don't I?" When asked whether Buck has provided for her, she lists her inheritance as a horse, a saddle, two guns, and fifteen dollars. Having led the same kind of life as his friend, Ringo realizes he is bound to end up the same way. The memory of Buck's sudden end and his insignificant legacy are all that are left to show he ever existed. His *geras* (a horse, a saddle, a gun, and fifteen dollars) at the end of his life does not amount to the *kleos* and *timê* that Ringo felt his friend's warrior past should have provided. It is as if Buck never lived, wiped out from the world's memory. While he was alive, he had an identity, a reputation, because he posed a problem for the law and those with whom he had contact. Dead he is forgotten because he no longer poses a threat to anyone. Whatever feats of excellence he performed while alive hold no meaning in death. What his reputation finally amounts to is that he left nothing of significance to be remembered by, he died an unheroic death, and, more devastating than both of these, he was not even able to provide security for his wife. His friend's fate drives the point home that Ringo's own life as "the fastest gun alive" has not produced the *timê* and the *kleos* that he expected.

The second crucial scene that leads Ringo to reevaluate his life occurs while he awaits Molly's return as an emissary to his wife. During his anxious wait in the saloon, the young farmer Tommy enters the Palace Bar for a drink. Tommy represents the first contact Ringo has had with someone who neither knows the gunfighter nor has any idea of his reputation. For him, Ringo is a mere stranger to whom the bartender Max has introduced him and with whom he strikes up a friendly conversation. The bartender tells Tommy's story to Ringo. Recently married to a girl who seems to have a strong hold on him, he is under strict orders from his wife to have only one drink while he is in town for farm supplies. Ringo's offer of a second is refused as Tommy cites his wife's admonition. Ringo, drawn to Tommy's simple and unassuming nature, listens attentively to his companion's idyllic tale of the life he and his wife lead on their farm and his catalogue of the cattle and horses their hard work has added to their stock. Held against the scene describing the legacy of a gunfighter's death and his wife's solitary struggle, this scene pictures a like-minded husband and wife, close and with a single purpose, oblivious to the world outside their farm. Ringo is touched by the harmony he senses in this couple, whose devotion provides all the fame and honor they need. Separated, Molly and Buck have nothing to show for their life. Together, Tommy and his wife, even at the beginning of their life, have already amassed a great deal. Domestic harmony like theirs expresses for Homer the complementarity of man and woman, the greatest gift one can bestow on another human being:

> And may the good gods give you all your heart desires:
> husband, and house, and lasting harmony too.
> No finer, greater gift in the world than that.
>
> (*Od.* 6.198–200)

The third scene occurs between Ringo and Marshal Strepp, a scene in which Ringo is already showing signs of the effect of his first two meetings. The death of the gunfighter and the life of the farmer prompt him to think about his own prospects. Instead of responding to Strepp's concern that it is time for him to leave town, he shares his thoughts about Buck:

> Ringo: "She told me about Buck; never heard it before."
> Strepp: "I guess he never knew what hit 'em."
> Ringo: "That's a fine life, ain't it? Just trying to stay alive not being able to live on and enjoy anything, not getting anywhere. Just trying to keep from getting killed. Just waiting to get knocked off by some tough kid like the kind of kid I was."
> Strepp: "And the truth of the matter is it don't pay much either."
> Ringo: "Here I am 35 years old and I ain't even got a little watch. How did you get out of it Mark?
> Strepp: "I just quit."

When Ringo first arrived in town, he was surprised his old friend Strepp was marshal of Cayenne. Too preoccupied with getting in touch with his wife to pursue the matter, and having had the benefit of his meetings with Molly and Tommy, Ringo is now intrigued to know how Strepp was able to leave behind his gunfighter past and end up on the side of the law. Here, Strepp's confession of his participation in a bank robbery and gunfight in which a child was killed reveals that he felt responsible for the death, although it could have been his bullet as well as anyone else's that killed the girl. He left the life of a gunfighter to wander through the West until he ended in Cayenne. There, he determined to build a new life, out of the same anonymity from which Peg constructed her new life, in an effort to prevent such innocent deaths in the future. In a signature statement that marks his new identity, Strepp has refused to wear a gun. No longer impressed with feats of valor, Strepp presents himself as a simple, quiet, unassuming man doing his duty. He has found contentment by leaving his reputation behind and by making sure that no one else tries to create one in his jurisdiction. His insistence that Ringo leave the town as soon as possible, and the care he takes in assuring that he is kept out of sight of the crowds eager to catch a glimpse of him, change the terms of the game from one where an individual's glory matters more than collective security, to one where the good of the many trumps that of the one.

Strepp's confession reveals that a gunfighter can change his life, but the change has to occur within. In Strepp's case, it occurs when he discovers his humanity, when he realizes that his actions could have caused the death of an innocent child. It is at that moment that he is willing to trade fame for anonymity. He acts in terms of what he believes to be right—an intrinsic human value—rather than what he might gain from the act—an assertion of utility value—relinquishing any kind of external fame. No one will know what he did or why he did it except he, an act for which Achilles provides the model when he reenters the battlefield to avenge his fallen friend Patroclus. No longer concerned about his fame or the many gifts offered by Agamemnon, he acts out of devotion and love for a friend. Similarly when he returns to Priam the body of Hector he previously dragged around Troy, he does so out of pity for an old man who reminds him of his own father, a father who, he realizes, will never again see his son. Achilles and Strepp have looked inward and discovered their humanity, the very obverse of the warrior/gunfighter who acts out of a need to be known, to be recognized, and to be remembered.

It takes all three experiences—the unexpected news of Buck's death, the conversation with Tommy, the confession of Mark Strepp—to jolt Ringo into a recognition of what it means to be "the fastest gun alive." The fame that accompanies this honor relates to the skill of the fast draw and not to the nature of the man who performs the act. Buck is expendable just as Ringo will be when someone faster at the draw comes along. In the world of the western film the performance (the drawing of the gun) takes precedence over the performer. While Buck was alive, he was admired for his act; dead and no longer able to act, he becomes inconsequential. Buck's death, and the way he died, enable Ringo to assess the two possibilities available to "the fastest gun alive," the Homeric equivalent of the *aristos Achaiôn:* remain the best and be admired as long as the act can be performed, but die young since others are waiting to acquire that act or remain unnoticed and live a long life. Achilles avails himself of the same thought in *Iliad* 9 when Odysseus, Phoenix, and Ajax approach to persuade him to return to their aid,

> two fates bear me on to the day of death.
> If I hold out here and I lay siege to Troy,
> my journey home is gone, but my glory never dies.
> If I voyage back to the fatherland I love,
> my pride, my glory dies . . .
> true, but the life that's left me will be long,
> the stroke of death will not come on me quickly.
>
> (*Il.* 9.499–505)

Buck's death is as shocking to Ringo as the death of Patroclus is to Achilles. But Achilles abandons his pride and focuses his anger on Hector in order to avenge his friend's death, while Ringo does not seek revenge. Rather, his friend's death seals for him the realization that *kleos,* the title of the best in the West, does not bestow undying fame on the warrior. Buck's fame lasted only during his short life. Once he was dead, his fame died with him; what remains is a corpse lying unattended in some back alley.

The emptiness of a gunfighter's fame is further reinforced by Tommy's honesty and forthrightness, which lead Ringo to consider the kind of life he himself would like to lead with his own wife and son. After his conversation with the farmer, Ringo knows what he wants to do with the rest of his life and is eager to meet with his wife to propose to her his idea of a small farm far away from the present territory where no one will have heard of him. There the three of them can begin the simple life he so admires in Tommy. The burden of the title he has been carrying all these years no longer seems to matter. It is better to be a farmer than have notoriety as a gunfighter: "I'd rather slave on earth for another man— / than rule down here over all the breathless dead," Achilles tells Odysseus when they meet in the underworld (*Od.* 11.556). When Peg is persuaded by Molly to meet him, Ringo proposes to her the idea of a small farm he would like to buy in California, an idea that he admits just came to him:

> "I wanna get away from here Peggy."
> "When did you get this idea Jim?"
> "Well I didn't get it. It kinda just came over me. . . . I changed you know. I'm different now."

By the conclusion of these three scenes, Ringo's character takes on new meaning. He has reached the conclusion that the greatest priority for a mortal is to stay alive and enjoy life as long as possible, since eventually all mortals must face death. He moves from uncertainty to certainty, from aimlessness to purpose. His weariness seems to disappear, and he is excited and once again interested in life. After all his years of running from place to place, he can now stop. He has discovered the solution he was seeking—a piece of ground for his wife and son far away from the world he presently inhabits. His fame has been nothing more than a form of entertainment for the public, a sport that they participate in as onlookers. Once dead, he will no longer be of any interest, for he will no longer provide the public with the thrill of a gunfight, the rush that they experience through him. Yet the life he chose gave him only two false alternatives: to fight and win glory for oneself or fight and die and give glory to one's opponent as Sarpedon remarks to Glaucus in the *Iliad,* "So in we go for attack! / Give our enemy glory or win it for ourselves!" (*Il.* 12.380–82). The western gunfighter is a Homeric warrior transposed from thirteenth-century B.C.E. Troy to the nineteenth-century American West. The life of the western gunfighter, so long as he remains within the margins set by the Homeric warrior, takes place in a world from which there is no escape, as Sarpedon tells Glaucus in the *Iliad:*

> Ah my friend, if you and I could escape this fray
> and live forever, never a trace of age, immortal.
> I would never fight on the front lines again
> or command you to the field where men win fame.
> But now, as it is, the fates of death await us
> (*Il.* 12. 374–78)

In a final twist on the *Iliad,* it is possible in some respects to consider Hector as a model for Ringo. Hector, unlike Achilles, is not aware of his fate. He clings to the hope that it might be possible to defeat Achilles, although he knows him to be a much greater warrior. Ringo too realizes his end cannot be much different from Buck's, but after his conversation with Strepp, he has hope for a way out of his dilemma. Considering Strepp's renunciation of his past and his acceptance of anonymity, Ringo too envisions a future with Peg and his son, Jimmy, as an unknown somewhere far from the territory where he might be recognized. When Hector is about to face Achilles and debates running away and being labeled a coward or standing up to an opponent stronger than he and losing his life, he decides, "Better to clash in battle, now, at once— / see which fighter Zeus awards the glory! (Il. 22.155–56). Even though in his heart he knows he is no match for Achilles, he still entertains the possibility of victory. After all, only Zeus knows for certain the final outcome, and it is just possible that the match might go his way. As mortals, both Ringo and Hector are able to face hopeless situations because they cannot predict their future.

Irony and Fate

These three scenes account for Ringo's ultimate act at the end of the film. Having reconciled with his wife and having reunited with his eight-and-one-half-year-old son, he has been assured by Peg that in one year's time, she and their son will accompany him to the new life he has proposed. His mission accomplished beyond his wildest dreams, he is now ecstatic and ready to begin his one-year trial. But as in Greek tragedy fate awaits him just outside the door he has to exit to mount his horse—the door that separates life from death. In the alley behind the Palace Bar, the marshal has made all the preparations for Ringo's departure and is ready and waiting. A deputy is busy canvassing the area for the three brothers who have pursued him throughout the film and who are now hiding in a barn directly across from the door from which Ringo is to exit. Ringo leaves the bar, having discovered the value of family (a private, unsung life with the few people who love him, as opposed to a public life in the spotlight as the fastest gun alive). As he mounts his horse, the audience expects that the three brothers will finally end his life. But fate is again averted, for the deputy spots the brothers and disarms them before they can act. Ringo is free. Although he has been guilty of hubris, the gods have forgiven him. He mounts and begins to ride out of town, when suddenly Hunt Bromley, the young town boaster eager to make a reputation for himself, emerges from behind a tree, his guns poised. He calls out Ringo's name and before Ringo can turn his head, Bromley shoots him from behind, back-shot just as Buck Harris was.

As the marshal arrests Bromley, who gloats over the kill that will bestow on him the reputation of having killed the fastest gun alive, the dying Ringo pleads with Strepp for Bromley's freedom, insisting that Bromley was faster on the draw and thus deserves his newly earned title. With his dying breath Ringo explains to the puzzled Strepp, who witnessed Bromley's cowardly act, that allowing Bromley to get away with the title is a greater punishment than a jail sentence or even a hanging could bestow on him. Bromley will have to learn the way Ringo has learned what it means to carry the burden of the "fastest gun alive." He will have to experience himself the short-lived fame that such a title carries. On the brink of death, the burden of the title he has been carrying has become for Ringo a deadly legacy, perhaps the only one he has to give. Setting Bromley free condemns him to wander as a lonely and hunted man as Ringo did. In death, Ringo understands that as a western Achilles he had chosen unwisely, that a long uneventful life is preferable to a short glorious one.

Ringo at the end of the film dies as the result of a cowardly act, which emphasizes the falseness of a title indicating that the new bearer is "the best." Bestowing this title on Bromley is comparable to Paris's taking on the title in the *Iliad,* as both, throughout the film and the epic, respectively, are shown to be inferior to the original holders. They belittle the whole idea of being "the best." *The Gunfighter* makes it clear that Bromley is not as fast as he believes himself to be and will discover this the hard way when some "squirt" guns him down for the title he has stolen. It is for this reason that Ringo pleads for his release. Like Bromley, Paris is not considered a major warrior, and he runs away from the fighting in the *Iliad* whenever he can. It takes his brother Hector's taunts and insults to push him back into the battle,

> your people dying around the city, the steep walls,
> dyng in arms—and all for you, the battle cries
> and the fighting flaring up around the citadel.
> You'd be the first to lash out at another—anywhere—
> you saw hanging back from this, this hateful war.
> Up with you—
> before all Troy is torched to a cinder here and now!
> (*Il.* 6.386–92)

In having Bromley/Paris be the ones who finally defeat Ringo/Achilles, the texts demean the idea of the struggle for a fame that ultimately amounts to nothing other than ignominious death. The true fame for which Achilles and Ringo will be remembered by the future is not that they were the best of the Achaians or the fastest gun alive but that the first died for a friend, asking nothing in return, and the other sought a simple life for his wife and son.

By exploring the themes of the hero's cunning, homecoming, and reunion *The Gunfighter* can be read as a western *Odyssey.* However, the film can also be seen as a western *Iliad* by placing the emphasis on the hero as a warrior striving to become "the fastest gun alive," a title he equates with the honor and glory that will give meaning to his life. But as in the Homeric epics, through self-discovery and self-recognition the hero ends by repudiating *timê, kleos,* and *geras,* the values through which the Homeric hero strives to become *aristos Achaiõn* (the best of the Achaians).

Notes

1. *The Gunfighter,* dir. Henry King, 85 minutes, b&w, 1950, Twentieth Century Fox, with Gregory Peck, Helen Westcott, Millard Mitchell, Jean Parker.

2. *Timê* (honor), *kleos* (fame), and *geras* (gifts) have been dealt with by numerous scholars. See especially Katz (1991), Rabel (1997), Zanker (1994), and McAulan and Walcott (1998).

3. For a discussion of *aristos Achaiôn* (the best of the Achaians) see Nagy (1979).

4. All translations from Homer's *Iliad* and *Odyssey* are taken from Robert Fagles's translations (1990, 1996).

5. All quotations from *The Gunfighter* are taken by the author directly from the film.

Works Cited

Adkins, A. W. *Merit and Responsibility: A Study of Greek Values.* Oxford: Oxford University Press, 1960.

Ahl, Frederick, and H. Roisman. *The Odyssey Re-Formed.* Ithaca: Cornell University Press, 1996.

Alden, M. *Homer beside Himself: Para-Narratives in the* Iliad. Oxford: Oxford University Press, 2000.

Austin, N. *Archery at the Dark of the Moon: Poetic Problems in Homer's* Odyssey. Berkeley: University of California, 1975.

Baker, Bob "Shame through Five Decades." In *Book of Westerns,* edited by Ian Cameron and Douglas Pye. New York: Continuum, 1996.

Baxin, Andre. "The Evolution of the Western." In *What Is Cinema?* Vol. II. Translated by Hugh Gray. Berkeley: University of California Press, 1971.

Bazin, André. "The Western, or the American Film Par Excellence." In *What Is Cinema?* Vol. II. Translated by Hugh Gray. Berkeley: University of California Press, 1971.

Belton, John. "Language, Oedipus, and Chinatown." *Modern Language Notes* 106 (1991): 933–950.

Bespaloff, Rachel. *On the* Iliad. Translated by Mary McCarthy. Princeton, NJ: Princeton University Press, 1970.

Blundell, Mary Whitlock, and Kirk Ormand. "Western Values, or the People's Homer: *Unforgiven* as a Reading of the *Iliad.*" *Poetics Today* 18, no. (4) (1997): 533–69.

Borges, J. L. "The Art of Fiction XXXIX." *Paris Review* 40 (1967): 116–64.

Bruce, Chris et al. *Myth of the West.* New York: Rizzoli, 1990.

Buchan, Mark. *The Limits of Heroism; Homer and the Ethics of Reading.* Ann Arbor: The University of Michigan Press, 2004.

Burrows, Jack. *John Ringo, the Gunfighter Who Never Was.* Tucson: University of Arizona Press, 1987.

Buscombe, Edward, ed. *The BFI Companion to the Western.* London: André Deutsch/ BFI, 1988.

Cairns, D. L. *Oxford Readings in Homer's* Iliad. Oxford: Oxford University Press, 2001.

Cameron, Ian, and Douglas Pye, eds. *The Book of Westerns.* New York: Continuum, 1996.

Clark, Matthew. "Fighting Words: How Heroes Argue." *Arethusa* 35, no. 1 (2002): 99–115.

Clark, Michael. "Images of the Hero in the *Iliad*." *Greek, Roman & Byzantine Studies* 36, no. 2 (Summer 1996): 137–58.

Clauss, James J. "Descent into Hell: Mythic Paradigms in *The Searchers*." *JPFT* 27, no. 3 (Fall 1999): 2–17.

Clay, Jenny Strauss. *The Wrath of Athena: Gods and Men in the* Odyssey. Princeton, NJ: Princeton University Press, 1983.

Cohen, Beth, ed. *The Distaff Side*. Oxford: Oxford University Press, 1995.

Curtin, Kevin Thomas. "The Natural; Our *Iliad* and *Odyssey*." *AR* 43, no. 2: 225–41.

Dalby, Andrew. *Rediscovering Homer; Inside the Origins of the Epic*. New York: W. W. Norton, 2006.

Dowell, Pat. "The Mythology of the Western; Hollywood Perspectives on Race and Gender in the Nineties." *Cineaste* 21, nos. 1–2 (1995): 6–10.

Eckstein, Arthur M. "Darkening Ethan: John Ford's *The Searchers* from Novel to Screenplay to Screen." *Cinema Journal* 38, no. 1 (1998): 3–24.

Edwards, M. *Homer: Poet of the* Iliad. Baltimore and London: The Johns Hopkins University Press, 1987.

Elley, Derek. *The Epic Film: Myth and History*. London: Routledge and Kegan Paul, 1984.

Fagles, Robert, trans. *Homer,* The Iliad. New York: Penguin, 1990.

———, trans. *Homer,* The Odyssey. New York: Penguin, 1996.

Finkelberg, Margalit. "Odysseus and the Genus 'Hero.'" *Greece and Rome* 42, no. 1 (April 1995): 1–14.

Finley, Moses. *The World of Odysseus*. New York: Viking Press, 1978.

Foley, John Miles. "'Reading' Homer through Oral Tradition." *College Literature* 34, no. 2 (Spring 2007): 1–28.

Folsom, James K. *The Western: A Collection of Critical Essays*. Englewood Cliffs, NJ: Prentice-Hall, 1979.

Ford, A. *Homer: The Poetry of the Past*. Ithaca, NY: Cornell University Press, 1992.

Ford, A. "Epic as Genre." In *A New Companion to Homer,* edited by I. Morris and B. Powell. Leiden: E.J. Brill, 1997.

French, Peter A. *Cowboy Metaphysics: Ethics and Death in Westerns*. Lanham, MD: Rowman & Littlefield, 1997.

French, Philip. *Westerns; Aspects of a Movie Genre*. New York: Viking, 1973.

Gallagher, Tag. "Shoot-Out at the Genre Corral." In *Film Genre Reader,* edited by Barry Keith Grant. Austin: University of Texas Press, 1986.

Garfield, Brian. *Western Films; A Complete Guide*. New York: Da Capo Press, 1982.

Gledhill, Christine. "Genre; the Western." In *The Cinema Book,* edited by Pam Cook. New York: Pantheon Books, 1985.

Grant, Michael. "The *Iliad* and the Heroic Ideal." In *Readings on Homer,* edited by Don Nardo. San Diego: Greenhaven Press, 1998.

Green, Peter. "Heroic Hype, New Style: Hollywood Pitted against Homer." *Arion* 12, no. 1 (2004): 171–87.

Griffin, Jasper. *Homer on Life and Death.* Oxford: Clarendon Press, 1980.

———. *The Odyssey.* Cambridge: Cambridge University Press, 1987.

———. "Homer's Epic Style." In *Readings on Homer,* edited by Don Nardo. San Diego: Greenhaven Press, 1998.

Grist, Leighton. "*Unforgiven.*" In *The Book of Westerns,* edited by Ian Cameron and Douglas Pye. New York: Continuum, 1996.

Hammond, Dorothy, and Alta Jablow. "Gilgamesh and the Sundance Kid." In *The Making of Masculinities,* edited by H. Brod. Boston: Allen & Unwin, 1987.

Henderson, Debbie. "Cowhand to Cowboy: Fabrication of Myth." *MAA* 6 (1997): 47–65.

Hofmeister, Timothy P. "Achillean Love and Honor in Ridley Scott's *Black Rain.*" *Classical and Modern Literature* 13, no. 1 (Fall 1992): 45–51.

Holtsmark, Erling B. *Tarzan and Tradition; Classical Myth in Popular Literature.* Westport, CT: Greenwood, 1981.

Jordan, Philip D. *Frontier Law and Order: Ten Essays.* Lincoln: University of Nebraska Press, 1970.

Katz, Marylin A. *Penelope's Renown.* Princeton, NJ: Princeton University Press, 1991.

Kitses, Jim. "Authorship and Genre: Notes on the Western." In *The Western Reader,* edited by Jim Kitses and Gregg Rickman. New York: Limelight Editions, 1969.

———. *Horizons West.* Bloomington: Indiana University Press, 1970.

Kitses, Jim, and Gregg Rickman, eds. *The Western Reader.* New York: Limelight Editions, 1999.

Koziak, Barbara. "Homeric Thumos: The Early History of Gender, Emotion, and Politics." *Journal of Politics* 61, no. 4 (November 1999): 1068–091.

Large, Ron. "Shane and the Death Wish: The Redemptive Hero in American Culture." *JEP* 13, nos. 3–4: 232–40.

Louden, Bruce. *The* Odyssey; *Structure, Narration, and Meaning.* Baltimore: Johns Hopkins University Press, 1999.

———. *The* Iliad; *Structure, Myth, and Meaning.* Baltimore: Johns Hopkins University Press, 2006.

Lovell, Alan. "The Western." In *Movies and Methods,* edited by Bill Nichols. Berkeley: University of California Press, 1976.

MacKinnon, Kenneth. *Greek Tragedy into Film.* Rutherford, NJ: Fairleigh Dickinson University Press, 1986.

Maronitis, D. N. *Homeric Megathemes; War, Homilia, Homecoming.* Lanham, MD: Rowman & Littlefield, 2004.

Marsden, Michael T. "Savior in the Saddle: The Sagebrush Testament." In *Focus on the Western,* edited by Jack Nachbar. Englewood Cliffs, NJ: Prentice-Hall, 1974.

Marston, V. "Epics and Westerns." *Classical Outlook* 54 (1976–77): 76–79.

Martin, R. *The Language of Heroes: Speech and Performance in the* Iliad. Ithaca, NY: Cornell University Press, 1989.

McAuslan, Ian, and Peter Walcot, eds. *Homer.* Oxford: Oxford University Press, 1998.

Mitchell, Lee Clark. *Westerns: Making the Man in Fiction and Film.* Chicago: University of Chicago Press, 1996.

Morris, Ian, and Barry Powell, eds. *A New Companion to Homer.* Leiden: Brill, 1997.

Morrison, James V. *Homeric Misdirection: False Predictions in the* Iliad. Ann Arbor: The University of Michigan Press, 1992.

Nachbar, Jack, ed. *Focus on the Western.* Englewood Cliffs: Prentice-Hall, 1974.

Nagy, Gregory. *The Best of the Achaeans: Concepts of the Hero in Archaic Greek Poetry.* Baltimore: The Johns Hopkins University Press, 1979.

Nichols, Bill, ed. *Movies and Methods.* Berkeley: University of California Press, 1976.

Nortwick, Thomas Van. *Somewhere I Have Never Travelled; The Hero's Journey.* New York: Oxford University Press, 1996.

Papovich, J. Frank. "Homeric Honor and Cultural Values." In *Readings on Homer,* edited by Don Nardo. San Diego: Greenhaven Press, 1998.

Rabel, Robert J. *Plot and Point of View in the* Iliad. Ann Arbor: University of Michigan Press, 1997.

Rainey, Buck. *The Reel Cowboy: Essays on the Myth in Movies and Literature.* Jefferson, NC: McFarland, 1996.

Redfield, J. *Nature and Culture in the* Iliad: *The Tragedy of Hector.* Chicago: Chicago Univesity Press, 1975.

Richardson, S. "The Devious Narrator of the *Odyssey.*" *Classical Journal* 101, no. 4 (2006): 337–60.

Rickman, Gregg. "The Western under Erasure: *Dead Man.*" In *The Western Reader,* edited by Jim Kitses and Gregg Rickman. New York: Limelight Editions, 1998.

Rosa, Joseph G. *The Gunfighter: Man or Myth?* Norman: University of Oklahoma Press, 1969.

Rosenbaum, Jonathan. *Dead Man.* London: BFI, 2000.

Scodel, Ruth. *Listening to Homer; Tradition, Narrative, and Audience.* Ann Arbor: University of Michigan Press, 2002.

Segal, Charles. *Singers, Heroes, and Gods in the* Odyssey. Ithaca, NY: Cornell University Press, 1994.

———. "*Kleos* and Its Ironies in the *Odyssey.*" In *Reading the Odyssey; Selected Interpretive Essays,* edited by Seth L. Schein. Princeton, NJ: Princeton University Press, 1996.

Shay, Jonathan. *Achilles in Vietnam.* New York: Atheneum, 1994.

Silk, M. S. "Achilles: An Exceptional Hero Gains Self-Awareness." In *Readings on Homer,* edited by Don Nardo. San Diego: Greenhaven Press, 1998.

Slotkin, Richard. *Gunfighter Nation; The Myth of the Frontier in Twentieth-Century America.* New York: Harper Perennial, 1992.

Smith, Nash. *Virgin Land: The American West as Symbol and Myth.* Cambridge, MA: Harvard University Press, 1978.

Sobchack, Thomas. "Genre Film: A Classical Experience." *Literature/Film Quarterly* 3 (1975): 196–204.

Solomon, Jon. *The Ancient World in the Cinema.* 2nd ed. New Haven, CT: Yale University Press, 2000.

Sragow, Michael. "The Homeric Power of Peckinpah's Violence." *Atlantic Monthly* 273, no. 6 (1994): 116–22.

Szaz, Ferenc M. "Homer and the Myth of the American West." *Journal of the West* 35, no. 3 (July 1996): 3–6.

Taplin, O. *Homeric Soundings: The Shaping of the* Iliad. Oxford: Clarendon Press, 1992.

Tomplins, Jane. *West of Everything; The Inner Life of Westerns.* Oxford: Oxford University Press, 1992.

Vandiver, Elizabeth. "From Noman to Inman: The *Odyssey* in Charles Frazier's *Cold Mountain.*" *Classical & Modern Literature* 24, no. 2 (Fall 2004): 125–48.

Vivante, Paolo. *The Iliad; Action as Poetry.* Boston: G. K. Hall, 1991.

Warshow, Robert. "The Westerner." 1954. Reprint. In *Film: An Anthology,* edited by Daniel Talbot. Berkeley: University of California Press, 1966.

———. "The Gangster as Tragic Hero." In *The Immediate Experience: Movies, Comics, Theatre and Other Aspects of Popular Culture.* New York: Atheneum.

Williams, Doug. "Pilgrims and the Promised Land: A Genealogy of the Western." In *The Western Reader,* edited by Jim Kitses and Gregg Rickman. New York: Limelight Editions, 1998.

Wills, Gary. "*The Searchers.*" In *John Wayne's America: The Politics of Celebrity.* New York: Simon & Schuster, 1998.

Wilson, Donna F. *Ransom, Revenge, and Heoic Identity in the* Iliad. Cambridge: Cambridge University Press, 2002.

Winkler, Martin M. "Classical Mythology and the Western Film." *Comparative Literature Studies* 22, no. 4 (1985): 517–40.

———. "Homeric *Kleos* and the Western Film." *Syllecta Classica* 7 (1996): 43–54.

———, ed. *Classical Myth and Culture in the Cinema.* New York: Oxford University Press, 2001.

———. "Homer's *Iliad* and John Ford's *The Searchers.* In *The Searchers: Essays and Reflections on John Ford's Classic Western,* edited by Arthur M. Eckstein and Peter Lehman. Detroit: Wayne State University Press, 2004.

Wright, Will. *Six Guns and Society: A Structural Study of the Western.* Berkeley: University of California Press, 1975.

Zanker, Graham. *The Heart of Achilles; Characterization and Personal Ethics in the* Iliad. Ann Arbor: The University of Michigan Press, 1994.

Contributors

JONATHAN S. BURGESS is professor of classics at the University of Toronto. He is the author of *The Tradition of the Trojan War in Homer and the Epic Cycle* (2001) and *The Death and Afterlife of Achilles* (2008), as well as numerous articles.

CHARLES CHIASSON is associate professor and director of the Classical Studies program at the University of Texas at Arlington. Among numerous publications on ancient Greek literature, his article on the Cleobis and Biton episode in Herodotus was awarded the Gildersleeve Prize for 2005.

JOEL CHRISTENSEN teaches in the Department of Classics and Philosophy at the University of Texas at San Antonio. He has published articles on the rhetoric of heroism in Homer and the *Gilgamesh* poems, the archaic poet Archilochus, and the poetics of rivalry in the *Odyssey.*

BRUCE LOUDEN is currently professor at the University of Texas at El Paso. He has published two books on Homer, completed a third (*The Odyssey and the Near East*), and has also published on topics including the Bible, the *Rig Veda,* Bacchylides, Euripides, Plautus, *Beowulf,* Shakespeare, and Milton.

KOSTAS MYRSIADES is professor of comparative literature and editor of *College Literature* at West Chester University (West Chester, Pennsylvania). He edited the *MLA*'s *Approaches to Teaching Homer's* Iliad *and* Odyssey and is the author/editor/translator of sixteen other books.

RICK M. NEWTON is Professor Emeritus of Classical Studies at Kent State University in Kent, Ohio. His articles on Homer's *Odyssey* have appeared in *Classical Journal, Classical World, Greek, Roman and Byzan-*

tine Studies, Classical and Modern Literature, and the MLA volume *Approaches to Teaching Homer's* Iliad *and* Odyssey.

SCOTT RICHARDSON is professor of classics at St. John's University (Collegeville, Minnesota) where he teaches courses in comparative literature and classical languages and literature. He has published *The Homeric Narrator* (1990) and articles on Homer.

SHAWN ROSS is a Lecturer in Ancient and World History at the University of New South Wales in Sydney, Australia. Specializing in preclassical Greece but with wider interests in the ancient world, Ross has published articles dealing with proto-Panhellenism in the Homeric epics, the post–Bronze Age archaeology of the Palace of Nestor at Pylos, and native revolts in the early Roman Empire.

JOHN B. VLAHOS is an independent scholar working in conjunction with Richard P. Martin and Mark W. Edwards at Stanford University.

Index